Uruguayan Theatre in Translation
Theory and Practice

LEGENDA

LEGENDA is the Modern Humanities Research Association's book imprint for new research in the Humanities. Founded in 1995 by Malcolm Bowie and others within the University of Oxford, Legenda has always been a collaborative publishing enterprise, directly governed by scholars. The Modern Humanities Research Association (MHRA) joined this collaboration in 1998, became half-owner in 2004, in partnership with Maney Publishing and then Routledge, and has since 2016 been sole owner. Titles range from medieval texts to contemporary cinema and form a widely comparative view of the modern humanities, including works on Arabic, Catalan, English, French, German, Greek, Italian, Portuguese, Russian, Spanish, and Yiddish literature. Editorial boards and committees of more than 60 leading academic specialists work in collaboration with bodies such as the Society for French Studies, the British Comparative Literature Association and the Association of Hispanists of Great Britain & Ireland.

The MHRA encourages and promotes advanced study and research in the field of the modern humanities, especially modern European languages and literature, including English, and also cinema. It aims to break down the barriers between scholars working in different disciplines and to maintain the unity of humanistic scholarship. The Association fulfils this purpose through the publication of journals, bibliographies, monographs, critical editions, and the MHRA Style Guide, and by making grants in support of research. Membership is open to all who work in the Humanities, whether independent or in a University post, and the participation of younger colleagues entering the field is especially welcomed.

ALSO PUBLISHED BY THE ASSOCIATION

Critical Texts
Tudor and Stuart Translations • *New Translations* • *European Translations*
MHRA Library of Medieval Welsh Literature

MHRA Bibliographies
Publications of the Modern Humanities Research Association

The Annual Bibliography of English Language & Literature
Austrian Studies
Modern Language Review
Portuguese Studies
The Slavonic and East European Review
Working Papers in the Humanities
The Yearbook of English Studies

www.mhra.org.uk
www.legendabooks.com

TRANSCRIPT

Transcript publishes books about all kinds of imagining across languages, media and cultures: translations and versions, inter-cultural and multi-lingual writing, illustrations and musical settings, adaptation for theatre, film, TV and new media, creative and critical responses. We are open to studies of any combination of languages and media, in any historical moments, and are keen to reach beyond Legenda's traditional focus on modern European languages to embrace anglophone and world cultures and the classics. We are interested in innovative critical approaches: we welcome not only the most rigorous scholarship and sharpest theory, but also modes of writing that stretch or cross the boundaries of those discourses.

www.legendabooks.com/series/transcript

TRANSCRIPT

1. *Adapting the Canon: Mediation, Visualization, Interpretation*, edited by Ann Lewis and Silke Arnold-de Simine
2. *Adapted Voices: Transpositions of Céline's Voyage au bout de la nuit and Queneau's Zazie dans le métro*, by Armelle Blin-Rolland
3. *Zola and the Art of Television: Adaptation, Recreation, Translation*, by Kate Griffiths
4. *Comparative Encounters between Artaud, Michaux and the Zhuangzi: Rationality, Cosmology and Ethics*, by Xiaofan Amy Li
5. *Minding Borders: Resilient Divisions in Literature, the Body and the Academy*, edited by Nicola Gardini, Adriana Jacobs, Ben Morgan, Mohamed-Salah Omri and Matthew Reynolds
6. *Memory Across Borders: Nabokov, Perec, Chamoiseau*, by Sara-Louise Cooper
7. *Erotic Literature in Adaptation and Translation*, edited by Johannes D. Kaminski
8. *Translating Petrarch's Poetry: L'Aura del Petrarca from the Quattrocento to the 21st Century*, edited by Carole Birkan-Berz, Guillaume Coatalen and Thomas Vuong
9. *Making Masud Khan: Psychoanalysis, Empire and Modernist Culture*, by Benjamin Poore
10. *Prismatic Translation*, edited by Matthew Reynolds
11. *The Patient, the Impostor and the Seducer: Medieval European Literature in Hebrew*, by Tovi Bibring
12. *Reading Dante and Proust by Analogy*, by Julia Caterina Hartley
13. *The First English Translations of Molière: Drama in Flux 1663-1732*, by Suzanne Jones
14. *After Clarice: Reading Lispector's Legacy in the Twenty-First Century*, edited by Adriana X. Jacobs and Claire Williams
15. *Uruguayan Theatre in Translation: Theory and Practice*, by Sophie Stevens
16. *Hamlet Translations: Prisms of Cultural Encounters across the Globe*, edited by Márta Minier and Lily Kahn
17. *The Foreign Connection: Writings on Poetry, Art and Translation*, by Jamie McKendrick
18. *Poetics, Performance and Politics in French and Italian Renaissance Comedy*, by Lucy Rayfield

Uruguayan Theatre in Translation

Theory and Practice

❖

Sophie Stevens

LEGENDA
Transcript 15
Modern Humanities Research Association
2022

Published by Legenda
an imprint of the Modern Humanities Research Association
Salisbury House, Station Road, Cambridge CB1 2LA

ISBN 978-1-78188-311-2 (HB)
ISBN 978-1-78188-314-3 (PB)

First published 2022

Copy-Editor: Richard Correll

CONTENTS

For Audrey, Oscar and Wilfred,
and a future filled with languages

ACKNOWLEDGEMENTS

❖

This book is the result of many years of research, practice, questioning, collaborating, listening, watching, learning and, perhaps above all, advocating for theatre translation as a creative part of the disciplines of Modern Languages, Theatre Studies and Latin American Studies. I want to thank Graham Nelson along with Matthew Reynolds in the Transcript Series for supporting this project. The fact that Legenda has published this book which contains chapters of analysis alongside three complete stage-ready translations of plays from Uruguay demonstrates that they also recognise the importance of connecting research and practice in cross-disciplinary publications. I am grateful to them for this opportunity and for the helpful feedback that they and the reviewers have given me throughout the process.

The primary research for this book was conducted whilst completing my PhD at King's College London. I was able to undertake the PhD thanks to a full studentship from the Arts and Humanities Research Council. I also received grants to carry out research, deliver workshops and attend conferences from the following: King's Graduate School; The Faculty of Arts and Humanities at King's; The Department of Spanish, Portuguese and Latin American Studies at King's; and the Collaborative Innovation Scheme for Early Career Researchers funded by The Cultural Institute at King's. The Association of Hispanists of Great Britain and Ireland also provided grants which enabled me to attend the annual conference and become part of a dynamic academic community.

I would like to thank the members of the vibrant and diverse academic community at King's, particularly the staff and students in Spanish, Portuguese and Latin American Studies where this work was developed. I had the joy and privilege of sharing the ups-and-downs of the PhD and Early Career Academic experiences with Dr Katie Brown who is the perfect conference buddy and friend. Professor Patrick ffrench, Dr Elisa Sampson Vera Tudela and Dr Tom Boll have provided guidance and mentorship during and since the PhD, including on my current research project.

I would like to thank Professor Catherine Boyle who has supported me in so many ways and in so many roles: as my tutor, my PhD Supervisor, my mentor, my colleague and my friend. She encouraged me to pursue a thesis on Uruguayan theatre in translation and provided guidance, tools and resources to equip me to develop the work on translation theory and practice which provides the foundation for this book. She has read and offered feedback on countless drafts and I have always benefitted greatly from our discussions about my writing. I'm grateful for what she has taught me about ways of working in (and beyond) academia and how through acts of collaboration, intellectual generosity, and creating spaces for research in practice we can transform the role of scholarship and universities in our world. I learnt how we might take steps to bring about this transformation whilst working with Catherine alongside a brilliant and inspiring team on the Arts and Humanities Research Council-funded project *Language Acts and Worldmaking* between 2017 and 2020. The project emerged from concerns and questions about the discipline of Modern Languages and actively demonstrated how languages intersect with research and practice taking place across the university, in schools, in arts organisations and in community groups. This has made me even more determined to show how theatre and translation create opportunities for us to understand and engage with the world that we inhabit. I hope that this book goes some way to enhancing that understanding. Chapter 3 draws in part on researches previously published in my article, 'Distance and Proximity in Analysing and Translating *Bailando sola cada noche* [Dancing Alone Every Night] into English', *The Mercurian: A Theatrical Translation Review*, 6 (2016), 81–99.

The Out of the Wings research project created by Professor Catherine Boyle, Professor David Johnston and Professor Jonathan Thacker in 2008 enabled me to encounter new plays from Spain and Latin America. The Out of the Wings Collective continues to develop this work and has provided an important forum in which to test my ideas and translations with a group of creative researchers and practitioners. I am especially grateful for the opportunities to share translations and collaborate with playwrights, directors and actors at the annual Out of the Wings Festival. Two of the plays included in this book premiered in English translation at the festival in 2016 and 2017 respectively. The process of working with a company to prepare the text for performance in front of an audience enhanced my translation process and so fed into the methodologies included in this book. It also enhanced the richness of the translations produced and published here.

I'm fortunate to have also been welcomed into other academic communities around the world. I am particularly grateful to Professor Adam Versényi at the University of North Carolina at Chapel Hill and Professor Gail Bulman at Syracuse University, NY, for providing opportunities for me to share and receive feedback on my work in the context of workshops, conferences and lectures. Gail and colleagues at the Department of Languages, Literatures, and Linguistics at Syracuse and Dr Sarah Booker in Romance Studies at UNC Chapel Hill created invaluable opportunities for me to work with their students. This enabled the texts I was working on to travel again; this time by experimenting with translating Uruguayan theatre for an audience in the US. These interactions allowed me to think through translation in different ways and from a different perspective. I am grateful to both Gail and Sarah for becoming such supportive friends.

My research visits to Uruguay have always been so uplifting, creative and intellectually stimulating. I am very thankful for the academics, playwrights and subject specialists who helped me to track down texts and who generously shared their time, insights and resources with me. I am especially grateful to: Professor Roger Mirza at the Universidad de la República; the staff at the Biblioteca Nacional; the team at the Centro de Investigación, Documentación y Difusión de las Artes Escénicas at the Teatro Solís and the team at the Museo y Centro de Investigación at the Asociación General de Autores del Uruguay. They all helped me to access first editions of plays, press archives and critical texts relating to Uruguayan theatre. Many of these colleagues also played an important role in recommending plays and helping me to get tickets which allowed me to see a diverse range of shows in a variety of performance spaces.

As part of this research, I met with and interviewed playwrights Raquel Diana, Estela Golovchenko and the late Carlos Maggi in 2013. The discussions in those interviews, and since then with both Raquel and Estela, helped me to understand more about how theatre is produced in Uruguay. Raquel and Estela have both generously welcomed me into their homes and shared aspects of their creative processes with me. I am grateful to them and other playwrights I have spoken to for making me feel so welcome and for encouraging me in my research. I'd like to thank the many friends in Uruguay and Argentina who have been wonderful hosts during the many return visits that I have made since living in Montevideo and Buenos Aires many years ago.

My good friends Dr Jessica Stacey and Dr Robert Stearn set up and invited me to join a writing group. This group helped to transform my writing practice and sustained me during months of lockdown due to the Coronavirus pandemic. The structure and support of that group played a big part in enabling me to finish this monograph. The group has also been a space to share insights and advice about the experience of Early Career Academics and I am grateful for the support and friendship I received. There are also many friends who have accompanied me to readings and performances of plays, including those in this book. Many of these are friends from my undergraduate days at King's and their ongoing love and support has been invaluable.

I am grateful to my parents, Margaret Stevens and Michael Stevens, for emphasising the importance of education, encouraging me to develop a love of languages and supporting me in pursuing opportunities to study and work abroad, even though those opportunities would have seemed unimaginable to them.

I would like to thank my husband, Chris Fowler, whose curiosity, generosity, support, good humour and optimism have been unfailing throughout this project. This book is dedicated to our godchildren and nephew in the hope that they will have a future filled with the joys of both theatre and languages.

s.s., August 2022

INTRODUCTION

Uruguayan Theatre in London

Uruguayan theatre is dynamic, distinctive and outward-looking. It takes a variety of forms, based on a diverse cultural heritage. Theatre in Uruguay is influenced by Latin American literary and performance traditions, classical European theatre, and carnival theatre linked to the African diaspora.[1] These inherited theatre narratives and styles are renewed, adapted and reinvigorated by contemporary Uruguayan theatre artists. The plays in this book illustrate the ways in which playwrights have been innovative in terms of form, the use of humour and their creativity when depicting characters in situations which challenge the audience's imagination. The six plays analysed here deal with a range of intriguing themes including the experience of women, generational differences, death and afterlife, political resistance, memory, resilience and the force of storytelling. These themes and concepts make Uruguayan theatre an exciting and relevant object of study today.

How and why might a playwright in Uruguay write about a woman who died alone in her London flat? I remember asking myself this question as I nervously downloaded the text for *Bailando sola cada noche* [*Dancing Alone Every Night*] (2008) by Raquel Diana from the online platform *Dramaturgia Uruguaya.*[2] I wondered what the play might say; what might Diana have to say about this story, woman and situation? It seemed that the life and death of the real Joyce Vincent (who inspired the play) were complicated by issues around exclusion, failures in the social welfare system and gender-based violence. What I found was that Diana took on all these issues in a thoughtful and creative way by using dark humour, song and two other characters to explore a period of Joyce's life about which very little can be ascertained — that is, the two and a half years between Joyce's death and the discovery of her (incredibly decomposed) corpse. Diana presents these issues in a way that is relevant to a Uruguayan audience and brings to the fore concerns affecting Uruguayan society: isolation in the city, women's and human rights and disappeared people. Diana acknowledges the link to the story of the real Joyce Vincent through a series of newspaper articles included as a prologue. She also points out the link to another Joyce Vincent who is a singer. The play is a lively, playful and critical imagining of a kind of afterlife in which the protagonist reflects on her relationships, ambitions and the significance of having her own flat which provided security and also isolation. The play shows how narratives travel across perceived boundaries and can be reinterpreted to tell a story that is relevant for a new context and audience whilst still maintaining links to the place where the narrative originated. The play, the research I undertook and the many meetings with Diana informed my thinking about how narratives become mobile, how links are created between two contexts and how plays can encompass both close and distant cultural realities. These ideas underpin this study; a full translation of *Dancing Alone Every Night* can be found in Chapter 4.

Until quite recently, Uruguayan theatre seemed to be relatively unknown in the United Kingdom. This has meant that it has been both interesting and challenging to work on theatre from Uruguay, even though Spanish-language theatre has gained an increased profile. Without wishing to discount the work of certain scholars and the opportunities created by festivals which will be mentioned in the pages that follow, until the recent increase in readings and productions of Uruguayan theatre, there had been few opportunities for actors, audiences and students to come into contact with it. Having introduced Uruguayan theatre into drama workshops, translation events, university teaching and theatre festivals, I have found that its relatively unknown status can be an advantage. It has meant that students, audiences and actors have often approached the plays openly and without making prior assumptions. They have frequently been surprised and fascinated by the questions provoked, the different theatrical styles and the connections to their own experiences in the UK. This study demonstrates how playwrights employ a range of techniques to engage with questions and issues affecting societies at both national and international levels. They achieve this in a variety of different ways: by using stories which originate outside Uruguay to reflect on local issues and challenges; by depicting intergenerational conflicts to question the personal and political legacy one leaves behind; by questioning the challenges of progress and the ways in which this transforms society. Through a detailed analysis of these features, I will demonstrate the international appeal of the six plays studied in this book.

This book focusses primarily on plays written in the period between 1957 and 2008 and examines a diverse range of theatre narratives which, I argue, are relevant to an audience in the UK, even though several of the playwrights included are not widely known there. The capacity of these plays to speak to audiences in the UK will be examined through an analysis of the process undertaken to present performances and rehearsed readings of English translations of three of the plays analysed in this book; two of these were my translations and are included in the book. Another of the plays that I study and translate in this book was developed through a series of workshops with youth theatre actors and details of the process of sharing the play are included in Chapter 1. Translation, both as a practice and a mode of analysis, is at the heart of each of the chapters that follows. I examine Uruguayan national theatre through a lens of translation for performance and propose a translation process which provides a framework for understanding theatre produced in a particular place, its cultural roots and references. The series of analyses undertaken means that the translator develops an in-depth knowledge of the play. This knowledge of the play's foundations, its cultural and historical context, and an awareness of where the voices in the play speak from is precisely what can enable it to become mobile and traverse national borders. The translator activates this knowledge to establish links with the target cultural context so that a play can be developed for performance in a new place, for a new audience. Through a detailed analysis of six plays, this study explores methodologies for creating new dramatic texts for the stage and includes full stage-ready translations of three of the plays. These translations have been through a long process of analysis, scholarly research and testing in a variety of forums: at table reads, in workshops with students and actors, in university seminars. All of the translations presented here have been tested in front of an audience.

My translation research and practice in London is the starting point for this book and so this constitutes the target context in the translation process. During the period of research and writing, beginning in 2012, Uruguayan theatre has gained an increased profile in the UK and this book provides the first extended study dedicated exclusively to Uruguayan theatre in English. This work has taken place at an interesting and challenging time of political change, marked on a national level by the referendum on the UK's membership of the European Union in 2016 and the resulting negotiations, leadership changes, conflicts, questions and protests to which this has given rise. It is not my intention to explore matters relating to the referendum in detail but where they relate to the themes of the plays studied, particularly in Chapter 5, I will make reference to aspects of the Brexit topic. At this introductory stage, I want to acknowledge that the vote which resulted in a decision to leave the EU and the following public reactions seem to indicate significant shifts in the way in which UK citizens view their relationship to others and their expectations around issues of diversity and integration in local and global communities. Running in parallel to this, there seems to be an increased awareness of and willingness to engage with voices, perspectives and ideas from elsewhere, to learn from narratives which originated in other countries and to see how they can shed light on our own situation. This is evident in the presence of theatre in translation on stage in London. There are several theatre companies such as Foreign Affairs, Global Voices and Legal Aliens which focus primarily on developing and creating international work.[3]

International theatre is present in the programmes of theatres in London such as the Gate Theatre, Royal Court, Orange Tree Theatre, KILN and Arcola Theatre, many of which have a long history of showcasing plays from across the world, including and sometimes focussing on work from Spain and Latin America. A growing interest in Spanish-language theatre in translation is demonstrated by the work of festivals such as Out of the Wings and CASA Latin American Theatre Festival, as well as the New Spanish Playwriting Season at the Cervantes Theatre. These festivals take place at a range of emerging and established theatres and may move from year to year. For example, in 2017 CASA Latin American Theatre Festival had two key venues, Arcola Theatre and Southwark Playhouse; in 2019 Out of the Wings Festival expanded its programme and took place at Omnibus Theatre in Clapham, following two years at the Cervantes Theatre in Southwark. This range of venues enables works to reach new audiences and local communities. In many cases, Uruguayan theatre in London has been part of festivals showcasing specifically Latin American theatre and works have been presented in the form of rehearsed readings as well as full performances. *Thebes Land* by Franco-Uruguayan playwright Sergio Blanco, based on a literal translation by Rob Cavazos, adapted and directed by Daniel Goldman, had two successful runs at Arcola Theatre in London in 2016 and 2017.[4] The second run was part of the CASA Festival; Goldman was Artistic Director of CASA at the time. This second run created an opportunity for rehearsed readings of other Latin American plays in translation at Arcola Theatre and Southwark Playhouse. These readings included (amongst others): *Pig Woman* by Argentine dramatist Santiago Loza and *Weathered* by Abel González Melo (Cuba), both translated by William Gregory; *Noise* by Peruvian author Mariana de Althaus, translated by Mary Ann Vargas; *Namíbia, Não! (I Can't Breathe!)* by Brazilian author Aldri Anunciação, translated by Almiro Andrade; and my translation of *Dancing Alone Every Night* by Raquel Diana (both *Noise* and *Dancing Alone Every Night* had previously been showcased at the Out of the Wings inaugural week of play readings at King's College London in 2016).

As in the case of *Dancing Alone Every Night*, some of these rehearsed readings came about through my initiative in proposing the plays included in this book as part of festival programmes. There is a constant connection between my work within the university and collaborations with practitioners and institutions outside the academy. These partnerships have enabled me to develop work which tests the translated texts in new ways, with directors, actors and audiences; this collaborative work generates a new set of questions and insights. The links between scholarship, practice and performance are central to my work on theatre translation. These fundamental connections underpin the format of this book which consists of three chapters of analysis, with each one focussing on two Uruguayan plays, to illuminate a particular aspect of the translation process (Chapters 1, 3 and 5). Following each of these chapters, one of the plays studied is included as a full-length stage-ready translation (Chapters 2, 4 and 6). The analytical chapters explore the types of reading and research carried out to be able to understand the original as a piece for performance and create a new text in the target language. They also illustrate the working partnerships that I have developed as well as the various roles that I have undertaken and activities that I have participated in as part of Uruguayan theatre productions. Beyond the role of translator, I've taken part in rehearsals as a Script Consultant, in post-show discussions in dialogue with theatre practitioners and I have facilitated theatre translation workshops.

Below I list readings and productions of Uruguayan plays which have taken place in London between 2016 and 2020. I have done my utmost to avoid omissions but there may be some, particularly in the case of readings or short runs where (in some cases) information about these is not archived. The list below is revealing as it indicates the repeated presence of certain authors and translators, the work of certain festivals and, in many cases, collaborations between academics and theatre companies. Of the Uruguayan dramatists included, many of them have had plays performed in other European countries and some of them reside or have resided in Europe: Denise Despeyroux in Spain, Sergio Blanco in France and Mario Benedetti in Spain. Uruguayan authors have also participated in the Royal Court International

Playwrights programme and taken part in workshops hosted by the Royal Court in Latin America; these initiatives were started by the late Elyse Dodgson, who co-founded the theatre's International Department and led its work for over twenty years. Contemporary Uruguayan playwrights Mariana Percovich and Gabriel Calderón have previously undertaken writing residences at the Royal Court.

Between 2016 and 2020, Uruguayan theatre has appeared on London stages as follows:

The Rage of Narcissus by Sergio Blanco, translated and directed by Daniel Goldman. Full production at the Pleasance Theatre, 2020. The text was published by Oberon Books in 2020.

Her Open Eyes by Raquel Diana, translated by Sophie Stevens, Out of the Wings Festival, Omnibus Theatre, 2019. Rehearsed reading directed by Fran Olivares. The translation was published in *The Mercurian: A Theatrical Translation Review* (8) in 2020.

The Reality by Denise Despeyroux, translated by Sarah Maitland, New Spanish Playwriting Season, Cervantes Theatre, 2019. Full production directed by Raymi Ortuse Quiroga. The text was published by Ediciones Antígona in 2019.

Thebes Land by Sergio Blanco, translated by Daniel Goldman from a literal translation by Rob Cavazos. Full production directed by Daniel Goldman, Arcola Theatre, 2016 and 2017. The text was published by Oberon Books in 2017.

Ready or Not by Estela Golovchenko, translated by Sophie Stevens, Out of the Wings Festival, Cervantes Theatre, 2017. Rehearsed reading directed by Camila Ymay González.

Dancing Alone Every Night by Raquel Diana, translated by Sophie Stevens, Out of the Wings Festival, King's College London, 2016 and CASA Latin American Theatre Festival, Southwark Playhouse, 2017. Both rehearsed readings directed by Camila Ymay González.

Pedro and the Captain by Mario Benedetti, translated by Adrianne Aron, The Vaults Festival, The Vaults Waterloo, 2016.[5] Full performance directed by Miguel Hernando Torres Umba.

Black Tenderness: The Passion of Mary Stuart, by Denise Despeyroux, translated by Simon Breden, Gate Theatre, 2016. Rehearsed reading directed by Tara Robinson. The text was published by Cue Press in 2017, edited and with an introduction by Margherita Laera.[6]

In the case of *Pedro and the Captain*, my role was Script Consultant and the work was similar to that of a dramaturge in that it involved explaining and contextualising the dramatic text and providing supplementary materials to support the work of the director and actors. It also involved working as part of a team to adapt aspects of the vocabulary of the script for an audience in the UK, with permission from Adrianne Aron. This work on a range of productions has created the opportunity to be in the rehearsal room for some or all of the time and this is always an enriching experience which, I believe, creates richer productions. For the Out of the Wings readings, this is standard practice, and where possible the translator participates throughout the rehearsal process. This is crucial because it allows for dialogue and exchange which increases awareness of the different roles played by translators, directors, actors and designers, as well as the intersections between each one. The types of analysis carried out in the translation process, and detailed in this book, prepared and equipped me for these discussions taking place in the rehearsal room, whether I was there as translator, dramaturge or acting on behalf of the author of the original (or a mixture of all three). These processes and experiences support one another because the experience of working with actors in workshops, table reads and rehearsals constantly feeds into my translation methodology. This means that the questions that they ask, the discussions that we have, and the types of negotiations that we explore as the text moves into the new context and is embodied by actors all inform and are incorporated into my own translation practice.

What This Book Proposes

This book proposes a framework of translation for performance which poses a set of questions and analyses that simultaneously and productively enable us to engage with both the rootedness and possible mobility of the dramatic text. These key questions focus on understanding the Uruguayan dramatic text as a text to be translated for performance. This mode of analysis places the source and target cultures and contexts in dialogue through an investigation of the relation of the play's place of origin to the new site of production. Therefore, it is a contextualised understanding of Uruguayan theatre which illuminates its international appeal. The chapters that follow demonstrate the types of research undertaken within this framework of translation for performance and the subsequent creative and critical responses that this generates from translators: the research process equips them to move the dramatic text into a new context and develop it for a new audience. It also equips them to explore and critique the original dramatic text and provide new readings of it which can lead to new scholarly research. This is particularly important in the case of plays where there is little existing scholarship, as in the case of many of those included in this study. It equips translators to take on roles as mediators, negotiators, instructors and advisors and thus enables them to support practitioners in developing plays for performance. Whilst this study focusses on Uruguayan theatre, the methodologies outlined in the framework of translation for performance can be applied to unlock new critical responses to and translations of theatre originating in other countries and languages.

The translation processes illustrated in this book demonstrate how the translator can work to identify a translation strategy for a particular text through a process of analysis and dialogue with the text. The selection of the approach to take is based on the processes of close reading, analysing the text in the original language and making connections to the target culture. These processes of reading and research undertaken to understand the dramatic text, often whilst the translator is based in the target context, constitute an interpretative act. This series of analyses enlivens the translation strategy. This book examines examples of how the analysis of the dramatic text for translation involves creating links across literary, translation and theatre scholarship as well as tracing links between concepts which arise both thematically and dramatically within the dramatic text. It explores, proposes and conceptualises methodologies for maintaining these links in the translated text. For each of the plays included as full translations, the translation strategy was not fixed but emerged from the study of the play itself. The analysis discusses how these strategies were identified and proposes methodologies which could be applied in the process of translating other dramatic texts, moving from and into other contexts.

The translator undertakes a series of tasks as 'intercultural informant',[7] dramaturge and author for the stage and this enables them to adopt a creative approach to the translation process. This creativity hinges, in part, on an awareness of and engagement with the writerly processes undertaken by the playwright, rather than any kind of original intention, which cannot be accessed or unlocked from within the text. Translation is always an interpretative act, based on the close reading and analysis of the dramatic text. This places the translator in constant dialogue with the text through a process of 'bombard[ing] it with questions'.[8] The translator uses a range of techniques and strategies to create a new performable play in the target language. This creative work is grounded in a critical understanding of where the text is from and the network of characters, conflicts and crises that arise from the dramatic text. At the same time, they identify the aspects of the dramatic text which resist connection, pose a challenge to the text's mobility and to its ability to establish contact with a new audience. This book proposes that familiar and remote cultural encounters can occur within one translated play and that cultural differences do not have to be erased entirely in order for a performable dramatic text to exist in a new language and cultural context. It examines strategies for enabling the audience to engage with both aspects of the play and to experience it 'in the blend'; both recognising themselves and something new and beyond themselves in the translated play.[9] It explores how the choice of language and development of characters within the translated play can assist the actors and audience in navigating these different aspects of the play so that it does not become fragmented and inconsistent but rather enables the audience to engage with it in multiple ways.

This book introduces Uruguayan plays and playwrights with international appeal to an English-speaking audience. By presenting analysis and translations within one study, it seeks to emphasise the role of translation practice as part of academic scholarship. It enables a rich engagement with these dramatic texts, their multiplicity, their relevance, the challenges they pose and the possible solutions they ask us to consider. It is my intention that, now they are available, the full translations of these plays should contribute to the work of scholars, students, practitioners, teachers, actors and directors with a range of experiences of translation for the stage. I hope that this might lead to future productions and that these new translations pave the way for these plays to be used in new and exciting ways.

Theatre Translation Theory and Practice

The framework for translation for performance that I propose begins with close reading based on the methodology posited by Patrice Pavis. This close reading entails dramaturgical and contextual analyses that underpin the translation process as well as a creative imagining and projection of the text to be performed within the target context. Pavis outlines preverbal and verbal phases in the creation of a new dramatic text in the target language. By delineating a preverbal stage, Pavis emphasises the work that the translator undertakes before writing the new dramatic text, which takes place in the verbal stage.[10] I demonstrate this work in practice and specify the types of analysis that it involves. The idea of the preverbal is useful in that it outlines a stage in the process which centres on the dramatic text as generating a range of instructions, networks, images and concepts that the translator identifies and works with throughout the translation process. Pavis aligns the process of the translator with that of the playwright and stresses that the preverbal phase crystallises the translator's work through a close engagement with the dramatic text, rather than with the intention of the author of the original. As David Johnston states, the 'translator works to a "theatrics" (by analogy with "poetics") at whose heart is the performability of the text', thus the process articulated by Pavis requires an engagement with the text as a text to be performed.[11] Pavis states that the translator first and foremost carries out a dramaturgical analysis of the play to be translated, which involves identifying the macro-structure of the play in order to understand the 'fiction conveyed by the text'.[12] This involves 'a coherent reading of the plot as well as the spatiotemporal indications contained in the text'.[13] This dramaturgical process begins with an analysis of the macro-structure but then necessarily entails an examination of the micro-structures and how these relate to the 'dramatic core' of the text, the macro-structure which holds the text together as the 'architecture of the piece'.[14] The core creates a trajectory for the drama and signals key themes and concepts which link the elements of the micro-structure.

Through a process of 'bombard[ing] it with questions', the translator enters into a dynamic dialogue with the text. This dialogue obliges them to engage with aspects of the text that are not intended to be spoken but which provide instruction to those creating the mise-en-scène.[15] This part of the process, as outlined by Pavis, places emphasis on the fact that the object of the written dramatic text constitutes one element of the final performance. The preverbal creates a space prior to the writing of the new dramatic text in the target language in which the translator engages with, visualises and pays particular attention to the essential instructions and indications for a mise-en-scène included in the dramatic text. The methodology proposed in this book adopts Pavis's approach as a way to underscore the significance of an awareness of the dramatic text as a text to be performed and it demonstrates how this awareness informs and enhances the translation process. Pavis proposes that as part of the dramaturgical analysis, the translator creates a preverbal image and that '[i]n this ante-textual magma, gesture and text coexist in an as yet undifferentiated way'.[16] What the translator imagines is one of many possible future performances. This is a projection, imagining or conceptualising of the way in which the text provides the basis for a mise-en-scène. The preverbal image encapsulates the multiplicity of elements present in the theatrical mise-en-scène. Within the eventual mise-en-scène in the target language and context, the translated text constitutes just one of the elements of the sign system of the stage. Whether or not the translator identifies with Pavis's idea of the projected image, what is essential in this part of the process is the in-depth understanding of the play-text as a text to be performed and the way in which it creates a 'a vision of life, a working model or paradigm of living rather than a simple reflection of it', constructed through a specific stage language which emerges from the cultural context and which can be transformed for the target context.[17]

The translator's work will always be based on an interpretation of the dramatic text. This is because there are no 'inherent fixed readings' and each text will contain a certain multiplicity.[18] Texts rarely say or speak about just one thing and it is important for the translator to be aware of this multiplicity in the translation process. Their interpretation of the dramatic text is informed by a rigorous process of analysis, which includes dramaturgical and contextual analyses. These oblige the translator to ask the questions: what is at stake in the dramatic text? What was at stake in the original context? The research that they undertake to answer these questions alerts them to the multiplicity within the original dramatic text whilst also enabling them to establish a framework of concepts and references in which to do their work. The research carried out equips them to identify the scope of the text, the emphasis it places on certain themes or ideas, and the functions of the different characters and events. This informs the translator's decisions as they work to 'rehearse and reassess, to reassemble and redress' the options available to them in the target language.[19] To understand further the interplay between the micro- and macro-structures, the interconnectedness of the multiple voices within the dramatic text, and how they affect the translator's work, the idea of the text functioning as a network is productive. For Barthes, 'the metaphor of the Text is that of the network'.[20] He suggests that the text defers the signified by constantly generating signifiers through 'a serial movement of disconnections, overlappings, variations'.[21] Rather than emphasising a network of meanings, Barthes's idea places emphasis on the series of connections, allusions and references that the text makes. Through the process of analysis, the translator works to identify how this network of interconnecting ideas, references and themes functions in the original text. This provides a basis for them to establish a meaning-generating network in which to work as they translate into the target language. The idea of the network demonstrates the links and connections within the text and the scope of meanings that it entails, the possibilities that it opens up and those which it restricts. The network reinforces the symbiotic relationship between the micro- and macro-structures of the dramatic text. It is essential to underscore that this network does not create vagueness or looseness; it does not mean that the translator can choose any word or forever defer their choice. Rather, by working to analyse and understand the source text as a network, the translator creates a network of references in the target language, based on the scope of possible meanings of the original, and this acts as a framework for their translation. They constantly engage with this framework to inform their choices throughout the translation process. They work to create a coherence within the logic, narrative and paradigm of the text itself.

Identifying and analysing the network of signifiers and the scope of the referents in the dramatic text is an essential part of the process of inhabiting the world of the text and understanding how the series of semantic fields, allusions, resonances and discourses interact with one another. Where there might be multiple possibilities, the task of the translator is to choose the one that will allow that network of meaning to be recreated in the target situation. The analysis which follows demonstrates that this concept of the network is particularly productive when making translation decisions where particular words or phrases are used to create connections across the text. It can help us visualise these connections and reflect on the significance of echoes from one part of the text in another which may be repeated by one character, in response to a recurring situation or as a way to link two moments in the text. This network can also be fruitful when faced with a challenging aspect of the translation, where a phrase or word in the original evokes multiple referents or ideas which cannot be captured in the same way in one word in the target language. By viewing the text as an interconnected web of signifiers, and seeking to replicate this in the target language, we are able to reconcile that what cannot be captured in the translation of one particular phrase may be captured at another point in the translation of the play. Another phrase or word may be able to do the work of capturing that meaning, resonance or idea at a different moment so it is still present and forms part of network of the play.

The dramatic text is a construct. It is a stage version of the reality about which it speaks and with which it interacts; it can reflect, critique and reveal aspects of the situation, culture or place that it depicts. In order to conceptualise and explore the work that the play does, I draw on Antoine Vitez's ideas of the concept of the stage as laboratory which provides a forum in which accepted norms can be tested. Vitez states that:

> Society knows more or less clearly that in these edifices we call theatres people work for hours on end in order to increase, purify and transform the actions and intonations of everyday life, also to question them, bring them to crisis point.[22]

Vitez presents the stage as a space for discovery. The stage may represent the language and actions of a particular nation through parody, comedy or folklore, to cite some of the examples of texts that I will examine in this book, but it always acts as a laboratory which reveals, uncovers and explores multiple aspects of the experiences portrayed. Vitez asserts that the stage does much more than represent; it goes beyond this to challenge, to question and to put these actions to the test. The stage is therefore a site of investigation; it is a space for experimentation, testing boundaries and for production. From this experimentation, new possibilities, questions and discourses can arise. If we consider the stage as laboratory in relation to the dramatic text in translation, in reference to the play brought into the new cultural and linguistic context, then the impact of increasing, purifying and transforming 'actions and intonations of everyday life' is potentially greatly increased.[23] How can a translated play serve to question the everyday reality of the target context? What insight can the play provide into the original culture? Are the language and actions presented in the theatrical laboratory a demonstration of the source culture and presented in the new context as a revelatory insight into a distant culture? Or are they in fact appropriated in some way through the actors in the new cultural context and through the script in the target language to challenge the language and actions *in* that new context? The stage is a space in which the dramatic texts from other cultures are brought to life and are scrutinised by the audience. But, significantly, the play is also able to put the audience to the test, to shed light on uncomfortable aspects of society and to create social and political repercussions. The resonances of the play in the original language are therefore extended but also transformed and renewed: the translation and its staging in the new context necessarily modifies the original and so constitutes its afterlife.

This book will illustrate how the dramaturgical analysis, research and process of creative imaginings enable the translator to extend the resonances of the original text without severing all contact with it. Throughout this study, this part of the process will be referred to as establishing 'points of contact' with the original dramatic text and its cultural context. A link between a play written in another language and the context in which the translator works may be what motivates them to translate it in the first place. They might identify a link in the way, for example, a political struggle is portrayed, a contemporary issue such as isolation, immigration or women's rights is treated, or the way in which a character disrupts the status quo. The initial stage of the dramaturgical analysis, which allows a creative imagining of the text in the target language and situation, involves exploring how these points of contact can be established so that the dramatic text can become mobile and move into the target language and context. At the same time, this contact reveals how difference and distance open up between the two texts and contexts. Just as one idea enables a sense of proximity to be established, another will reveal distance and difference and both of these will form part of the translation process. Jean-Luc Nancy's conceptualisation of touch as establishing contact between two entities whilst recognising a distance in between will be employed to theorise and articulate this aspect of the process in which closeness can simultaneously reveal difference.[24] In this way, I argue that translation can be transformative as it enables audiences to encounter both the familiar and a sense of difference through experiencing a play originally written in another language in translation. Nancy's theory enables us to specify how translation is not a process of absorbing, assimilating, penetrating or modifying a cultural product, in this case a Uruguayan play, but rather it is about facilitating a sense of proximity which allows a dialogue to occur through the process and performance of the translated play. This study will demonstrate the ways in which the dialogue occurs and how this enables familiar and distant cultural realities, points of reference and concepts to coexist.

The translation into the target language is the first part of a series of 'collective hermeneutic acts', which constitutes the process of preparing the text for performance in the new context.[25] Unless commissioned to work on a particular project, for a specific production, translators will translate a dramatic text to create the possibility of any number of future performances. The creative teams of these future productions will then bring their own interpretations to bear on the dramatic text. Awareness of multiplicity in terms of the multiple readings, interpretations and processes that the translated text will go through as it is prepared for performance is important for the translator's work. The dramaturgical and contextual analyses enable the translator to fulfil the roles of dramaturge in the rehearsal room, to articulate the possibilities and to explore them with actors and collaborators. This creates a symbiotic relationship between the research process and the rehearsal room. By conducting the dramaturgical analysis, the translator is already projecting, conceiving and imagining the play in performance. The range of research and the multiple revisions of the text created as part of the process of creating a performable translation equip them to explore, explain and articulate the contextual research and analysis within the rehearsal room. At the same time, those experiences of working collaboratively with actors, of trying and testing through table reads and workshops, as well as rehearsals, enable the translator to develop an awareness of the questions posed by actors, directors, technicians and theatre practitioners. These experiences and exposure to the type of questions asked by creative teams then feed into the translator's future work as they carry out the dramaturgical analysis. We can productively think of translators and creative teams as practitioners who move into the text. I demonstrate how Aaltonen's ideas of these teams as 'tenants' who temporarily occupy the text and interact with the 'sediment' left behind by the previous occupants allows us to conceptualise how we work with a text that simultaneously speaks of a situation in a different context which has gone before as well as speaking for the here and now.[26] The translator, actors and directors work to transform the play for a new audience but this does not mean that it cannot maintain resonances and references from the original context. I argue that by creating a robust stage language, the translator is able to open up a possibility for the audience to experience the translated play in 'the blend'.[27] This allows them experience the play as multiple and as containing multiple voices which, within one performance, can provoke the audience to step back and see the piece as representing otherness whilst also being drawn into it and seeing themselves.

An Analysis of Six Uruguayan Plays

The analysis of each of the plays studied in this book provides an insight into the different stages of the theatre translation process and draws on the theoretical concepts already outlined. The six plays studied are: *M'hijo el dotor* [*My Son the Doc*] by Florencio Sánchez (1903); *La biblioteca* [*The Library*] by Carlos Maggi (1957); *Pedro y el capitán* [*Pedro and the Captain*] by Mario Benedetti (1979); *El Herrero y la Muerte* [*Death and the Blacksmith*] by Mercedes Rein and Jorge Curi (1979); *Punto y coma* [*Ready or Not*] by Estela Golovchenko (2003) and *Bailando sola cada noche* [*Dancing Alone Every Night*] by Raquel Diana (2008).[28] I demonstrate how the thematic and theoretical are linked in order to show how, for each of the plays, a translation strategy informed by translation theory emerged as a result of the in-depth analysis of the original play. The objective is to identify strategies, techniques and approaches that can be adopted by other translators. This study does not seek to compare the plays but to place them in dialogue with one another. It discusses the connecting themes, concepts and questions which link them to a Uruguayan theatre tradition whilst also enabling them to become mobile through translation. Therefore, the two plays written since the year 2000 have each been placed in dialogue with a play written before the year 2000, and two plays written in the same year are studied in different chapters. This creates a dialogue across time and demonstrates how the process of translation can be used to understand a range of texts.

This book takes as a starting point a theatre anthology published in two volumes by the Uruguayan Ministry of Education and Culture in 1988 and 1990 entitled *50 años de teatro uruguayo* [*50 Years of Uruguayan Theatre*].[29] These two volumes each contain eight plays which were all staged in Uruguay, including *La biblioteca* (vol. I, pp. 113–60) and *El Herrero y la Muerte* (vol. II, pp. 429–64). They celebrate Uruguayan playwrights and the dynamic range of plays produced in Uruguay in the period between 1933 and 1981. The significance of these dates should not be underestimated because the anthology was published shortly after the return to democracy in March 1985. Uruguay had experienced a repressive civic-military dictatorship beginning in June 1973 and citizens had been severely affected by the dictatorship in neighbouring Argentina (1976–83) where many Uruguayans were forcibly disappeared. The civic-military dictatorship entailed the curtailing of civil liberties, the banning of public meetings and the intense and violent interrogation of anyone who posed a threat to this regime. The dictatorship threatened artists and theatres that were seen to be aligned with the Communist Party and many theatre spaces were closed down and practitioners went into exile. A notable case is the independent producing theatre El Galpón founded in 1949 in Montevideo, which trained actors and directors and had a reputation for creating politically engaged work. In 1976 the theatre and its company were classified as illegal; the theatre's space was seized by the authorities and many of its members took refuge in the Mexican Embassy and then went into exile in Mexico where they continued to perform. They were able to return and reclaim their space following the re-establishment of democracy in Uruguay and the theatre still exists today.[30] The prologue to the two volumes of *50 años de teatro uruguayo* acknowledges this hiatus due to the dictatorship but asserts that dramatic creativity had begun to flourish once again in Uruguay. The prologue states that its objective is to re-launch the production of dramatic texts.[31] The plays included in *50 años de teatro uruguayo* trace key aspects of and influences upon the development of Uruguayan theatre, including the importance of the rural drama. Rural dramas were shaped in some ways by the Spanish *sainete* tradition, particularly in Sánchez's work, and depicted the challenges facing landowners as Uruguay modernised and people moved to the capital city. The anthology includes plays which adapt classic European narratives thus demonstrating how they were modified by Uruguayan playwrights.[32] It also includes several works by members of the *Generación del 45* or *Generación crítica*; a generation of authors who began writing around the year 1945 and who, through their work, reflected on, critiqued and produced satirical responses to the challenges facing Uruguayan society. This book studies six Uruguayan plays, including two from the anthology, in order to explore the following questions which underpin the analysis in Chapters 1, 3 and 5: if the aim of the anthology was to celebrate and promote national theatre then how did Uruguayan theatre continue to develop and were there trends and traces that linked these plays to contemporary works?

Chapter 1 demonstrates close reading informed by the dramaturgical and contextual analysis of the dramatic text as the essential first step in the process of translation for performance. It shows in practice how the question 'what is at stake in the dramatic text?' guides a critical analysis which enables the translator to identify the micro- and macro-structures of the play and how these are interconnected. It demonstrates how the translator expands the scope of the question to explore what was at stake in the source context at the time when the play was written. The chapter argues that a detailed understanding of the source culture is precisely what enables the text to become mobile because this equips the translator to embark upon a process of forming links between source and target cultures, an idea which will be explored in Chapter 3. Through the dramaturgical analysis, which is enhanced by knowledge of the cultural history of the source culture, the translator understands the scope of possible meanings generated by the text: the ideas, references and character relationships which create the network of the text. Emphasis is therefore placed on 'meaning as becoming [which] makes the translation of that text a performative constituent of the mise-en-scène'.[33] In order to demonstrate this process, Chapter 1 analyses *M'hijo el dotor* by Florencio Sánchez and *La biblioteca* by Carlos Maggi to interrogate two plays which deal with themes of progress, work ethic and the value of public service. Both of these plays take place over three acts and I show how analysing of the structure of the plays, including the passage of time, is particularly useful in illuminating the series of dramaturgical and contextual analyses.

Sánchez's movement between the two capital cities of Montevideo and Buenos Aires, as well as the themes he addresses, places his work within the tradition of *Teatro rioplatense* (theatre created in the region surrounding the Río de la Plata [River Plate], primarily in Montevideo and Buenos Aires; the river, or estuary, runs between Argentina and Uruguay forming part of the border and opens into the Atlantic Ocean). Scholar Griselda Castro states that this shared theatre tradition is where we can begin to trace the origins of Uruguayan national theatre.[34] It is for this reason that Sánchez's work is included in this study. *M'hijo el dotor* is less studied than *Barranca Abajo* [*Downhill*] (1905), probably Sánchez's most well-known play, but the two share some key themes. *M'hijo el dotor* explores the tensions that arise when a man moves from his parents' ranch to pursue studies in Montevideo. The play traces the conflicts that arise as ideologies, ways of earning a living and moral behaviours are called into question. The second play, *La biblioteca*, follows the lives of the employees of Montevideo's national library as they undertake the endless project of reducing the size of the library to allow for it to be demolished in stages. The intention is that this will pave the way for the construction of a new library building on the same site. The proposed modern, technologically sophisticated and spacious library also promises to create new opportunities for the employees. My analysis will demonstrate how the relationship between the library building and the library employees is at the core of the play; as this relationship extends and intensifies over a period of twenty-five years, they become increasingly dependent on one another. The result is a satirical play which critiques the stagnant state of public service and the disregard for cultural projects. This indicates a broader critique of the importance of funding for arts and culture in society. *La biblioteca* hints at the type of unrest, disquiet and dissatisfaction which preceded the collapse of democracy in Uruguay.

Chapter 2, *The Library*, is a full translation of this play. *La biblioteca* has previously been translated into English by William Oliver in the US but this is the first translation for an audience in the UK.[35] I had the opportunity to develop this translation through table reads with colleagues and actors from the Out of the Wings Collective, and through a series of workshops with young actors at the Arcola Youth Theatre. These workshops were developed in partnership with a theatre practitioner and were supported by the Collaborative Innovation Scheme for Early Career Researchers funded by the Cultural Institute at King's College London.[36] The workshops particularly revealed the significance of the library building and how it becomes like another character within the play. This informed my understanding of the relationship that the employees have with the building. Both the workshops and readings enabled me to explore and discuss how the play makes connections to the target context of the UK and how the themes and ideas, particularly relating to bureaucracy, resonate with a London audience; these experiences informed the choices in my English translation.

Chapter 3 specifies how the translator engages in a process of establishing points of contact between source and target cultures to identify the links which enable the play to move across into the UK target context. It illustrates this process by developing the ideas of Jean-Luc Nancy on touch in order to specify how theatre translate translation instigates a relationship between two texts and cultures; this relationship entails both a sense of distance and proximity. The chapter explores strategies for analysing this relationship between cultures and maintaining a sense of close and distant cultural realities in the translated text. It investigates the concept of afterlife both thematically and conceptually to propose a strategy for the translation of *Pedro y el capitán* and *Bailando sola cada noche*. Both plays place characters in liminal zones as they experience a type of afterlife. The chapter examines how the uniqueness of these unknown spaces can pave the way for developing a translation strategy which focusses on the idea of extension (after Benjamin).[37] By placing the characters at the limits of known human experience, the playwrights challenge preconceived ideas to portray both familiar and remote experiences and this creates possibilities for the translator and translated text to do the same. The plays analysed in this chapter demonstrate how, through theatre, we can enter into worlds which test our understanding and provoke us to ask: what if this were happening right now?

Pedro y el capitán deals explicitly with the horror of the civic-military dictatorship by placing an encounter between an interrogator and a political prisoner centre stage; they engage in a long and destructive dialogue over several encounters as the play is divided into four parts. *Pedro y el capitán* received an award from Amnesty International for raising awareness of human rights violations. Benedetti was a member of the *Generación crítica* and one of Uruguay's best-known authors, although he is more renowned for his prose and poetry. He went into exile during the civic-military dictatorship and wrote *Pedro y el capitán* in Cuba after hearing stories of the experiences of human rights violations occurring in Uruguay and throughout Latin America.

Benedetti's awareness that the experiences of interrogation and torture represented in the play created connections between Uruguay and other Latin American countries was significant because the civic-military dictatorship experienced between 1973 and 1985 in Uruguay was not an isolated case in the region. At a similar time, repressive regimes also seized power in the neighbouring countries of Brazil (1964), Chile (1973) and Argentina (1976). The respective regimes identified citizens who posed a threat to the type of society that they sought to create and applied violent measures as a way to maintain order. These included abduction, torture, imprisonment, assassination and disappearance (the latter usually involved one or more of the aforementioned types of violence and meant the victim could not be located). In Uruguay it was those affiliated with the Communist Party and the left-wing urban guerrilla group Movimiento de Liberación Nacional — Tupamaros, often referred to as Tupamaros, who were initially identified as subversives, but this category was later expanded to encompass a broader spectrum of society. Plan Cóndor or Operación Cóndor [Operation Condor] expanded the territory in which subversives could be targeted by facilitating violent repression across the national borders of Uruguay, Argentina, Chile, Brazil, Paraguay, Bolivia and later Peru and Ecuador.[38] *Pedro y el capitán* has been performed throughout the world and was staged in English (as *Pedro and the Captain*) in London in 2016, directed by Miguel Hernando Torres Umba as part of the Vaults Festival. My role as Script Consultant will illustrate how the scholarly and dramaturgical analyses I carried out enabled me to work on developing the script for an audience in London and enabled the actors to understand the context in which it was created.

Bailando sola cada noche takes as a starting point the story of a woman who died alone in London in 2006. The real Joyce Vincent (also the name of the protagonist) was discovered in her flat in Wood Green, north London, two years after her death and surrounded by Christmas gifts. Raquel Diana imagines and dramatises Joyce's death by ascribing actions, gestures, words and songs to the period of time between her death and the discovery of her corpse. Some aspects of the experience of the protagonist coincide with the story of the real Joyce Vincent, in particular that both women experience domestic violence. Both Benedetti and Diana take inspiration from situations occurring elsewhere; if these stories originate elsewhere then how might the Uruguayan audience connect with them and how, through translation, might an audience in London engage with them? Chapter 3 explores the significance of these distances between contexts and refutes the idea that this leads to the creation of a universal dramatic text. It will demonstrate how the interplay between distance and proximity present in the original Spanish can be transferred into the English translation to provide an insight into familiar and unfamiliar cultural contexts. It proposes that if we understand and work creatively with the concept of afterlife as a 'productive opening of meaning' then this allows the questions posed by and through the original dramatic text to be transformed for the target context, generate new meanings and interact with specific discourses in the UK.[39]

Chapter 4, *Dancing Alone Every Night*, is a full translation of this play which has been presented as a rehearsed reading at the Out of the Wings Festival (2016) and the CASA Latin American Theatre Festival (2017). Both readings were directed by Camila Ymay González.

Chapter 5 addresses two distinct styles of theatre narrative: the folkloric and the flashback. Through a detailed analysis of *El Herrero y la Muerte* and *Punto y coma*, it demonstrates how the theatre translator develops an understanding of forms of theatre which draw on particular cultural, historical and literary traditions. It illustrates how close attention to the ways in which these theatre narratives are created can inform and enhance the translation process, enabling the theatre narratives to become a creative tool to reach new audiences. This chapter will argue that the imagined encounters presented in these plays use the theatre stage as a site of resistance where everyday life reaches a 'crisis point'.[40] *El Herrero y la Muerte* is one of just two plays in the anthology *50 años de teatro uruguayo* written by a woman; Rein co-wrote the play with Jorge Curi.[41] It is a dramatic representation and adaptation of a legend about an encounter between Jesus and a humble blacksmith, which results in the latter being granted three wishes. It is based on Chapter 21 of the Argentine novel *Don Segundo Sombra* (1926) by Ricardo Güiraldes. In the play, the blacksmith skilfully employs his wishes to outsmart his neighbours, the local authorities and even Death, disrupting heavenly and earthly order as he makes simple requests in order to keep his humble patch of land. Performed over 500 times during the dictatorship period, the play communicated a message about integrity, resilience and humble forms of resistance at a time when public gatherings and the exchanging of ideas were banned.

Punto y coma depicts an encounter between a father and daughter who were estranged during the Uruguayan civic-military dictatorship. Their meeting takes place in the Palacio Legislativo, the Uruguayan parliament, because the character of the father is now a Senator, having adopted a political role in the newly formed democracy. The play therefore deals with the challenges of the transition to democracy and reintegration into society. These were important issues in Uruguay, particularly because during the dictatorship period it had the highest number of political prisoners per capita of any country in the world.[42] This meant that, following the return to democracy, there was a question as to how former prisoners might find a place in society. The intense 'reunion' in the play is disrupted by flashbacks to the woman as a young girl in hiding with her mother. As the characters recount their stories and experiences, filling in the gaps for one another, the play highlights the pernicious effect of silencing these stories and the significance of dialogue around memory and past experiences. It therefore actively poses a challenge to the silence and impunity surrounding human rights violations committed during the dictatorship and perpetuated by the introduction of the Ley de Caducidad de la Pretensión Punitiva del Estado [Law of Expiration of Punitive Claims of the State]. Introduced in 1986 by President Julio María Sanguinetti in response to the increasing number of reports of cases of human rights violations in the aftermath of the dictatorship, the law was a way to maintain peace and avoid unrest in the military by restricting possibilities within society and the judicial system of holding military and police officers accountable for these crimes. Written in 2003, at a time when there seemed to be a shift in attitudes towards the memory of the dictatorship period, at both personal and political levels, Golovchenko uses flashbacks as a way to demonstrate these gaps in memory formally as well as to illustrate how past and present are intertwined. She creates a dramatic narrative and a stage language which enable the actor and the audience to make these connections and to move between past and present.

Chapter 6, *Ready or Not*, is a full English translation of this play which was presented as a rehearsed reading at the Out of the Wings Festival at the Cervantes Theatre, Southwark, London in 2017 and directed by Camila Ymay González. In terms of the scope of this study, Golovchenko's work is significant as she is one of just two Uruguayan women playwrights who are based outside the capital city Montevideo.[43] Golovchenko is a playwright, teacher, and co-director of the Teatro Sin Fogón company in Fray Bentos (a city in the west of Uruguay). Between 2015 and 2020 she was Director of Culture for the Departamento de Río Negro, one of the nineteen provinces into which Uruguay is divided.

The study of Uruguayan theatre in motion, through translation, allows for a creative way of engaging with and understanding national theatre. For me, the processes of translating theatre, writing about those translation processes and writing about theatre are inseparable. This is, in part, because I started to do these three things at the same time as a graduate student, when I had the opportunity to engage with and participate in the research of the Arts and Humanities Research Council-funded Out of the Wings project.[44] The project began in 2008 and since 2015 the Out of the Wings Collective has continued this work by creating, reading and performing new plays in translation. This book demonstrates theatre translation research both as practice and in practice. It illustrates productive and creative partnerships between academics, academic institutions and theatre practitioners and reinforces the importance of these partnerships. This study provides new insights into the processes for developing performances of translated plays and it identifies considerations, collaborations and opportunities that have been instrumental in the sharing of plays in translation in London. I hope that these opportunities continue to exist and that more emerge as translated theatre gains an increased profile. My research and practice are always in dialogue with each other. Dialogue, both as a concept and as practice, is at the heart of my approach to theatre translation work. I understand that as a translator I am in constant dialogue with the dramatic text, which activates scholarly research and brings it into the dialogue to create new insights and paint a more detailed image of the text. This paves the way for a dialogue with a range of other interlocutors. These include actors and directors in workshops and rehearsals; students and scholars in seminars; playwrights in theatres and bars; audience members at performances of translations. The six plays included in this book provoke the investigation and articulation of questions and issues which are central to theatre translation. In specifying these questions, this book seeks to open a dialogue about Uruguayan theatre in translation which will involve students, researchers, practitioners and theatre-makers.

Notes to the Introduction

1. For a study of carnival theatre, including translations of *murgas* (satirical carnival shows), see Gustavo Remedi, *Carnival Theater: Uruguay's Popular Performers and National Culture*, trans. by Amy Ferlazzo (Minneapolis: University of Minnesota Press, 2004).
2. Raquel Diana, *Bailando sola cada noche*, *Dramaturgia Uruguaya*, (2008) <http://www.dramaturgiauruguaya.uy/obras/bailando-sola-toda-la-noche/> [accessed 17 September 2020]. On *Dramaturgia Uruguaya*, the link to the play is called 'Bailando sola toda la noche' but the text is entitled *Bailando sola cada noche* and Raquel Diana confirmed this to be the title in an interview on 30 October 2013. The text was published under the title *Bailando sola cada noche: comedia más bien negra y patética* (Montevideo: Yaugurú, 2013).
3. For more information see: *Foreign Affairs*, <http://www.foreignaffairs.org.uk/> [accessed 31 July 2021]; *Global Voices Theatre*, <https://globalvoicestheatre.com/> [accessed 31 July 2021]; *Legal Aliens Theatre*, <https://www.legalalienstheatre.com/> [accessed 31 July 2021].
4. Rob Cavazos is credited with producing a literal English translation of the Spanish text in both production materials and the published play. There are many debates and discussions amongst translators about how these literal translations are produced. Often a translator is called upon to produce a literal translation from the source language. This literal version in the target language is then passed on to a playwright (who often does not speak the source language) to adapt it for the stage. This was not the case for *Thebes Land* as Daniel Goldman is fluent in Spanish. There are many issues that can arise with literal translations so I'll underscore what I consider to be the two most important ones: how is the translator of the literal version credited, acknowledged and paid for their work? Can a translation ever be literal if a certain amount of interpretation is always involved? For more insight into this process in practice see Geraldine Brodie, *The Translator on Stage* (London: Bloomsbury, 2018). I asked Goldman about the literal translation of *Thebes Land* and he said that it was created by Cavazos (with whom he had worked before) in order to have a translation to share with the theatre to enable the play to be programmed. This literal version then provided a basis for Goldman's work in translating and adapting it for the performance (shared with permission).
5. Mario Benedetti, *Pedro and the Captain: A Play in Four Parts*, trans. and intro. by Adrianne Aron (San Francisco, CA: Cadmus Editions, 2009).
6. This was part of a research project directed by Laera entitled *Translation, Adaptation, Otherness: 'Foreignisation' in Theatre Practice* (2016–19). More information about the project can be found on the project website <www.translatingtheatre.com> [accessed 26 October 2020].
7. Adam Versényi, 'The Dissemination of Theatrical Translation', in *The Routledge Companion to Dramaturgy*, ed. by Magda Romanska (Oxford: Routledge, 2015), pp. 288–93 (p. 289).
8. Patrice Pavis, *Theatre at the Crossroads of Culture*, trans. by Loren Kruger (London: Routledge, 1992), p. 138.
9. David Johnston, 'Professing Translation: The Acts-in-between', *Target*, 25.3 (2013), 365–84 <doi.org/10.1075/target.25.3.04joh> (p. 381).
10. Pavis, 'Toward Specifying Theatre Translation' in *Theatre at the Crossroads*, pp. 136–59.
11. David Johnston, 'Translation for the Stage: Product and Process', *NUI Maynooth Papers in Spanish, Portuguese and Latin American Studies*, 6 (2002), 1–28 (p. 12).
12. Pavis, *Theatre at the Crossroads*, p. 139.
13. Ibid., p. 140.
14. Johnston, 'Product and Process', p. 14.
15. Pavis, *Theatre at the Crossroads*, p. 138.
16. Ibid., p. 148.
17. Johnston, 'Product and Process', p. 14.
18. Sirkku Aaltonen, *Time-Sharing on Stage: Drama Translation in Theatre and Society* (Clevedon: Multilingual Matters Ltd, 2000), p. 28.
19. Adam Versényi, 'Translation as an Epistemological Paradigm for Theatre in the Americas', *Theatre Journal*, 59.3 (2007), 431–47 <http://dx.doi.org/10.1353/tj.2007.0173> (p. 433).
20. Roland Barthes, *Image, Music, Text: Essays Selected and Translated by Stephen Heath* (London: Fontana Press, 1977), p. 161.

21. Ibid., p. 158.
22. Patrice Pavis, ed., 'The Duty to Translate: An Interview with Antoine Vitez', in *The Intercultural Performance Reader* (London: Routledge, 1996), pp. 121–30 (p. 127).
23. Ibid.
24. Jean-Luc Nancy, *Being Singular Plural*, trans. by Robert D. Richardson and Anne E. O'Byrne (Stanford, CA: Stanford University Press, 2000).
25. Catherine Boyle, 'On Mining Performance: Marginality, Memory and Cultural Translation in the Extreme', in *Differences on Stage*, ed. by Alessandra De Martino, Paolo Puppa and Paola Toninato (Newcastle upon Tyne: Cambridge Scholars Publishing, 2013), pp. 207–23 (p. 207).
26. Aaltonen, p. 47.
27. Johnston, 'Professing Translation', p. 381.
28. Dates refer to year the play was written.
29. Laura Escalante, ed., *50 años de teatro uruguayo: antología*, 2 vols (Montevideo: Ministerio de Educación y Cultura, 1988–90).
30. 'Historia', *Teatro El Galpón*, <https://www.teatroelgalpon.org.uy/historia/> [accessed 6 September 2020].
31. Dra. Adela Reta, 'Prólogo', in *50 años*, ed. by Escalante, I, 5.
32. The anthology includes *Orfeo* [*Orpheus*] by Denis Carlos Molina (1950, vol. I, pp. 67–106).
33. Johnston, 'Professing Translation', p. 366.
34. Griselda Castro, *Sainetes: análisis de obras de Florencio Sánchez y Armando Discépolo* (Montevideo: Editorial Técnica S.R.L., 1988), p. 5.
35. Carlos Maggi, *The Library*, in *Voices of Change in the Spanish American Theater: An Anthology*, ed. and trans. by William Oliver (Austin: University of Texas Press, 1971), pp. 105–69.
36. An overview of the project can be found here: 'Translation Plays, Intercultural Workshops', *King's College London*, <https://www.kcl.ac.uk/Cultural/-/Projects/Translation-Plays> [accessed 13 October 2020].
37. Walter Benjamin, 'The Task of the Translator: An Introduction to the Translation of Baudelaire's *Tableaux Parisiens*', trans. by Harry Zohn, in *The Translation Studies Reader*, ed. by Lawrence Venuti, 2nd edn (New York: Routledge, 2004), pp. 75–85.
38. Operation Condor was a transnational system based on an unprecedented level of cooperation and coordination between these countries and, as a result, it amplified the power of the individual regimes by enabling them to track, arrest and kill dissidents beyond their borders. J. Patrice McSherry identifies three levels to the Condor system: the first was 'mutual cooperation among military intelligence services'; the second was 'a form of offensive unconventional warfare' carried out by '[m]ultinational Condor squadrons' to forcefully disappear people who had gone into exile. Finally, '[u]nder Phase III, special teams of assassins from member countries were formed to travel worldwide to eliminate "subversive enemies"' (pp. 4–5). McSherry's study also demonstrates the types of 'organizational, intelligence, financial, and technological' support for Operation Condor from the US, as well as training in methods of abduction and torture provided to those working as part of the operation (p. 4). J. Patrice McSherry, *Predatory States: Operation Condor and Covert War in Latin America* (Lanham, MD: Rowman & Littlefield, 2005).
39. Colin Davis, *Haunted Subjects: Deconstruction, Psychoanalysis and the Return of the Dead* (Basingstoke: Palgrave Macmillan, 2007), p. 11.
40. Pavis, ed., 'The Duty to Translate', in *The Intercultural*, p. 127.
41. The other is *Acorobino* by Amalia Nieto, vol. I, pp. 287–304.
42. Beatriz Walker, *Benedetti, Rosencof, Varela: el teatro como guardián de la memoria colectiva* (Buenos Aires: Ediciones Corregidor, 2007), p. 38.
43. *Las Hermanas de Shakespeare: perspectivas de género en el teatro* (Montevideo: Intendencia de Montevideo, 2018), p. 32; available online at <https://montevideo.gub.uy/sites/default/files/biblioteca/publicacionsimposiolashermanasdeshakespeare_0.pdf>.
44. *Out of the Wings*, <http://www.outofthewings.org> [accessed 9 September 2020].

CHAPTER 1

❖

Frames of Analysis for Theatre Translation: A Dramaturgical Study of *M'hijo el dotor* and *La biblioteca*

What is at stake in the dramatic text?

This chapter illustrates the types of analysis, research and creative work that the theatre translator undertakes in order to answer the question: 'What is at stake in the dramatic text?' I propose that this question serve as a starting point for the dramaturgical analysis, which will be detailed in this chapter, and which underpins the theatre translation process. This question provokes many other questions as the translator 'bombard[s] it [the text] with questions from the target language's point of view'.[1] These questions will be articulated and illustrated through examining key examples from two Uruguayan plays in order to propose a framework for the initial stages of theatre translation. By expanding the scope of this question to ask, 'what was at stake in Uruguay at the time?', the translator researches, contextualises and establishes links to experiences in Uruguayan society, points of reference and voices of criticism or praise. To demonstrate the dramaturgical and contextual research in practice, this chapter presents analyses of two Uruguayan plays: *M'hijo el dotor* [*My Son the Doc*] (1903) by Florencio Sánchez and *La biblioteca* [*The Library*] (1957) by Carlos Maggi.[2] The analysis of *M'hijo el dotor* allows for an introduction to the *rioplatense* [River Plate] theatre tradition and a presentation of some of the main influences which shaped the development of Uruguayan national theatre. This play therefore provides the foundation for this study, firstly by introducing Uruguayan theatre traditions and secondly by demonstrating how knowledge of these traditions can inform and enhance the translation process. I present a close reading of the play in which I show how an understanding of the micro- and macro-structures informs the translator's work by enabling them to identify the ways in which the text functions as a network and the ways in which this network can be created in English. In the second part of the chapter, I provide accounts of the work carried out to create a stage-ready English translation of *La biblioteca* [*The Library*] in order to specify how a translation strategy emerges from an understanding of the original dramatic text. The translation process of *The Library* involved researching and specifying the concept of bureaucracy as a disease in the play, creating images of the intricate set designs to understand the relationship between the Library and its employees and how this would affect the movement of the actors, and working with a group of actors to test how the English translation conveyed the fast pace and increasing pressure of Act 1.

M'hijo el dotor deals with the tension created between the traditional rural economy and the modernisation taking place in the capital city at the start of the twentieth century in Uruguay. This included occupations based on study and research, which is what the protagonist, Julio, pursues as he leaves the family ranch to train to become a doctor in Montevideo. *La biblioteca* presents the functioning and failing of a public institution in order to explore what constitutes public service and how this type of work is valued. During the period of the 1950s, the relationship between the state and society was scrutinised and critiqued by scholars, artists, politicians and global powers. This chapter explores how the themes of learning, study, progress and identity (personal and professional) are depicted in *M'hijo el dotor* and *La biblioteca* across two different periods of Uruguayan history because the plays were written fifty years apart, both at critical moments of change in Uruguayan society. As this list demonstrates, one of the features of these plays is that they illuminate and explore themes which are identifiable as universal so a key concern in my translation process and this chapter is to examine what role cultural specificity has to play in the translation process. Why does the contact with the cultural context of the original matter? How does it affect the translation process and the new dramatic text created in the target language?

By working to understand how the play functions as a piece of drama, resonates with discourses in society and generates meaning in the source language and culture, the translator engages with the richness and multiplicity of the play and is able to imagine how it can connect to the target context. Whilst some of this engagement may occur through actually seeing the play, and some instant connections to the target culture may be what motivates the translator to undertake the translation in the first place, they still embark on a process of research. A key aspect of this research process is to understand the space in which the play operates in the source culture and identify how a space might be created for it in the target culture. This process enables the translator to project the play into the target context, perhaps to construct a preverbal image as they imagine the future mise-en-scène (after Pavis), and to make the links that will enable it to become mobile and travel across into the target language. The emphasis placed by Pavis on the preverbal, on the work undertaken prior to the writing of the dramatic script is significant. This is because it delineates a stage in the process in which both 'gesture and text coexist in an as yet undifferentiated way' as the translator imagines a future possible performance, which is just one of many possible performances of the dramatic text that they will write.[3] In this way, Pavis aligns the translator's creative process with that of the playwright of the play in the original language, rather than their intention, and this paves the way for the creative work that the translator will do as writer for the stage in the target context.

This chapter shows how the research process allows the translator to understand the possibilities for meaning generated by the source dramatic text so that they create a framework of concepts and meanings for the play in the target language. Through the dramaturgical analysis, informed by knowledge of the cultural history of the source culture, the translator understands the scope of possible meanings that are generated through the complex network of ideas, references and character relationships in the original. They then work creatively to establish this network in the target language to inform their translation. As they create a framework of possible meanings for the text, the translator identifies a translation strategy which emerges from the text and which sustains the relationships between its micro- and macro-structures by working to emphasise and accentuate the key aspects revealed in the dramaturgical analysis. This framework surrounds and sustains the dramatic text, locating it in a space where there are multiple meanings with which the translator works. It is therefore important to recognise that the cultural contextual analysis of the original dramatic text does not fix meaning. Throughout this process, emphasis is placed on 'meaning as becoming [which] makes the translation of that text a performative constituent of the mise-en-scène'.[4] This process is one of establishing the range of meanings, of understanding what a text can mean, precisely because the emphasis on the multiplicity of meanings does not mean that there is an infinite range of meanings for any given text: there are judgements to be made about the text which will guide the translator's decision-making in the translation process.[5]

This is where multiplicity intersects with interpretation: every judgement made about the text is based on an interpretation but this is one that has to give space to other future interpretations. The translation process is a balance between specifying meaning and creating an openness which allows actors and directors to occupy the text in order to develop it for performance. The process outlined in this book demonstrates how the translator's work is informed by scholarly research which equips them to take on the role of dramaturge in the rehearsal room. As Johnston states, the translated text

> reflects the sense of a process which the translation has undergone — from first reading, through reader appropriation and, of course, scholarly analysis, and subsequently via the various strategies, tactics, resignation to losses and decisions as to compensations, which together form the translation, to the writing of a new playscript.[6]

Translation for performance is necessarily a collaborative process and this has an impact on the ways in which the dramatic text is studied and questioned from multiple viewpoints. The contributions of these collaborators serve to enhance the robustness of the translated dramatic text as it is tested against the expectations of a culturally specific stage language in the target language. In this way, the exploration of the theatre translator as dramaturge and practitioner does not seek to eliminate or undermine this collaborative project but to understand how the theatre translator as dramaturge can pave a constructive pathway for their later work.

Uruguayan Theatre Traditions: *M'hijo el dotor* in Context

M'hijo el dotor by Florencio Sánchez was first performed at the Teatro Comedia in Buenos Aires in 1903 by the Jerónimo Podestá theatre company.[7] This theatre company, along with several others established by the Podestá family, were central to the development of a *rioplatense* theatre tradition which existed across Uruguay and Argentina and which, as Griselda Castro states, should be considered as the foundation for a Uruguayan theatre tradition.[8] The cultural histories of Uruguay and Argentina are inextricably linked and many playwrights and theatre companies viewed working in both countries, and in particular in the two capital cities, Montevideo and Buenos Aires, as essential to establishing and maintaining their success. In the case of Florencio Sánchez, he had moved between Buenos Aires and different cities in Uruguay to secure work, primarily as a journalist, and to make contact with literary circles. Following his dismissal from the Argentine newspaper *La República* for expressing views in which he aligned himself with a workers' strike in 1902, he relocated from Rosario to Buenos Aires and wrote *M'hijo el dotor.*[9]

The Podestá theatre company were a family of Argentine and Uruguayan circus actors living in the Chivilcoy area of the province of Buenos Aires.[10] In 1884, a European theatre company, directed by the Carlo brothers, planned to create a performance based on a short story entitled *Juan Moreira* by Argentine author Eduardo Gutiérrez, which was published as an insert to the newspaper *La Patria Argentina* in 1878.[11] The performance was planned as part of the Carlo brothers company's farewell tour of the region and so they wanted it to be successful. When they consulted Gutiérrez about the adaptation, the author responded that, in order for it to work, they would need a performer who could skilfully ride a horse, fight, sing, dance, play guitar and work a knife, namely a *criollo* (native of Uruguay) and a *gaucho*, but the Carlo brothers were European and did not have the expertise in their company of actors for this role.[12] Gauchos were independent, nomadic herdsmen who would possess all of the skills enumerated by Gutiérrez. They were able to move freely throughout the Uruguayan countryside with their cattle before the land was divided up into farms and ranches for cultivation. Many participated in the wars of independence against the Spanish. These nomadic gauchos were often the protagonists of theatre and circus performances, and were also the subject of literature and folklore, causing Juan Carlos Legido to refer to this period, immediately before Sánchez started writing, as the foundation of Uruguayan national theatre and 'la edad de cuero' [the age of leather] in reference to the significance of their cattle and the use of this material in their clothes and equipment.[13]

The Carlo brothers invited José Podestá to play the role of the gaucho, Juan Moreira, at the Politeama Argentino and transform Gutiérrez's work for the stage. The story was performed as a pantomime with music to accompany the actions. Two years later, José Podesta decided to restage the production. Adam Versényi views this as a turning point in the development of Uruguayan national theatre because hotel-owner M. León Beaupuy saw this new production and suggested adding dialogue to the piece.[14] In 1886, two years after first performing the play,

José Podestá added dialogue to the performance, based on the original story.[15] The growing popularity of *Juan Moreira* meant that the show transitioned from large circuses on the outskirts of the city to smaller inner-city theatres in Montevideo in 1889 and Buenos Aires in 1891. Therefore, the addition of dialogue marked a change in form for the play as it was adapted for these new performance spaces.[16] As Versényi explains, the changes in the style and form of theatre, which enabled the transition to stages in the city, were another indication of growing tensions in society surrounding the rural–city divide:

> What gave the circus performance its vitality was the innocence of its audience that participated in the story wholeheartedly, seeing its own destiny in that of the preindustrial hero. At the other end of the scale were the established city theatres, inheritors of European culture who, with marked delay, offered their audiences all the innovations of neoclassicism, romanticism, naturalism, and realism [...]. The concerns of these two theatrical currents — the cultured and the popular, the city and the country — mirror the bifurcated social structure following independence and were gradually to be joined in the late nineteenth and early twentieth centuries as Latin America became integrated into the political–economic system of the modern world.[17]

The early development of theatre for the Uruguayan and Argentine stages, particularly in the capital cities of Montevideo and Buenos Aires, was strongly influenced by theatre from Spain and Italy. *Sainetes were* short, one-act plays originating in Spain which were created to entertain theatre audiences as an interlude in longer plays. They comprise three scenes which usually correspond to the formula 'planteo-desarrollo-desenlace' [exposition-development-dénouement] and include popular songs. In the Spanish theatre tradition examples can be found from Cervantes, Lope de Vega and Tirso de Molina. The *sainete criollo* took aspects of this inherited theatre tradition and rooted it in the Río de la Plata. *Sainetes* often included marginalised characters such as immigrants; Castro states that the large-scale European immigration to Uruguay and Argentina between 1857 and 1908 gave rise to character types which were included in these short plays. The language employed was colloquial and included the use of slang, inflected by the languages spoken by Spanish and Italian immigrants.[18]

Sánchez's work depicted the conflicts experienced throughout society, whilst theatre and theatre spaces were also undergoing a transformation. As a result of the confluence of both these changes, the focus shifted from that of the noble, nomadic gaucho as depicted in the stage version of *Juan Moreira*, to the peasant or farmer who sought to maintain their land and livestock in the face of challenges. This is a topic which Florencio Sánchez would develop in his plays and which he chooses to present in particular through the lens of the family and the inter-generational conflict as seen in both *M'hijo el dotor* and *Barranca Abajo* (1905), which are referred to as rural dramas. Sánchez also wrote several *sainetes* over the course of his short writing career; he produced the majority of his twenty plays between 1903 and 1909.[19] Whilst often viewed as entertainment, Sánchez adapted the style for his audience so whilst his *sainetes* often included humour, this was underpinned by a commitment to tackling social issues which evoked the everyday struggles experienced by the audience.[20] Legido adds that Sánchez's ability to depict familiar challenges that the audience identified with was key to his success. This was amplified by the fact that in his *sainetes* and other works Sánchez did not shy away from portraying the challenges faced by people marginalised by society and also marginalised by the transformations to industry experienced at the turn of the century.[21] Oscar Brando draws on the work of Freire to suggest that one of the features of Sánchez's work, which distinguishes it from that of his predecessors, is the creation of an underlying violence or tension, rather than an emphasis on physical violence (although this is not excluded entirely) as a way to depict conflict.[22] This creates an uncomfortable tension which underpins the dramatic action, making the audience aware of the violence without it always being depicted physically, and simultaneously drawing them into the dramatic action by enabling them to recognise aspects of their own experience in that of the protagonists. This adds a layer of complexity to his work which implies both the difficulty and the deep rootedness of the problems that the characters must face.

Frames of Analysis for Theatre Translation

The first stage of the dramaturgical analysis of *M'hijo el dotor* focusses on engaging with the dramatic core of the text: 'everything on stage is part of various patterns of significance that enable the theatrical actions to underscore and vivify the dramatic core'.[23] Therefore, it is important to recognise that there is a sense of interdependence around the idea of the dramatic core: as the architecture of the piece, the dramatic core holds the other elements of the play in place and sustains them as part of the network of signifiers, themes and concepts but these different 'theatrical discourses' also serve to reinforce the dramatic core.[24] According to Pavis, the first stage of the dramaturgical analysis is a macro-textual translation, undertaken by the translator as 'reader and a dramaturge'.[25] At the same time, there is a constant interplay between the macro-textual and micro-textual elements which includes the characters, their traits, 'the system of echoes, repetition, responses and correspondences that maintain the cohesion of the source text', meaning that the macro-textual analysis requires and implies the analysis of the micro-structures.[26] Together these elements enable the translator to understand the different 'sign systems that make up the theatrical situation of enunciation' which enable the dramatic text to function as a text to be performed.[27] As the 'architecture' and 'narrative core' of the play, the dramatic core establishes a specific trajectory for the play as it moves from start to finish and this is unique to each play.[28] In order to identify the elements of this dramatic core, first of all I pose the question: what is at stake in the dramatic action of the play? To answer this, I break the play into sections, usually using the scenes or acts of the play as a way to conduct an initial analysis of structure to identify what is at stake in each one. This is because what is at stake in the play changes as the dramatic action progresses. This question obliges me to focus on the heart of the dramatic action and, crucially, to focus on it as a driving force, which propels the action of the play forward. It is essential in this analysis to interrogate the play as a whole; this part of the process, although it begins to separate the dramatic text into sections, still focusses on the text as a whole in order to understand its movement from start to finish and the 'fiction',[29] 'vision of life' or 'paradigm'[30] that the play creates.

M'hijo el dotor is presented in three acts: the action begins at the courtyard of Don Olegario's ranch, the second act takes place in a hotel room in the capital, Montevideo, and the final act returns to the ranch, although the action moves from outside (as in the first act) to inside the house. In Act 1, Julio has returned home to his parents, who are also caring for their goddaughter Jesusa, during a break in his studies in Montevideo. His father, Don Olegario, criticises his son for behaving like royalty, referring to Julio as '[e]l príncipe' [the prince] (Act 1, Scene 2, p. 247) for adopting new tastes in the city and making demands on his mother, Mariquita. Don Olegario mocks and criticises his son's choices, including Julio's adoption of a new name to hide his actual name, Robustiano: '¡Un mozo que se ha mudao hasta el nombre pa que no le tomen olor a campero, hace bien en tomar chocolate!' [A boy who has even gone so far as to change his name so that there isn't the slightest whiff of country air about him should, of course, drink hot chocolate!] (Act 1, Scene 2, p. 247). Julio's attempts to distance himself from the countryside and to show that he is superior to the people who live there (including his family) are demonstrated by his willingness to modify and adapt his preferences to fit into his new environment and this extends to changing his name. In this way, Sánchez instantly draws our attention to Julio's tendency and ability to rapidly change his ideas and actions whilst maintaining a sense of conviction that he is justified in doing so, something which Julio will articulate at crucial moments of conflict throughout the play.

One of these moments of conflict between Julio and Don Olegario arises when it is revealed that, during his time studying in Montevideo, Julio has accumulated debts and behaved poorly. When Don Olegario learns of this he asks, ¿quién nos quita de encima esta mancha?' [Who will remove this stain from us?] (Act 1, Scene 11, p. 255). This question encapsulates what is at stake in Act 1 and the question as to how amends can be made propels the dramatic action forward and prompts Olegario to give Jesusa's hand in marriage to Don Eloy, who brought news of Julio's actions via a letter. Julio's abuse of his father's trust and money introduces the theme of earning a living, again creating tension between the father, who works hard to maintain his ranch and livestock and support his family, and the son, who studies in the city but behaves like a libertine. When Olegario confronts Julio, the latter explains that Olegario's morals and conduct are outdated and seeks to affirm his freedom (Act 1, Scene 13, pp. 258–59). Julio emphasises the significance of change and progress and underscores the idea that this is at the heart of the differences between him and his father: 'Todo evoluciona, viejo; y estos tiempos han mandado archivar la moral, los hábitos, los estilos de la época en que usted se educó' [Everything moves on, old man; the morals, ways and customs with which you were raised, today, they are a thing of the past] (Act 1, Scene 13, pp. 258–59). The divide between the two generations is patent and Julio's efforts to forge a new way of life and secure his own independence are undermined by his financial instability, which highlights the fragility of his situation and his inability to transition entirely into life in the city. Brando underscores the dual nature of the conflicts at the heart of Sánchez's work: the clash between moral codes is yet another indication of the opposition between new and old, which is part of the conflict between countryside and city.[31] *M'hijo el dotor* stages the conflict between rural lifestyle and livelihood and a new way of life offered by new roles, accessed through university study in Montevideo. The play proposes an exploration of tensions between father and son for the patriarchal power to command, between the older and younger generations about changing morals, and also between the attitudes of men and women, which shows the conflict arising from the roles that they were ascribed in society at the time.

Manacorda de Rosetti and Palma de Carpinetti identify the questioning of the value of new types of education as the trigger for the dramatic action in *M'hijo el dotor* because Julio's studies have provoked a change in attitude, morals and ideals.[32] This is revealed in terms of the form and the microstructures of the play because the majority of verbal utterances in the play are short, which gives rise to a rapid dialogue, but Julio's speeches in which he elaborates his theories break this rapid rhythm because they are convoluted.[33] Therefore, the differing principles presented in the play are also apparent through their mode of presentation and this serves a dramatic function in heightening the sense of distance between Julio and the rural community. This emphasises a growing distance between the characters in the play which is sometimes constructed, such as when Julio elaborates his ideas, a key example of which is illustrated below, but at other times it is reflective of the difficulty in communication between the characters and their lack of willingness to understand one another, often as a reaction to change.

Act II takes place in Montevideo where Don Olegario, who is sick, has gone to see a doctor. Jesusa reveals that she is pregnant and Julio is the father. In this act, what is at stake is, who will make a sacrifice for the future? The idea of sacrifice is presented explicitly in Julio's speech to Jesusa in which he appeals to a morality of sacrifice regarding her pregnancy, the news of which she discloses initially to Julio alone. He states that their union would be false if he sacrificed his future to be with her because he does not love her and that she would be seen as an exemplary mother for her sacrifice to her child. Julio blames merciless natural law for their illicit union, which is the reason why he acted in such a way, mistaking for love '¡lo que no era más que una vil manifestación del instinto! [...] He padecido más por ti que por el desdichado incidente con mi padre' [what was nothing more than a vile demonstration of human instinct! [...] I have suffered more because of you than because of that unfortunate business with my father] (Act II, Scene 5, pp. 266–67). He explains that neither of them is to blame because 'Fué un accidente' [It was an accident] (Act II, Scene 5, p. 267) and so distances himself from Jesusa and responsibility for their child. In this scene Julio frames his argument against Jesusa so that the language he employs to present his rationale is used to elevate his status and create a hierarchy in which reason (embodied in Julio) is at the top; his understanding of natural law makes him superior to Jesusa, even if he cannot prevent himself from succumbing to its dictates. He once again emphasises the way in which his understanding, attitudes and beliefs differ from those of Jesusa and his parents, and implies that this sets him apart from them when he says 'mi moral es distinta de esa moral que anda por ahí' [my morals are different from those around here] (Act II, Scene 5, p. 267). This is an example of how individual relationships, exchanges and tensions underscore the dramatic core of the play. The complexities of these exchanges are part of the micro-textual analysis and some of these will be illuminated during the rehearsal process where actors might make a choice as to whether the distancing created is intentional or not. It is not the work of the translator to somehow make visible the intention of the author, or the character, in these exchanges. For the translator, an awareness of how the theme of opposition between rural and city is conveyed in the form of the exchanges between characters, as well as the words that they speak, and the impact that this has on the rhythm of the dramatic text informs their translation decisions so that aspects of this rhythm can be created in the target language.

Act III returns to the rural setting as Olegario, now on his death bed, is cared for by a witch doctor. In this act, the future of the characters is at stake and, crucially, the question of how the decisions of Julio and Jesusa could affect Olegario's survival rises to the surface when Olegario requests that Julio marry Jesusa. Should Julio condemn Olegario to death for his outdated morals? Jesusa asks Julio if dying is the end of everything; if this is the case then they do not need to fulfil their promise to marry as it will not actually return Olegario to life but simply allow him to die happy. She states that she does not want Julio to sacrifice himself in this way and that the original reasons for them not to marry remain (Act III, Scene 12, p. 281). At the end of the act, it seems that Jesusa, whom Julio rejected for her affiliation with the outdated morals of the countryside, is shown to think practically about her future and to have the ability to take on ideas and appropriate them for herself as she repeats some of Julio's points in her arguments against him. This suggests that Jesusa gains freedom through the knowledge that she has acquired from Julio and she is able to view her own future in a different light. However, this repetition could signal a different type of learning — learning by rote — through which ideas might be taken on and verbalised without being fully understood, thus potentially creating pernicious repercussions within society when an ideology is adopted without fostering the knowledge to support it, interrogate it and modify it. The repetition serves to problematise the theme of learning, which is an essential element of the dramatic core of the play, whilst serving the dramatic function of creating another link between Jesusa and Julio as she echoes his words.

In my analysis so far, I have identified what is at stake in each of the three acts of the play and the key elements of the dramatic core as: the tension between rural and city life; the justification of beliefs and professions, including what it means to earn a living; and the issues around ways of gaining knowledge. The next stage is to extend the scope of the question 'what is at stake?' beyond the boundaries of the dramatic action in order to examine the context in which the play was created. What was at stake in Uruguay at the time when Florencio Sánchez was writing this play? Through exploring this question, the contextual analysis broadens the scope of my understanding of the situation in which the play was written. This allows the translator to examine some of the factors shaping the themes and ideas presented in the play and the way in which the questions provoked by the text might have resonated at the time and engaged with discourses present in society. This is an essential part of the dramaturgical work of the translator as 'intercultural informant'[34] and 'cultural liaison'[35] who uses their culturally specific knowledge to inform the translation decisions that they make in creating the new dramatic text, which itself can become a site of intercultural encounter.

Historical Context

As already identified, at the time when Florencio Sánchez was writing there were growing tensions between traditional rural industries and emerging industries established in Montevideo. Uruguay had already endured a civil war in 1897 and would face another in 1904. The second uprising, led by Blanco caudillo Aparicio Saravia, was provoked by an economic crisis, which caused rural communities to become increasingly poor and there was unease about how they would fit into a newly shaped economic structure for the country.[36] These communities also sought greater and fairer representation in parliament, which was an ongoing issue from the war in 1897 and would lead to a series of parliamentary reforms during the first two decades of the twentieth century.[37] In 1903, when President José Batlle y Ordóñez (centre/centre-right, Colorado party) first came to power, he promised to make significant social reforms to improve the working and living standards of all social classes in Uruguay by providing access to education and healthcare for everyone. He also sought to develop an urban-industrial model to establish financial stability, nationalise public services and manage foreign investment more effectively in order to support the development of industry and factories in Uruguay. The government focussed on generating new types of industry within the city of Montevideo. Although the majority of Batlle's proposed reforms would be introduced during his second term as president (1911–15), and many would be adapted in response to opposition from groups within Uruguay or to changes in the global situation in the build-up to the First World War, the start of the twentieth century nevertheless marked a period of important change. This would eventually lead to compulsory primary education and the creation of secondary schools throughout the rural *interior* of the country, resulting in increased literacy levels, new industries and training to support their development, eight-hour working days (although not across all sectors) and initiatives to increase tourism, particularly from Argentina.[38]

Manacorda de Rosetti and Palma de Carpinetti specify that Sánchez wrote *M'hijo el dotor* at this time when change was greatly anticipated yet many people lacked clarity as to how it would occur: 'Sánchez, a través de Julio, expone ese estado de ánimo de los grupos renovadores que se agitaban sin conocer bien los rumbos, ni siquiera las metas' [Through Julio, Sánchez reveals the mentality of reformist groups who began to act without really knowing their course of action or even their goals].[39] The inconsistency in Julio's behaviour is indicative of this anxiety which surrounded the transformations society was undergoing at the time.

It captures the urgency of the need for change and the emergence of an incipient socialism which was not yet well-defined and whose advocates may not have had opportunities to adequately study existing models and patterns.[40] Sánchez succeeds in capturing the ambivalence surrounding this shift in some of the criticisms voiced by Julio's parents about his behaviour: they hope that their son will progress in his career but they do not want their own livelihood to be undermined. The sense of opportunity is met with one of apprehension, particularly about how the changes might have an impact on accepted morals. However, the play does not clearly depict a shift to a new attitude, rather it explores some of the factors which have led up to this moment of change or crisis in order to question its impact on society whilst leaving the audience to decide what the future might hold for the characters and the society in which they live. The importance of learning and study is a prominent theme throughout the play and the dramatic action provokes questions around how instruction is received, who has the power to teach and how to identify reliable sources of knowledge. These questions are raised forcefully and explicitly in the exchanges between Don Olegario and Julio; for example, at the end of Act II, after learning of Jesusa's pregnancy, Don Olegario asks his son: '¿Eso es lo que te han enseñao los libros, gran sinvergüenza? [Is this what you learnt from your books, you rogue?] (Act II, Scene 7, p. 270). These questions are coupled with an exploration of how knowledge can be applied, how it equips the characters to question accepted ideas, as with Jesusa, and the extent to which it enables them to modify their actions or those of others. Through the contextual analysis, the translator is able to root the play in the context in which it was written by creating links from that context to the themes that emerge through the dramaturgical analysis.

If these themes emerge as prominent from the dramaturgical analysis and have been identified as connecting to issues and discourses present in the source culture when the text was written and performed, how can this inform and enhance the translation process? The dramaturgical and contextual analyses enable the translator to imagine and engage with the dramatic text as a piece of drama to be performed, and to understand the types of resonances and ideas that it might generate in the source language and culture. This process enables them to understand the types of work that the play does as a cultural object and this understanding equips them with knowledge and ideas to transform the text into the target language. It provides a crucial insight into what the 'experience of theatre' might have been like for the audience of the original play.[41] Once again, this is multiple because each performance and each audience member is different. Through a study of the historical and cultural context, as detailed in this chapter, the translator identifies some of the connections that the audience of the original might make to their own experience and the kind of questions or debates that the play might generate, contribute to, or seek to influence. An important part of the dramaturgical analysis is interacting with the network of meanings created by the original play, which is created through the internal logic of the play and the connections to the context, in order to establish the network of meanings in the target context. This network of meanings enables the translator to establish the potential scope of the text and it also provides a framework for their work as they make choices about the translation in the target language.

The dramaturgical analysis constitutes an essential stage in what Pavis refers to as the 'preverbal' phase in the construction of a dramatic text before the play is committed to writing.[42] The text is a script for the performance and not just the words to be spoken. Therefore, the preverbal does not exclude the verbal but contains all the theatrical sign systems that make up the dramatic text which, as well as dialogue, provide instruction to the actor.[43] Pavis proposes that just as the writer of the original dramatic text undergoes this preverbal stage in which they creatively imagine the future possible performance of the text, so does the translator as an essential step in the creation of the dramatic text in which 'we are left with only the linguistic trace of the preceding gestural and preverbal processes'.[44] The translator's process evidently differs in that they depart from an existing dramatic text, which informs and instructs their preverbal dramatic image; this anticipates their own verbal phase when the translator must begin to make choices and fix words onto a page to create and develop the new dramatic text in the target context as a written piece. If the translator creates a preverbal image, then it is necessarily unique and new, firstly because it projects one of many possible performances and secondly because it projects that image in the target context, thus creating an image of a new play which is rooted there and is informed by the dramaturgical, cultural and contextual analyses. These processes of analysis enable the creation of an informed imagining of the play in the source culture which underpins how the translator is able to imagine it in the target culture. The processes of research feed into the framework of possible meanings that the translator creates for the play and equips them with knowledge which will enable them to locate the play in the target context.

By considering the resonances in the original context and the impact that they might have on the audience, the translator gains an insight into the type of resonances that they might want to create in the target context, through the choices they make in the target language. This process also enables the translator to develop an awareness of the fact that whilst they specify the words that make up the dramatic text, this is not the end of the meaning-making process. Therefore, it is essential to recognise that, as Aaltonen points out, it is not up to the translator to specify the final meaning of the dramatic text in the target language because meanings are always 'context generated': they 'arise from relations and differences among signifiers but also from the interaction between signifiers and readers/ audiences'.[45] David Hare states that the play is performance: it is not actors or script but what is 'in the air' between the actors on stage and the audience.[46] The action on stage connects with ideas, questions and discourses present in society and brought into the theatre laboratory by the audience. The process of creating meaning occurs in the encounter between the audience and the translated dramatic text in performance as the audience create, extract and question meaning generated through the performance of the text. The words chosen by the translator create this encounter and can cultivate awareness of new perspectives, untold stories or issues affecting specific groups in society.

The dramatic action does not occur in a vacuum and the questions that it provokes interact with and arise from discourses present in society.[47] In the same way, concerns and issues present in the target culture influence the construction of concepts and meanings in the new dramatic text. What the contextualisation of the original allows the translator to do is to understand the play in its original context and the ways in which it might have connected with the original audience. This informs the translation process as the translator works to create strategies to evoke discourses present in the target society in order to enable the play to have a similar impact in the target context. This creates a connection between the function of the play in the source and target cultures and, in doing this, the play establishes a connection between the source and target cultures. This connection can be productive in providing the audience with insight into close and distant cultural realties. The significance of these links will be expanded upon in Chapter 3, which builds on the work of Jean-Luc Nancy to examine points of contact between cultures which enable texts to become mobile. The relationship created between cultures will be examined to discuss how distance and proximity provide a useful conceptual framework for understanding the possibilities offered through the theatre laboratory.

The question of what is at stake is complex and requires different levels of examination: by working through a dramaturgical analysis, which necessarily involves a contextual analysis, the translator understands and works with the original play as a construct created within a specific cultural and historical context. The questions that drive the dramatic action, like those identified above for *M'hijo el dotor*, are not static and are inextricably linked to the characters and their roles, which hinge on and illuminate the dramatic core. During the performance, the dramatic action on stage, the interactions between characters and the ways in which the play develops provoke further questions. For example, in the case of *M'hijo el dotor*: what happens to attitudes in society at a crucial moment of change? Where do we seek knowledge? What is the relationship between rural and city life, particularly for those, like Julio, who have a foot in both? These questions extend beyond the dramatic action as the play reverberates in the auditorium and the action on stage begins to interact with the societal concerns represented through the presence of the audience. In the next section, I present an analysis of *La biblioteca* as a way to demonstrate how a creative imagining of the relationship between the micro- and macro-structures of the dramatic text creates the framework of possible meanings and has an impact upon the decisions made in the translation process resulting in the creation of a robust dramatic text in the target language.

The Library: Staging a Shrinking Institution

La biblioteca was written by Carlos Maggi in 1957 and provides a satirical insight into the functioning of a public institution and the life of its employees in Montevideo during the extensive period of the construction of a new library building. It was first performed in 1959 at the Teatro del Pueblo, which is part of the Federación de Teatros Independientes [Association of Independent Theatres], and was directed by

Ruben Yáñez. Maggi was born in 1922 and belonged to the generation of writers known in Uruguay as the *Generación del 45* (in reference to the year when many of them began to write and publish) or the *Generación crítica*. The critical lens through which they examined Uruguay and, in particular, the characteristics of its people and their everyday lives is exemplified in Mario Benedetti's work *Montevideanos*.[48] Maggi inserts himself in a self-aware manner into the literary and theatre traditions of Uruguay: he recognised himself as part of the 1945 Generation and in an interview he also made reference to *La biblioteca* as 'un sainete con pretensiones' [an ambitious *sainete*].[49] Benedetti also aligns Maggi's earlier plays with the *sainete* tradition,[50] an idea which is echoed in a 1962 review from *Espectáculos* magazine where *La biblioteca* is described as an updated *sainete*, in which Maggi uses a range of imaginative techniques to provoke the audience's laughter.[51] Maggi, his contemporaries and his critics recognise and acknowledge the influence that the inherited Spanish and Italian theatre traditions had upon the early stages of his work, particularly the *sainete*, which also forms a link to Florencio Sánchez.

La biblioteca opens with a parody of the speech the workers anticipate that the Director of the Library will deliver before the Secretary General in a ceremony to mark the laying of the foundation stone of the new library building. In fact, Martínez's parody is the only version of the Director's speech that the audience ever hear; we never witness the Director's version but instead see his vain attempts to write it throughout Act I amidst distractions from employees requesting leave, readers in search of ancient tomes, a magazine editor, a young admirer, his fiancée and a very persistent tailor. At the mercy of the plans of two different Secretaries General over a period of twenty-five years, the employees must move the contents of the Library inwards, reducing the size of the Library by half, in order to create space for the demolition and reconstruction of the new building on the same site. The transfer of books and the subsequent shrinking of the Library are shown throughout Act II. The employees look to a bright future of promotions, higher salaries and a complex security system. Questions linger throughout the play as to whether the ambitious plans for the Library will ever come to fruition, to what extent the employees believe in the plans, and whether their efforts are actually contributing to the bigger picture. These questions constitute the macro-structure of the dramatic text.[52]

There is further evidence of the influence of Spanish playwriting on the creation of *La biblioteca* because Maggi explained in an interview that in the early conceptual stages of his play he saw *Doña Rosita la soltera* [*Doña Rosita the Spinster*] by Federico García Lorca. He realised that the story of the Library, like that of Rosita, was about constant waiting and, like the dramatisation of the story of Doña Rosita, he wrote it in three acts, which distinguished the passage of time.[53] In Lorca's play, at the beginning of each act the audience is confronted with the image of the ageing Rosita, which forms a stark contrast to the previous act, and as the dramatic action unfolds the audience learn of the gradual decline of her hopes for the future.[54] In this way, the structure of *La biblioteca* can be mapped onto that of Lorca's play and the two plays share key elements of their respective dramatic cores: in both plays the first two acts take place ten years apart and then a further ten years pass before the next scene (in *La biblioteca*) and act (in *Doña Rosita*). The dramatic structure of *La biblioteca* contains more elements and a total of twenty-five years pass during the play. *La biblioteca* comprises three acts and an interlude: Act II, Scene I takes place ten years after Act I; the Interlude takes place in the middle of Act II; at the start of Act II, Scene 2 a further ten years have passed; Act III occurs five years later.[55] At the start of each act, the library building has changed significantly and as the employees go about their work, talk about their aspirations, slowly age and lose hope (some of them even die), the drama communicates the impact that the changes, and lack of changes, to the Library, have had on their lives. The initial impact that the transformation of the building creates on the audience at the start of each act is developed and embodied through the experiences of the characters on stage. In a similar way to Rosita, the employees are awaiting news, instructions and indications of progress, in their case from the Secretary General, and so the sense of the lack of control over their own destiny is poignant throughout the play. Despite a lingering sense of uncertainty around the plans, there are crucial moments in the play when the employees demonstrate a sense of agency as they work to make preparations for the new building through elaborate processes of moving and storing books. As the play develops, there is an increasing sense that they have lost any agency that they might have had in the process, that their efforts have been wasted, and the idea that the new Library will never be built becomes potent. The dependency both on the Secretary General and on the Library itself are central to the dramatic core and establish a relationship between the employees and their place of work which makes it impossible for them to leave due to both a physical and a psychological connection to it.

The play is complex and the dramaturgical analysis enables the translator to identify the dramatic core and the different levels of action and interaction, occurring on a micro-textual level. The micro-structures hinge on the relationships between the ten library employees that we encounter, the ways in which they carry out their work, the changing attitudes of the employees towards their respective roles and their understanding of how the plan for the new library will affect their work and their lives. At the beginning of each of the three acts, there are long stage directions which detail the appearance of the Library, the scenography and demonstrate the effect of this movement inwards. A palpable tension is established between the individual aspirations of the employees and their roles as part of an institution which is due to be transformed. A striking way in which this tension is exemplified and dramatised is in Act II when the employees create a human chain to move the boxes into the specified reading room as quickly as possible. The stage directions state that:

> A partir de este momento todos entrarán vertiginosamente de a uno o en parejas trayendo y trayendo libros; paquetes y cajones que irán dejando en orden sobre el trazado hecho a tiza. Los utileros participarán así mismo y así se levantarán verdaderas paredes que irán obstruyendo la puerta principal, cegando la ventana y reduciendo la sala de dirección a dos compartimentos rodeados de un corredor estrecho. Los diálogos se traban entre los transportadores pero con independencia del movimiento incesante del acarreo que se abastece por

> ambas puertas y al final también por la ventana. Puede hacerse rematar un in crescendo, una cadena de envíos como la de los obreros que suben ladrillo, boleándolos de uno a otro. (*La biblioteca*, Act II, p. 130)
>
> [From this moment onwards they all enter very rapidly, either alone or in pairs, continuously bringing in more and more books, parcels and boxes that they leave in order on the floor, according to the outline marked in chalk. The Props Managers take part in the task as well, and in this way actual walls are erected which gradually obstruct the main door, block the window and reduce the Director's Office to two compartments surrounded by a narrow corridor. The people carrying start conversations with each other, irrespective of their incessant transportation of books through both doors and eventually through the window. The movement of the books becomes faster and faster and ends up with the characters creating a supply chain like workmen passing bricks from one person to the next.]

The conversations largely focus on their ambitions: Monteiro talks about being on the brink of making the Olympic team, if only he works a bit harder; the Deputy Director has plans for an aviary when he retires, but he is waiting for the promised salary increase before taking his leave; when he does retire, the Secretary hopes to be promoted to Deputy Director, with the help of a recommendation from the Director. As the employees rapidly and joyfully complete their task, making a bet as to who can move the most boxes in the shortest time, they raise their expectations and aspirations for the future. The initial reduction in size of the Library is the first step in its planned transformation but, paradoxically, as the play progresses and the Library gets smaller, thus creating the impression that the employees are getting closer to realising their goals, the themes of their discussions become increasingly negative. This is because the library building gradually becomes more distorted, which has an impact on the employees because they realise that the ultimate goal might never happen and that they will remain stuck in their current roles in the building.

One of the key tensions in *La biblioteca* is that whilst there are activities and changes in relation to the shape of the building, and this is a central element of the narrative drive of the play, the process and slow progress of transforming the library building constantly place obstacles in the way of its successful functioning. This is illustrated by the encounters and exchanges that occur each time a reader arrives at the Library and it becomes increasingly difficult for the employees to locate books, meaning that we never actually witness a reader successfully accessing the material that they are looking for. The exchanges between the staff and visitors often involve misunderstandings, result in humorous dialogue and sometimes even involve mocking others, as is the case with the researcher looking for a book in German (Interlude). It is significant that each of the readers seems to arrive at an inopportune moment: the Spanish Reader enters as the Director is preparing his speech (Act I); the Researcher arrives when the Library has been without electricity for several days (Interlude); the Critic arrives when the books have been removed (Act III). This provokes complaints from the employees about how difficult these readers are: 'Aunque le digo si no hubiera sido por los lectores que venían a veces, este edificio era muy bueno. Usted le saca los lectores a esta biblioteca y le queda perfecto' [Although, I'm telling you, if it hadn't been for the readers who used to come here sometimes, this building was pretty good. If you take out all the readers, this library would be perfect] (Martínez, Act II, Scene I, *La biblioteca*, p. 131). 'Hacía años que no venía un cargoso de éstos' [It's been years since someone this annoying has come] (Monteiro, Act III, *La biblioteca*, p. 151). The audience are left wondering if these farcical exchanges are repeated every time a reader arrives or if the few visitors that we see during the play are, in fact, the only people to enter the Library in this twenty-five-year period. Whether some visits are just poorly timed or the Library is rarely used, it shows a big gap between the expectations of the readers and the library staff. Whilst this is amusing, the challenges in accessing the material reveal both the way in which the Library has become dysfunctional and also an extreme sense of disconnect with the outside world, which means that access to the knowledge that the Library contains is severely restricted and its role in society is called into question. The Library becomes increasingly insular, the sense of distance from the outside world is amplified and the third and final act, in which the employees complete their working hours amongst the rubble of a building site in winter, reveals the outside world to be bleak and unpromising. At the end of the play, the employees and the contents of the Library are set to move into a shipping container whilst the site will be repurposed, which leaves the future of the Library uncertain and calls into question the value of the work of its employees.

The dramaturgical analysis reveals the relationship between the employees and their place of work as central to the dramatic core of the play. This is because the library building affects both the work they are able to do and also the pace of their exchanges; as their workplace becomes more restrictive, the ways in which they operate and communicate become slower and more complex. This forms a stark contrast to the buzzing Library that we see in the first half of the play. Act I is fast paced; as visitors begin to arrive, the stage directions state that 'A partir de este instante el ritmo se hace progresivamente vertiginoso' [From this moment onwards, the pace becomes increasingly rapid] and eventually several characters enter at once, voicing their competing and conflicting objectives (*La biblioteca*, p. 116). The sense of increasing pace is communicated in multiple ways through the language of the original play; the situation is intensified by the Secretary who, looming at the door of the Director's office, frequently announces the time, counting down the minutes until the Secretary General makes his appearance whilst the Director becomes increasingly embroiled in the requests and issues of the library staff and visitors. One of the ways in which I was able to consolidate the significance of the fast pace of Act I in the English translation was through a series of workshops carried out with young adults at the Arcola Youth Theatre and in schools connected to Widening Participation initiatives at King's College London.[56] By developing activities which used an extract from the very end of Act I to explore the multiple ways in which time pressure is created throughout the first act, I was able to gain a greater understanding of how this could be interpreted by actors. The workshop participants followed a series of activities beginning by focussing on communicating without using any discernible language and prioritising gestural communication. One of the ways in which this was explored was through participants working in small groups to create a one-minute performance of a fairy-tale using gobbledegook (a combination of invented sounds and words). This activity prioritised two key concerns of the workshop: how do language and action interact when we communicate both on and off stage? How can we identify the objective of a character and use that as a way to portray them and develop their actions when they are under pressure? Participants then moved through a series of exercises which enabled them to experiment with the dramatic text, and, finally, to recreate a short scene from *The Library* in a setting and language which would be relevant to their context in east London in 2015. This created opportunities for students to encounter aspects of the culture of Uruguay through theatre translation and to take on the role of a character from another culture. Participants engaged in a process of experimentation, reflection and improvisation to recreate the scene in a familiar context within their own community.

In addition to the stage directions quoted above, a series of lengthy explanations are met with short interjections and interruptions, particularly from the Secretary and the Director, which creates a rapid pace of dialogue. There are also frequent references to the heat in the room and one of the interpretations of the scene by workshop participants focussed on the ways in which trying to deal with the heat, whilst in a room full of people, would intensify the pressure. One of the characters who enters the Director's office is the Tailor, who does not speak but tirelessly and precisely takes measurements creating a humorous mismatch between words and actions as he takes control of the Director's movements. One of the workshop activities focussed on the way in which the Tailor manipulates the Director's actions as he seeks to impress Estela (the young woman seeking employment) by reciting his unfinished poem to her. This provided a way to begin to explore how conflicting objectives in the scene could result in humour. These aspects of the dramatic text add to the increasing pace and pressure of the act, which I had identified in the original language. The process of experimenting with this section of the text with actors in workshops enabled me to test if this also existed in the English translation and enhanced my understanding of the way in which the text functions to build up to the climax at the end of Act 1.

In terms of the context, the period after the Second World War in Uruguay, when the play was written, was very stable. Uruguay held significant reserves in foreign currency and politicians were seeking to improve the economy through agroindustry and manufacturing, which would create exportable products rather than raw materials. During the 1950s period of 'neobatllismo', Uruguay had an advanced political and social security system while workers received high salaries and had security in their jobs, leading to the common expression 'como el Uruguay no hay' [there's no place like Uruguay].[57] However, the impact of the Marshall Plan in Europe meant that opportunities to export were greatly reduced, making the economic model unsustainable. Writing in 1957, Maggi's work depicts aspects of the relationship between the state and its employees at a time when many people sought change and wanted to improve their economic status, which had declined as the country suffered an economic downturn, evidenced through a growing trade union movement and protests in Montevideo at the end of the 1950s. A sense of unrest and the need for change was manifested in other parts of Latin America, particularly through the Cuban revolution in 1959, which had repercussions throughout Latin America. Within Uruguay, the fact that society was not content with the economic and political situation was marked by the right-wing Partido Nacional winning the general elections in 1958 after almost a century of administration by the centre-right Partido Colorado.[58] The relationship between the state and its employees and society would become increasingly significant at the onset of the civic-military dictatorship in 1973 during which time certain government roles were repurposed to serve repressive ends. *Pedro y el capitán*, studied in Chapter 3, provides an insight into aspects of this problematic relationship.

Through the exploration of the role of the public functionary, *La biblioteca* depicts aspects of the relationship between the state and its employees. Reading *La biblioteca* alongside *M'hijo el dotor* provides an insight into Uruguayan theatre and culture: *M'hijo el dotor* calls into question the idea of progress linked to the new posts created in the city at the start of the century, and through his depiction of a state-run institution in *La biblioteca*, Maggi presents the experience of people undertaking these roles fifty-four years later. In *M'hijo el dotor*, the modernisation process presented by Sánchez is questioned and depicted at its early stages as nascent and incomplete; this is evidenced through the frequent changes in Julio's behaviour and attitudes. In contrast, Maggi depicts a scenario in which, for the employees of the Library, institutional bureaucracy has become an entrenched way of life which has resulted in a bureaucratic system that is so rigid it actually hinders progress. The fact that *La biblioteca* focusses on a public institution at a time when many people in Uruguay were employed by state-run organisations as a result of the new types of jobs and industries created in the first half of the twentieth century, means that many members of the audience would identify with the situation presented, which calls into question the role of the functionary. Critics identify that whilst Maggi draws on experience, including his own experience of working at the Biblioteca Nacional, he does not seek to present the Library through the lens of realism but rather to apply techniques taken from satire, *sainetes* and even the grotesque to use the dramatic space to shed light on the absurd, contradictory and intolerable aspects of institutions and experiences.[59] By depicting the case of a recognisable public institution over a long period of time, which is condensed in the performance, Maggi is able to demonstrate the lack of fulfilment for the employees, which may not be perceptible on a daily basis.

Maggi's own experience of having worked in the Biblioteca Nacional in Montevideo and his fascination with what he described in an interview with me as 'una cosa muy curiosa y muy concreta' [a very strange and specific thing], a photograph of the Library on the day that the foundation stone was laid, strongly influenced his ideas for the play. He explained that in the photograph, the employees of the Library appear full of hope for the future and amongst them was a small boy of around twelve years old, wearing short trousers. Maggi realised that the young boy in the photograph was the current Chief of Staff at the Library and so had spent his entire life within its walls.[60] Maggi was fascinated by this constancy which he referred to as 'esa enfermedad suave, a ese olor, a esa especie de vértigo, sueño y mareo que contagia cualquier órgano burocrático de cualquier país en cualquier mundo' [that kind of slow illness, that smell, that vertigo-like feeling, tiredness and dizziness transmitted by any bureaucratic organ in any country in the world].[61] He ascribes both a universal and a biological quality to the idea of bureaucracy, both of which serve to imply a limitless, living and human quality to it. Maggi's idea of a universal bureaucracy is recognisable; within the UK context, there are examples of state institutions with a bureaucratic system which seems impenetrable and a hindrance, particularly in regard to access to support via the welfare state. This also links to the ideas of access presented within the play; in *La biblioteca* the issue is access to knowledge, but bureaucracy can also prevent access to resources and support and so this concept can be extended through making connections to the target context. The Director explicitly discusses the nature of this bureaucratic disease and its simultaneous life-giving and life-destroying qualities when he makes a speech to his colleagues in which he focusses on the stagnation that occurs. He delivers this at the end of the play, when the library building is about to be flattened and José Luis asks for the card of the director of a different department so that he can apply for a promotion. The Director responds by extolling the virtues of 'La antigüedad' [seniority]:

> DIRECTOR La antigüedad es lo más importante. Una momia fresca no vale nada, en cambio si un ser vivo se va envolviendo con metros y metros de vendajes y rutina, si durante años se ha cocinado a trámite lento, hasta que el aburrimiento y el cansancio le sazonaron bien la carne, entonces, ya es diferente, ya hay mérito para ascender. (*La biblioteca*, Act III, p. 158)
>
> [DIRECTOR Seniority is of the utmost importance. A fresh mummy isn't worth anything at all, whereas if a living being gradually wraps themselves in metres and metres of bandages and routine, if for years they have cooked on a slow heat, until boredom and weariness have fully seasoned their flesh, well then it's different, then there is merit for promotion.]

The idea that the employees are infected by a disease, which slowly takes control of their physical abilities and consumes their positive outlook, rendering them negative and bitter, was essential to the network of meaning that I established in order to create the new dramatic text in English. This enabled me to ensure that the translation would mirror this gradual yet evident decline. The biological quality is attributed to the bureaucratic disease, which infects the employees, and is also attributed to institutions, which Maggi refers to as organs in the quotation above. This reinforces the idea of a mutual dependency and a kind of parasitic relationship in which the employees, seemingly nurtured by the larger organism are, in fact, infected, dependent on it for what little strength they have and so are unable to escape. Therefore, through these employees the institution is sustained. This idea has underpinned my understanding of the play and the concepts of bureaucracy, disease and the Library as a living organism were essential in establishing the network of meanings and referents of the dramatic text. I drew on this network throughout the translation process to inform my choice of words when creating the new dramatic text in English. It is through the analysis of the text and an understanding of the diverse ways in which bureaucracy is explored that I identified this as a central concept in the translation strategy.

In the Interlude, this parasitic relationship between the library building and staff is illustrated when Martínez and the Cleaner search for a book in the dark. The shrinking of the Library has turned the reading room into a catacomb, suggesting an oppressive and lifeless space. It also reinforces the sense of disconnection with the outside world as the Library gradually gets smaller and more impenetrable. As Martínez and the Cleaner search for a book in the dark, moving around like flies, they conjure up the image of parasites surviving on a rotting corpse:

> Martínez y el Limpiador trepan por los anaqueles apoyándose en escalas de cuerda no visibles para el espectador; suben, bajan y se desplazan hacia los costados como las moscas por sobre la pared. Estela va al escritorio y toma la linterna eléctrica. Los rayos de sol que iluminaban la escena han bajado del todo y el redondel de luz que ahora proyecta Estela corre sobre los anaqueles e ilumina con nitidez alternativamente, a Martínez y al Limpiador en sus actitudes de insectos, dando sucesivas instantáneas de las posiciones torturadas que ellos deben adoptar. (*La biblioteca*, Interlude, p. 138)
>
> [Martínez and the Cleaner climb up the shelves using rope ladders which are hidden from the audience; they go up and down and move towards the sides like flies on a wall. Estela goes to the desk and takes the lamp. The rays of sunlight which were illuminating the stage have faded entirely and the circle of light that is now cast by Estela passes over the bookshelves, clearly illuminating Martínez and then the Cleaner in their insect-like poses, giving successive snapshots of the tortured positions that they must adopt.]

The fact that their positions are 'tortured' and they can only try to complete their task by relying on Estela to project lamplight onto them reinforces the futile, frustrating and painful nature of their work. In order to engage with the physicality of the decline as a disease, I closely analysed the stage directions to create specific and detailed sketches of the scenery, scenography and the shape of the Library so that I could establish a picture of the arena in which the verbal exchanges between the characters occur. This allowed me to understand how the Library shapes the employees and is shaped by them as the dramatic action develops.[62]

The physical effect of the downsizing of the building is further evidenced in Act II, Scene 2 in which the Library has become intensely claustrophobic, like the 'interior de un submarino, de la panza de una ballena' [inside a submarine or the belly of a whale], and split into compartments through which the actors must crawl in order to communicate with one another (*La biblioteca*, Act II, p. 139). Furthermore, the working conditions make for a humorous yet intolerable experience as the employees work by candlelight or in absurd positions:

> Al levantarse el telón están a oscuras los compartimentos C y D, y los corredores laterales. En el compartimento A trabaja José Luis, retrepado en la punta de su banco como una cucaracha. En el compartimento B circulan de fichero a fichero, agachados, Ema Fontes y Monteiro. (*La biblioteca*, Act II, p. 140)

> [When the curtain rises compartments C and D and the side corridors are in darkness. In compartment A, José Luis is working whilst leaning back on the edge of the bench, like a cockroach. In compartment B, Ema Fontes and Monteiro move, bending over, from one filing cabinet to another.]

In this scene, which occurs twenty years after the first act, we see that the Library, far from being a spectacular, multi-functioning new space is just smaller and more restrictive; both physically to the movements of the staff and to their progress. José Luis is leaning backwards like a helpless, crushed cockroach, which adds to the sense, already established in the Interlude by the references to Martínez and the Cleaner as flies, that the transformation of the Library dehumanises its employees. Ema and Monteiro are the only characters who we witness carrying out a task relating to the upkeep of the Library as they are organising record cards in a filing cabinet. Monteiro refers to the cabinet as an animal for its capacity to consume the cards and make them disappear, thus suggesting that their task is pointless and reinforcing the idea that the Library has living, animal-like qualities for devouring the record cards rather than preserving them (*La biblioteca*, Act II, p. 140). It also emphasises the idea that the Library somehow sustains itself, and, in doing so, generates work for the employees which keeps them there. However, this cannot continue indefinitely, as the end of the play demonstrates. In the final act, there are frequent references to the infestation of pests caused by the demolition of the library building; as the workmen describe how the pests have remained in the dusty buildings and now must be forcefully evicted, the audience cannot help but make comparisons to the experience of the library employees.

The majority of Act II, Scene 2, is taken up by the tea break, which all employees attend, despite the complicated journeys that they must take to enter the kitchen. During the negative and pathetic exchanges which ensue, the audience learn that Estela has separated from her husband, a new and seemingly unreliable Deputy Director has been employed and Monteiro has missed out on his Olympic victory because he caught a fever days before training started. Monteiro states that in order for him to be able to get a promotion (and also make it possible for Estela to be promoted), Martínez would have to either die or retire within the next two years. Martínez responds, 'Jubilarme no pienso' [I'm not thinking of retiring] (*La biblioteca*, p. 143) and in Act III, he has passed away. Their discussions are interspersed by fragments of the conversation taking place in the Director's office where he discusses his depressed and suicidal state with a friend who offers little advice. Therefore, this penultimate scene emphasises the way in which the employees have been unable to progress and, like the temporary walls that they erected from books and boxes, they have become fixed in their current roles and unable to leave.

In the final act, despite the activity occurring around them, the lack of progress is blatant as the building is prepared for demolition. This is further emphasised by phrases and exchanges which evoke those which occurred in Act I. For example, the discussion over the lack of an item in the budget which would allow for the purchase of the spittoon in Act I provokes the Deputy Director to say, 'Si no hay rubro, no hay rubro. Para algo existen los rubros' [If there isn't a regulation then there isn't a regulation. Regulations exist for a reason] (*La biblioteca*, p. 115).[63] This is echoed by the Director in Act III: 'Perdóneme. Pero los horarios son los horarios y por algo existen' [I'm sorry but working hours are working hours and they exist for a reason] (*La biblioteca*, p. 153). This is the explanation given by the Director as to why the employees must remain at the building site until 5.30pm, despite the demolition occurring around them. In the translation, I worked to ensure that these repetitions in the structure of phrases in the dialogue were maintained so that the audience would make connections with the events of the first act. Once again, in both cases, it is significant that the rationale seems absurd and pointless and this is one of the sources of humour in the play. Yet it also reveals ingrained issues and ways of working: the dependency between the employees and their workplace, the stifling nature of the bureaucratic system, and their lack of agency and control.

The stage directions are extremely lengthy and by exploring the relationship between characters and their environment, I gained an understanding of how one shaped the other and this was essential to the translation strategy that I adopted. My analysis of the dramatic text brought to light a mutual dependency between the characters and their working environment and so it was essential to conceptualise this interaction and the way in which one sustains the other as part of the preverbal dramatic image which would inform my translation into English. It was necessary to ensure that I had a concrete understanding of the changing shape of the library building at the start of each act so that I could then analyse its impact upon the employees in terms of their work, attitudes and movements. I paid particular attention to the stage directions throughout the translation process and always ensured that they were incorporated into the different workshops and readings that I carried out as part of the development of the text in English (even when working with an extract of the text) in order to understand how they shaped the work of the actors. Also, given their significance in the play, it was very useful to hear the stage directions and scenography descriptions read aloud by actors, which helped me to think of the library building as a character. Through the idea of the bureaucratic disease, I was able to specify the function of the Library in cultivating this disease and transmitting it to the characters and how, through them, aspects of this lethargy would be transmitted to the audience. This process of conceptualising the interaction with the space in which the play occurs has been central to my understanding of movement within this play as the library building, and different aspects of waiting for its transformation, constitutes the dramatic core. The bureaucracy, which is essential thematically and as part of the dramatic core, becomes a way of life for the employees and this modifies their movements as it is expressed through their bodies.

Conclusion

This chapter has analysed the play as a construct which communicates a 'fiction'[64] or 'paradigm'[65] with which the translator must interact in order to move the text into the target language. It has shown how the dramaturgical analysis, prompted by the question of what is at stake in the dramatic text, enables the translator to adopt an approach which allows them to engage with the play as a piece to be performed, identify the micro-structures and macro-structures of the dramatic text which illuminate the dramatic core, and to situate the text within its context. I have argued that this is the first stage of the translation process and that it necessarily entails scholarly research to inform and enhance the translation process. This is because the dramatic construct of the play emerges from a particular context and I have shown how an awareness of the source context enhances an understanding of how the discourses, questions and ideas present in the play might interact with concerns in the air in the theatre and in society. Through undertaking this research, the translator is able to understand the network of meanings generated by the source text and work to establish a network for the text in translation. This becomes a framework which informs and guides their translation strategy as they identify key concepts with which to work and ways of working with them through language in order to create the new text in the target language. Chapter 3 expands the process of close reading of the play to demonstrate how an understanding of the ways in which the play relates to its original context is a productive way to create points of contact with the target culture. In this way, the translated play establishes connections in the target context, where it can also generate new meanings. I demonstrate how the translator can conceptualise and produce creative links between source and target cultures by embarking upon a creative process in which they seek to extend the resonances of the original and raise awareness of both close and distant cultural realties.

Notes to Chapter 1

1. Patrice Pavis, *Theatre at the Crossroads of Culture*, trans. by Loren Kruger (London: Routledge, 1992), p. 138.
2. Florencio Sánchez, *M'hijo el dotor*, in *Teatro*, 7th edn (Buenos Aires: Editorial Sopena Argentina, 1972), pp. 243–82; Carlos Maggi, *La biblioteca*, in *50 años de teatro uruguayo: antología*, ed. by Laura Escalante, 2 vols (Montevideo: Ministerio de Educación y Cultura, 1988–90), I, 113–60. Page references throughout the chapter are to these editions of the plays. All translations are my own.
3. Pavis, *Theatre at the Crossroads*, p. 148.
4. David Johnston, 'Professing Translation: The Acts-in-between', *Target*, 25.3 (2013), 365–84 <doi.org/10.1075/target.25.3.04joh> (p. 366).
5. David Johnston, 'Securing the Performability of the Play in Translation', in *Drama Translation and Theatre Practice*, ed. by Sabine Coelsch-Foisner and Holger Klein (Frankfurt a.M.: Peter Lang, 2004), pp. 25–38 (p. 32).
6. Ibid.
7. There is an existing translation of *M'hijo el Dotor* included in *Representative Plays of Florencio Sánchez*, trans. from the Spanish by Willis Knapp Jones, UNESCO Collection of Representative Works, Latin American Series (Washington, DC: Pan American Union, 1961), pp. 15–56.
8. Griselda Castro, *Sainetes: análisis de obras de Florencio Sánchez y Armando Discépolo* (Montevideo: Editorial Técnica S.R.L., 1988), p. 5.
9. Ibid., pp. 27–28.
10. María Nélida Riccetto states that Jerónimo and Luis were Argentine, while José and Pablo were Uruguayan. María Nélida Riccetto (ed.), *Teatro uruguayo contemporáneo: antología*, ed. and intro. by María Nélida Riccetto (Buenos Aires: Colihue, 1993), p. 26.
11. Castro, p. 7. Some scholars place the publication of the serials at later dates. Versényi gives the date as 1879. Adam Versényi, *Theatre in Latin America: Religion, Politics, and Culture from Cortés to the 1980s* (Cambridge: Cambridge University Press, 1993), p. 74. Lauren Rea says that the

publication dates were between 1879 and 1880 (p. 114). Both Versényi and Rea include an account of the way in which the Podestá company transformed the narrative for the stage. Rea discusses how by 1890 in Buenos Aires, *Juan Moreira* had been adapted into two different stage versions, each portraying the gaucho protagonist in a different way, and incorporated into a nation-building project, which would extend into the first three decades of the twentieth century. Lauren Rea, *Argentine Serialised Radio Drama in the Infamous Decade, 1930–1943: Transmitting Nationhood* (Farnham, Surrey: Ashgate, 2013), p. 117.

12. José J. Podestá, *Medio siglo de farándula: memorias* (Córdoba: Rio de la Plata, 1930), p. 42.

13. Juan Carlos Legido, *El teatro uruguayo: de Juan Moreira a los independientes, 1886–1967* (Montevideo: Ediciones Tauro, 1968), p. 12.

14. Versényi, *Theatre in Latin America*, p. 76.

15. Castro, pp. 7–8.

16. Versényi, *Theatre in Latin America*, p. 77.

17. Ibid., pp. 80–81.

18. Castro, pp. 22–23.

19. Florencio Sánchez, *M'hijo el dotor*, study and notes by Mabel V. Manacorda de Rosetti and Rosa Palma de Carpinetti, ed. by María Hortensia Lacau, 7th edn (Buenos Aires: Editorial Kapelusz, 1979), p. 14.

20. Castro, p. 34.

21. Legido, p. 15.

22. Oscar Brando, 'Florencio Sánchez: vida y obra en tres actos', in *El 900*, ed. by Oscar Brando, 2 vols (Montevideo: Cal y Canto, 1999), I, 239–52 (p. 244).

23. David Johnston, 'Translation for the Stage: Product and Process', *NUI Maynooth Papers in Spanish, Portuguese and Latin American Studies*, 6 (2002), 1–28 (p. 14).

24. Ibid.

25. Pavis, *Theatre at the Crossroads*, p. 139.

26. Ibid, p. 140.

27. Ibid, p. 148.

28. Johnston, 'Product and Process', p. 14.

29. Pavis, *Theatre at the Crossroads*, p. 139.

30. Johnston, 'Product and Process', p. 14.

31. Brando, I, 244.

32. Manacorda de Rosetti and Palma de Carpinetti in Sánchez, *M'hijo el dotor*, estudio preliminar, p. 21.

33. Ibid., p. 38.

34. Adam Versényi, 'The Dissemination of Theatrical Translation', in *The Routledge Companion to Dramaturgy*, ed. by Magda Romanska (Oxford: Routledge, 2015), pp. 288–93 (p. 289).

35. Walter Byongsok Chon, 'Intercultural Dramaturgy: The Dramaturg as Cultural Liaison', in *The Routledge Companion to Dramaturgy*, ed. by Magda Romanska (Oxford: Routledge, 2015), pp. 136–40 (p. 140).

36. In contemporary politics, the Partido Nacional is often referred to as Partido Blanco (white) in contrast to the Colorados (red) and these parties have their origins in the period of the civil wars in Uruguay and the different colour headbands worn by the two opposing factions. The Blancos are a right/centre-right party and came to represent the interests of the countryside and rural development. The Partido Colorado are centre/centre-right and represented the interests of Montevideo. Whilst sometimes today both parties can be referred to as centre-right, depending on the leadership at the time, the National Party is generally more conservative. Uruguay did not have a left/centre-left party until the formation of the Frente Amplio (Broad Front) in 1971.

37. Ana Frega, 'La formulación de un modelo: 1890–1918', in *Historia del Uruguay en el siglo XX (1890–2005)*, ed. by Ana Frega and others, 2nd edn (Montevideo: Ediciones de la Banda Oriental S.R.L; Ministerio de Relaciones Exteriores; Facultad de Humanidades y Ciencias de la Educación, 2008), pp. 17–50 (pp. 25–30).

38. José Batlle y Ordóñez was President of Uruguay 1903–07 and 1911–15. Frega points out that the majority of reformist projects were evidenced in his second term (p. 31) and she gives a detailed

account of the projects and laws introduced (pp. 31–39) in her chapter 'La formulación de un modelo' in *Historia del Uruguay*, ed. by Frega and others, pp. 17–50. A note on the term *interior*: this is used to refer to the majority of the rural areas of the country, excluding the coast and the capital, Montevideo, which is the largest city.

39. Manacorda de Rosetti and Palma de Carpinetti in Sánchez, *M'hijo el dotor*, estudio preliminar, ed. by Lacau, p. 22.
40. Ibid., pp. 22–23.
41. Johnston, 'Product and Process', p. 12.
42. Pavis, *Theatre at the Crossroads*, p. 148.
43. Ibid.
44. Ibid.
45. Sirkku Aaltonen, *Time-Sharing on Stage: Drama Translation in Theatre and Society* (Clevedon: Multilingual Matters, 2000), p. 28.
46. David Hare, *Writing Left-Handed* (London: Faber and Faber, 1991), p. 24.
47. Susan Bassnett, 'Still Trapped in the Labyrinth: Further Reflections on Translation and Theatre', in *Constructing Cultures: Essays on Literary Translation*, ed. by Susan Bassnett and André Lefevere (Clevedon: Multilingual Matters, 1998), pp. 90–108 (p. 93).
48. Mario Benedetti, *Montevideanos* (Montevideo: Centro Editor de América Latina, 1968).
49. Carlos Maggi, Interview conducted in Spanish, Montevideo, 15 November 2013.
50. Mario Benedetti, *Literatura uruguaya siglo XX* (Montevideo: Arca, 1988), pp. 312–13.
51. [Emir Rodríguez Monegal (?)], 'Dramaturgo con ambiciones', *Espectáculos*, 21 December 1962 (n.pag.).
52. There is one existing translation of *La biblioteca* for a US audience: Carlos Maggi, *The Library*, in *Voices of Change in the Spanish American Theater: An Anthology*, ed. and trans. by William Oliver (Austin: University of Texas Press, 1971), pp. 105–69.
53. Maggi, Interview.
54. Federico García Lorca, *Doña Rosita the Spinster*, ed. and trans. by Gwynne Edwards (London: Methuen Drama; A. & C. Black, 2008) (parallel text). Lorca had visited Argentina where he delivered a series of lectures and attended performances of his plays in Buenos Aires in 1933. (*Doña Rosita*, p. ix)
55. The Interlude takes place in Act II between Scenes 1 and 2. The stage directions at the beginning of the Interlude state that 'Han pasado diez años' [Ten years have passed] (p. 135). In my analysis, I understand this as a repetition of the time passed stated at the start of the act: 'Diez años después' [Ten years later] (p. 128). This is partly because the Interlude takes place in a different location — the rest of the play occurs in the Director's office (even as the Library changes shape) — and so the repetition of the passage of time introduces the idea that the reading room space has also aged and changed. Furthermore, in Act II, Scene 2 (when a further ten years have passed, according to the stage directions), the Director states that he is 47 years old. Therefore, I understand that only twenty years have passed since the start of the play, rather than thirty, because this would have made the Director seventeen at the start of the play. I have interpreted the Interlude, and the change of space that it demands, as a scene in a different location to Act II, Scene 1 but occurring in the same time period. There is then a jump in time for Act II, Scene 2 — this is my interpretation and understanding of the passage of time. The translation states the number of years that have passed at the start of each act and scene as in the original; I have not made any additions to clarify the passage of time. This is because, as translator, it is not my job to resolve this difficulty in the text and my way of understanding it is just one possible interpretation. Ultimately, the director of the play would make a decision about the passage of time in the play and how this relates to the age of the Library Director, as well as other elements in the play. I conceived of it in this way in order to be able to work with the idea of the passage of time in my translation. I was also able to discuss it with actors in the various workshops detailed in this chapter. For them, this information and instruction enabled them to imagine the ageing of their characters, as obviously the passage of time does not only relate to the building but also to the characters. We also discussed how the Interlude could serve a practical function in the play by allowing a change of scenography to occur behind the curtain which forms the backdrop to the Interlude.

56. This work was supported by funding awarded by the Cultural Institute at King's as part of their inaugural Collaboration Award for Early Career Researchers. The funding allowed me to plan, develop and deliver workshops in collaboration with theatre director and practitioner William Donaldson. The objectives of the workshop were: to develop techniques for taking on the role of a character from a different culture; to experiment with different types of language and the relationship between language and action; to explore how a play from Uruguay could be performed in London today in a way that is culturally relevant to participants' communities, youth theatre group, school or family. Through this collaboration, we were able to develop activities to explore the pace and rhythm of the play and the creative ways in which the play could be adapted for a contemporary audience. In this way, we explored aspects of the text identified in the dramaturgical analysis in practice through games and activities. An overview of the project can be found here: 'Translation Plays, Intercultural Workshops', *King's College London*, <https://www.kcl.ac.uk/Cultural/-/Projects/Translation-Plays> [accessed 13 October 2020].
57. Neobatllismo refers to the period 1946–58 during which president Luis Batlle Berres (Partido Colorado) sought to continue with the economic and social reforms to improve welfare, education and working opportunities implemented at the start of the century. Esther Ruiz, 'El "Uruguay próspero" y sus crisis. 1946–1964', in *Historia del Uruguay en el siglo XX (1890–2005)*, ed. by Ana Frega and others, 2nd edn (Montevideo: Ediciones de la Banda Oriental S.R.L; Ministerio de Relaciones Exteriores; Facultad de Humanidades y Ciencias de la Educación, 2008), pp. 123–62 (p. 125).
58. Ruiz, pp. 150–53.
59. Ruben Yáñez, 'El teatro actual', *Capitulo oriental: la historia de la literatura uruguaya*, 31 (1968–69), 479–98 (p. 489). Juanamaría Cordones-Cook, 'Entrevista a Carlos Maggi', *Latin American Theatre Review*, 20.2 (1986–87), 107–12 (p. 107).
60. Maggi, Interview.
61. Benedetti, *Literatura uruguaya*, p. 314.
62. The practice of drawing the stage layout and scenography was a really fruitful exercise for this play and it is one that I have often used in undergraduate seminars with students of Spanish, Theatre, and Translation (using the text in both the original Spanish and in English translation). The type of reading required and the visualisation of the stage underscores the importance of close reading, attention to detail and different types of languages for the stage. Having an image with which to work can enable and equip students to confidently approach the translation of the text.
63. *Rubro* translates as 'heading' or 'section'. In the *Diccionario del español del Uruguay* (Montevideo: Ediciones de la Banda Oriental, 2011), it is defined as 'partida financiera de un presupuesto' (p. 487) meaning the individual section/item/heading in a budget. Therefore, the issue and ensuing argument in the original is about the lack of a relevant section in the budget, defined by a heading, referring to purchasing extraordinary objects, including spittoons. In English, the force of the argument and the references to a specific rule were not fully captured in the word 'heading' or 'section'; in fact, I actually felt that this became quite vague and obscure unless it was qualified or expanded upon e.g. a section of the budget. This is why, for this part of the translation, I chose to translate 'rubro' as 'regulation' because it captures in one word the specificity and significance of the information that they are looking for. Using this word allowed me to maintain the rhythm of the argument and both its specificity and absurdity. The term appears later in the same discussion 'trasponer rubros' in reference to moving money around in the budget to pay for the spittoon and I chose to translate this as 'swindling' (p. 115). It also appears at the end of the scene when Martínez states: 'La sala se trasladó a 21 hasta que en el próximo presupuesto haya rubro para vaciar inundaciones' [The room was moved into 21 until there's a provision for draining floods in the next budget] (p. 126). For this final instance, the term 'section' (in the next budget) could work in English but for the other instances it was too vague. I decided that I would select a different word to capture the meaning when the term is used at three points in the act. Whilst this meant losing some of the repetition of this term throughout the act, I had maintained it where it was significant during the exchange about the spittoon.

64. Pavis, *Theatre at the Crossroads*, p. 139.
65. Johnston, 'Product and Process', p. 14.

CHAPTER 2

❖

The Library by Carlos Maggi

Information about workshops to develop and
share the translation can be found on pp. 37–38.
For details of the original text in Spanish, see p. 44 n. 2.

Characters

MARTÍNEZ (m)	Acts I and II
DEPUTY DIRECTOR, Don Esteban Fattori (m)	Acts I and II
SECRETARY, Mrs de Luppi (f)	Acts I and II
MONTEIRO (m)	
CLEANER, Aquiles (m)	Acts I and II
DIRECTOR, Schopenhauer Pérez (m)	
MARÍA ZULEMA (f)	Act I
SPANISH READER (m)	Act I
ESTELA (f)	
TAILOR (m)	Act I
EMPLOYEE 1	
EMPLOYEE 2	
MARCUCIANO PERLUCHINO (m)	Act II
JOSÉ LUIS (m)	Acts II and III
RESEARCHER (m)	Interlude
EMA (f)	Acts II and III
DIRECTOR'S FRIEND (m)	Act II
CRITIC (m)	Act III
ENGINEER (m)	Act III
WORKMAN 1 (m)	Act III
WORKMAN 2 (m)	Act III
ORATOR (invisible) (m)	Act III

Act 1

The height of summer around the year 1917 or 1918. The managerial office of the Library. A double door on the back wall, a small door on the wall to the right and a bright window on the left-hand side. The DIRECTOR*'s writing desk, small secretary's desk, several large comfy chairs etc. Before the curtain rises, a few beats of a military march can be heard. On stage there is the general apathetic air of any public office but suddenly, when the band stops playing,* MARTÍNEZ *positions himself behind the desk in a pompous manner and begins to parody a speaker. The* DEPUTY DIRECTOR*, the* SECRETARY*,* MONTEIRO *and the* CLEANER *encourage him with their laughter and shouts of support: Bravo! Hear hear! Hurrah! Etc.*

MARTÍNEZ My esteemed Director, Mr Schopenhauer Pérez, and Deputy Director, Mr Esteban Fattori (*the* DEPUTY DIRECTOR *nods*), also known as the Old Fox (*the* DEPUTY DIRECTOR *makes an expression to show his annoyance*), it is a pleasure to welcome you here today, Ladies and Gentlemen (*very good etc.*). Today we will lay the foundation stone of the new library building. What is the foundation stone? It is a stone that, once placed, does not mark the start of the construction of a building; and if it is removed at a later date, the building lacks nothing. Ladies and Gentlemen, the foundation stone is the only stone which is not fundamental at all. (*Cheers of approval. The* CLEANER *takes a flag, which is leaning against the wall in the corner of the room; he unfolds it and places it in its stand next to the speaker and beside the desk.*) Citizens... Citizens! (*He searches in his pockets.*) Citizens of this city, here I have it, (*he places his thumb and forefinger together and shows them*) upon this stone, I will build my library (*shouting and cheering in response*). Our country is a country of justice, democracy and freedom. Therefore, this stone is dedicated freely to the library that will be built upon it (*he flicks the imaginary stone into the air*). The stone is dedicated freely to the Old Fox hiding behind his cunning eyes (*the* DEPUTY DIRECTOR *makes an expression to show his annoyance*) and heaven forbid you should cross the Fox Cub hiding behind his little desk (*applauding and cheering*).

CLEANER Watch out! The Cub! (*Brief silence.*)

DIRECTOR (*Entering*) Good afternoon. (*He is an efficient, decisive and authoritative man.*)

ALL Good afternoon.

DEPUTY DIRECTOR How are you, sir?

DIRECTOR Fine thank you. There were noises coming from in here... I suppose that it must be the preparations for the ceremony.

DEPUTY DIRECTOR Yes, sir, the preparations... the band...

CLEANER I put the flag in place.

DIRECTOR I'd never have thought that such a small flag would cause such a racket. Martínez, go upstairs and ask to borrow a carpet from the Progress Society: the red one that they provided us with for the Menéndez donation. Lay it out in the hallway and close the main door until the ceremony starts. I don't want there to be footprints on it when we receive the Secretary General.

MARTÍNEZ It will be like new, sir. (*He leaves.*)

DIRECTOR Monteiro, see that the band sends someone to stand at the corner to give the signal. As soon as the Secretary General's car stops, the music must start. Not before or after. It has to be at that exact moment. One must seek to create a certain emotional effect. (*MONTEIRO leaves. To the DEPUTY DIRECTOR*) Don Esteban, I need you to...

CLEANER If I may, sir...

DIRECTOR Yes...

CLEANER We have a problem. There isn't a spittoon.

DIRECTOR Good heavens man!

CLEANER I'm telling you because the Secretary General is a spitter. I've seen him myself. He speaks for a while and... thp.

DIRECTOR Whatever happened to the ones we used to have?

CLEANER We never had any. Nobody spits here.

DEPUTY DIRECTOR Here we have manners, sir.

DIRECTOR Mrs de Luppi, would you do me a favour? Send someone to buy... one of those receptacles. See to it that it's done quickly. I have my speech, and I think that it still...

DEPUTY DIRECTOR Excuse me, Director, but I don't think it will be possible to buy one of those receptacles. There are no means for it.

DIRECTOR Well, it isn't important, things can stay as they are.

CLEANER I'm telling you, the Secretary General is a spitter and I'm not kidding, you know. He's going to leave our carpet in a terrible state.

DIRECTOR These are merely insignificant details. We must focus on what is fundamental and the rest doesn't matter.

DEPUTY DIRECTOR (*Almost to himself*) I wouldn't go as far as that.

DIRECTOR (*Worrying*) Don't you agree, Don Esteban?

DEPUTY DIRECTOR It would be good to have one. It's essential. It's correct. It's courteous.

CLEANER If you like, I can take the lampshade down, turn it over and put it on the floor. It's almost identical.

DIRECTOR For heaven's sake! That would be completely improper. Besides, the lampshade has a hole in the middle. Mrs de Luppi, are you sure there isn't anything in the till?

SECRETARY There is money. We have around one hundred pesos, but...

DIRECTOR Send someone to buy one then.

DEPUTY DIRECTOR But there's no regulation for it.

DIRECTOR We need an object and one buys objects with money. We have money. We pay for it and that's the end of the matter.

DEPUTY DIRECTOR If there isn't a regulation then there isn't a regulation. Regulations exist for a reason.

DIRECTOR This is absurd, Don Esteban...

DEPUTY DIRECTOR It might be. But the alternative constitutes classic misappropriation of public funds and I do not want to be an accomplice in it. It's a serious offence.

DIRECTOR And what are we to do, then? Do we choke the Secretary General or do we simply allow him to leave our carpet in ruins?

DEPUTY DIRECTOR There must be a solution other than swindling. It is clearly forbidden in article 96, section 9 of the financial legislation. Classic misappropriation. If there isn't a regulation, there isn't a regulation. They exist for a reason. (*Short pause*)

DIRECTOR Aquiles, go and buy one. Give him four or five pesos from the till please, Mrs de Luppi. It won't cost more than that. (*The CLEANER and the SECRETARY leave.*)

DEPUTY DIRECTOR If you don't mind, I would prefer to go home. I don't think I'm feeling too well, today, I am...

DIRECTOR Mr Fattori, you started off as a porter and today you are Deputy Director of the Library. Thirty-four years of service means that your good reputation precedes you.

DEPUTY DIRECTOR Yes, but I...

DIRECTOR How about you go to the Head Office and accompany the Secretary back here? I had it in mind to ask you to assist me with this important duty. Remember that a lot depends on the Secretary's visit today.

DEPUTY DIRECTOR Director, don't forget, I swear that this is misappropriation. Your youth will be your ruin yet.

DIRECTOR It is more likely that I will ruin my youth than it will ruin me. Go on Don Esteban, don't be anxious, go and meet the Secretary General and bring him back here. And do not be alarmed by this purchase. We must concern ourselves with achieving the fundamental things, fundamental, just like the foundation stone.

The DEPUTY DIRECTOR leaves and the DIRECTOR sits at his table, takes the draft of his speech out of his pocket and starts to go over it. He reads quietly but makes large gestures.

SECRETARY (*Entering the room*) Sir... there is...

DIRECTOR Shhhhhh (*in relation to his speech*) which sounds better? At this crucial moment or at this significant moment?

SECRETARY Crucial is shorter.

DIRECTOR (*Editing*) So it is. (*Oratorical*) At this crucial moment...!

SECRETARY Sir... There is...

DIRECTOR I don't have time to see anyone. Look at the time. The ceremony starts at six and I have to edit this and write up the final version.

SECRETARY But it's the editor from the magazine. If I tell her that you're busy she'll come in anyway.

DIRECTOR Who?

SECRETARY (*Imitating the pretentiousness of MARÍA ZULEMA*). Mrs María Zulema Alcanfor de Strauch.

DIRECTOR Oh!... It's her...Yes, tell her to come through.

SECRETARY (*From the door*) Come through please.

From this moment onwards the pace becomes increasingly rapid.

MARÍA ZULEMA Director... (*familiar tone*) How are you, sweetie?

DIRECTOR And this *Blue Vocation*?

MARÍA ZULEMA Divine. We're almost ready to go to print with issue 14. Previously unpublished works of two young French poets. Unfortunately, one of them lives in Buenos Aires (*the telephone starts ringing*), but he writes perfectly in French. So his work is in translation as well. We have an epic from Lower Normandy, which is delightful, all in modernist hendecasyllables, evident influence of Rubén in France given...

DIRECTOR Excuse me (*he goes to answer the telephone*). Yes, Schopenhauer Pérez speaking. Yes, Isabel... yes... (*Pause*) Yes of course, of course... (*Pause*) Yes, with a border on the inside...exactly, that's what I thou... (*Pause*) Yes, darling, of course. The very smallest border. Perfect. Yes... yes... well... now it's? It's almost half past five. Let's say seven. (*Pause*) Because of the ceremony, remem...? Yes, Isabel, yes, yes, yes. (*Pause*) Seven on the dot, as soon as the Secretary leaves, OK. See you soon, darling. See you... later, we'll talk about it, I have to look at my speech for... (*Pause*) See you very soon. Of course, silly, lots. See you very soon. Mmmmwaa , mmmwaa...

MARÍA ZULEMA Love! I call you not love
as that name is not fitting
but there is no matter where
love does not create form and beauty

DIRECTOR (*Taking the picture from the desk*) It was Isabel... we're getting married on Saturday... she is an angel.

MARÍA ZULEMA Love! I call you not love
as that name is not fitting
but there is no matter where...

DIRECTOR I don't think those lines scan correctly.

MARÍA ZULEMA But sweetie! They're from Calderón.

DIRECTOR From Calderón?

MARÍA ZULEMA Well... from him or from Lope... Or are they from Gracián?

DIRECTOR The syllables... hmm... If I weren't so pressed...

SECRETARY (*From the doorway*) Sir, if you can give me the draft of the speech, I can type it up for you.

DIRECTOR No, it needs a few finishing touches. I'll finish it right away. (*The* SECRETARY *leaves.*)

MARÍA ZULEMA You're busy, darling. I'm leaving. I'll come back another day. I didn't think that today of all days...

DIRECTOR Well, it's just that, today...

MARÍA ZULEMA I was coming to collect your ever so beautiful poem! So beautiful and so sincere, so...

DIRECTOR Yes, darling, but today, I don't know if you are aware...

MARÍA ZULEMA For me, that poem was simply unforgettable. It was something of a homage to the Belgian people, who were invaded! I remember it perfectly. Never has the invasion of Belgium moved me so! What was it called? The plaint of the saint? The bellow of the cello? What was it, sweetie? It seemed so musical. So... So... I have it on the tip of my tongue... The harpy of the harp? The brute of the flute? The grace of the double bass? What was it? I can almost see it. The scorn of the horn? The threat of the clarinet?

DIRECTOR I entitled it; 'The hero of the oboe.' (*Adopting a poetic tone*) A modernist impressionist view: a melancholy meditation on the Belgian ruins.

MARÍA ZULEMA How beautiful, sweetie! How beautiful!

DIRECTOR Do you remember in the portico? Two years ago, I told you the first lines... 'Beside the marsh a trace; a sign of starry space, symphonising'...

CLEANER (*Interrupting, he enters with a parcel which he carries like a trophy*) Sir! We bought the spit...

DIRECTOR (*Startled*) Aquiles!

CLEANER What?

DIRECTOR What are you bringing in here?

CLEANER I'm bringing the spit...

DIRECTOR (*Furious*) That will do! Leave it there and get out.

CLEANER (*Muttering*) He tells me to buy it, I buy it. She tells me to go in, I go in. So why is he shouting at me? Who can make sense of them?

DIRECTOR (*Conciliatory*) Aquiles: you have done nothing wrong. Just leave the parcel up there.

SECRETARY (*From the doorway*) Sir, it's less than half an hour until six.

DIRECTOR Oh, yes, the speech! I really need to get a move on!

MARÍA ZULEMA Sweetie... you have so much to do!... I ought to leave, I know, but your words are so beautiful that they captivate me. I swear to you, they captivate me. They are so... so... How shall I put it? So beautiful! So, so...

DIRECTOR (*To the SECRETARY*) We will take care of the speech right away, Mrs de Luppi. Aquiles, is the band ready?

CLEANER They have been ready for hours, and they've sent someone to stand at the corner to give the signal. I bought the... And so everything's set.

DIRECTOR Right, María Zulema, you can see, really, now I...

MARÍA ZULEMA I understand. You're busy. Can you give me the poem? I wanted it for this issue of *Blue Vocation* because... it is so... so...

CLEANER (*Leaving*) It is so, so, so, so, so... sounds like a broken record. (*The telephone rings.*)

DIRECTOR (*While he goes to answer*) To be honest with you, María Zulema, it isn't, what I would call, finished. (*To the telephone*) Hello...yes, it's me, me darling. I can't hear you very well at all, speak up. Yes, Isabel... yes. (*Short pause*) Yes... with the border on the inside, but sma... (*short pause*) Why?... I think on the inside... Do you think? Yes? (*To MARÍA ZULEMA*) I wanted to revise it. There are some verses which still... (*To the telephone*) Yes, Isabel, of course. (*To MARÍA ZULEMA*) I don't know, but I think I don't entirely have a feeling for some of the lines. (*To the telephone*) Of course, I said yes, yes of course... on the outside! (*Short pause*) All right, call her. I said yes. Yes, I'll speak to your mother! (*To MARÍA ZULEMA*) I think one of the lines has the wrong number of syllables.

(*To the* SECRETARY *who is at the door and shows him the blank sheets of paper*) Yes Mrs de Luppi, I think that we have enough time. I'll get to it in just one minute. (*To the* CLEANER *who enters and goes to open the box that he was previously carrying*) Aquiles. Do not open that. (*To the telephone*) Yes, yes, yes. Fine, thank you. And you? I said fine, thank you, and you? I asked you how you are today. I'm glad. Yes, yes, hello, hello! Miss, miss, please don't disconnect... Yes, we're talking, yes. Don't disconnect, miss. Yes, hello, hello. Oh, it's you Mrs... yes, yes, yes, yes, yes, of course (*short pause*) yes, yes (*short pause*). All right, with the very small, tiny border on the outside (*short pause*). Large? I also... of course. (*Short pause*) Yes... (*Meanwhile the* CLEANER *has taken the spittoon, which is made of blue glass, from the packet and cleaned it;* MARÍA ZULEMA *goes over to the desk and takes the spittoon in her hands as if it were a bouquet of flowers.*) (*To* MARÍA ZULEMA) But María Zulema! Aquiles, take it please.

MARÍA ZULEMA How beautiful sweetie! How beautiful! A blue vase! It's like something imagined by Amado Nervo.

DIRECTOR Yes, a blue vase to put roses in. (*To the telephone*) Sorry? No... I said yes, that it is going to look lovely. (*Short pause*) Of course... with the tiny border that's large and on the outside. Of course... yes, yes... (*short pause*). Well... at seven, when the Secretary General leaves... Of course, the found... (*short pause*). Yes, because it's already exp... (*Short pause*). Today, yes at six — no! I'll come at seven. Yes. See you later. See you later. See you later... mother.

SECRETARY (*She has been waiting by the door in full view.*) Doctor José Carlos de Guiñazul, Marquis of Cierraceño is here; he arrived a while ago and is getting impatient. Monteiro has a pressing matter to discuss with you. Also, a young lady has just come in and she wants to wait. I have already told her that you must finish your speech (*looking at* MARÍA ZULEMA) and that the ceremony is almost upon us. But she insists. She's the sort who enjoys pestering.

DIRECTOR And... what... what time is it?

SECRETARY After half past five.

DIRECTOR I really have to get a move on. Close those shutters, that light is painfully bright.

MARÍA ZULEMA You're busy...

DIRECTOR No, it's not that. It's just I'm busy.

MARÍA ZULEMA I had better go, hadn't I?

SECRETARY This way please.

MARÍA ZULEMA And the originals? Give them to me as they are, won't you? Give them to me, sweetie.

DIRECTOR Mrs de Luppi, show those people in. All of them. Go on. I'll tilt the shutters myself.

SECRETARY All of them?

DIRECTOR Yes, all at the same time, that way I'll deal with them faster. If only it weren't so hot! What time is it?

He tilts the shutters, the SECRETARY, *the* SPANISH READER, MONTEIRO *and* ESTELA *enter. Behind them is the* CLEANER *who carries a container of water. During the following scene he pours the water into the spittoon and takes it down from the desk, where* MARÍA ZULEMA *had placed it, and puts it on the floor.*

DIRECTOR Pleased to meet you, sir.

SPANISH READER (*Correcting him*) Doctor, Doctor José Carlos de Guiñazul, Marquis of Cierraceño, Spanish, of course.

DIRECTOR Pleased to meet you, take a seat. (*Aside*) What's the matter, Monteiro?

MONTEIRO The final, sir. The match is on Saturday.

DIRECTOR What final?

MONTEIRO We're playing for promotion to the second division.

DIRECTOR The what?

MONTEIRO The second division. Today is training and I have to go. Think of what's riding on Saturday.

DIRECTOR Look at me. Completely cool and I'm getting married on Saturday.

MONTEIRO And you aren't training? I mean... aren't you... aren't you making preparations?

DIRECTOR I am up to here with preparations.

MONTEIRO You see. You have to prepare. Can I go, sir? It's for promotion to the second division.

DIRECTOR And who will attend the reading room when the Secretary General arrives?

MONTEIRO It would be best to close the reading room this evening: who's going to read with a band playing in the courtyard? Anyway, I don't think that there will be any readers. No one has come for three or four days. If this were nightclub it would have gone bust already. Also, sir, if the Secretary General sees that it is empty, he's going to take note of it... It's going to make things worse.

DIRECTOR Very well, leave; off you go. Close up the reading room before you go and leave.

MONTEIRO I can't wait to go in dribbling amongst the defenders. (*He leaves as if dancing with an imaginary ball.*)

DIRECTOR I'm sorry about the interruption. Miss, I don't think that we have made our introductions. Forgive me.

ESTELA Estela Grisel, I brought this card for you sir.

DIRECTOR (*Greeting her*) Pleased to meet you Mis... (*He hears murmurings and sees the* CLEANER *and* MARÍA ZULEMA, *who have been arguing about the spittoon for a short while: he insists on leaving it on the floor and she is returning it to its place on the desk. The* DIRECTOR *interrupts his introduction and makes a gesture for them to stop.*)

CLEANER (*He abandons the to and fro of the spittoon*) But, Director! The Secretary is going to have to stand up every time. And what if he misses, with it here on the table?

MARÍA ZULEMA (*Putting it on the table*) Here, right? For your infinite talent, the blue vase is another source of inspiration.

SECRETARY (*Spitefully*) Put it right next to the picture.

DIRECTOR It makes no difference. Wherever it is. I'm so pressed for time and it's so hot! (*The* CLEANER *leaves, muttering under his breath.*) You had given me this card hadn't you, sir? (*To the* SECRETARY) What time is it? (*To* ESTELA) No. It was you who gave me the card (*he reads it*). Mmm. Mmm, mm. Oh! Pleased to meet you, Miss Grisel.

MARTÍNEZ (*From the doorway*) There is someone here with something for you, Mr Director, and he wants to see you.

DIRECTOR Tell him to leave it. I'm busy (MARTÍNEZ *leaves*). (*To* ESTELA) So you are...

ESTELA (*Too loudly*) A childhood friend of the Costa Rican Ambassador's sister.

MARTÍNEZ (*From the doorway*) The messenger says that it's the tailcoat you hired for Saturday and that you have to try it on and sign for it.

DIRECTOR (*To the* SECRETARY) Please can you take care of that. (*To* ESTELA) So you are...

SECRETARY She is a childhood friend of the Costa Rican Ambassador's sister (*She leaves*).

SPANISH READER Please excuse me... but I am in a bit of a hurry and they are already starting...

DIRECTOR (*To the* READER) Pleased to meet you. Pleased to meet you, sir.

SPANISH READER Doctor. Doctor José Carlos de Guiñazul, Marquis of Cierraceño at your service.

DIRECTOR Pleased to meet you. Have a seat.

SPANISH READER I was coming to see you, my director — if I may — I was coming to see you, because in this repository there is, without a doubt, a rare copy of the collection of etchings by the artist who was, at one time, the great master of his art, needless to say...

MARÍA ZULEMA Sweetie!... Sweetie! You seem busy. I had better go, hadn't I?

DIRECTOR (*He runs towards her*) Yes, darling. It would be better if you came another day. Tomorrow. Whenever you like. You can see them all, I'm swamped.

MARÍA ZULEMA And your poem? I won't leave without your marvellous, 'Paladin of the Violin'.

DIRECTOR 'Hero of the oboe'... (*Accompanying her*) Tomorrow, María Zulema. Come back tomorrow. You can see, I'm rushed off my feet.

MARÍA ZULEMA (*To the visitors*) He is a marvellous, marvellous poet. A great poet, although he is getting married on Saturday. See you tomorrow. Sweetie, you really won't give me the poem now? Sweetie... (*gesture of refusal from the* DIRECTOR). So stubborn! (*She leaves.*)

SECRETARY (*Taking him aside*) Director, the man with the tailcoat insists. He can't leave it without doing a fitting for you.

DIRECTOR Tell him to wait. That's all I need.

SECRETARY The tailor's shop closes at six and he has to be back before then. He says that unless you do the fitting today, they can't guarantee that it will be ready for Saturday.

DIRECTOR He can wait for a few minutes at least; what time is it? I'm dripping with sweat. (*Approaching them whilst wiping his face and neck.*) So you are...

At the same time.

SPANISH READER Doctor José Carlos de Guiñazul, Marquis of Cierraceño, at your service.

ESTELA A childhood friend of the Costa Rican Ambassador's sister.

SPANISH READER Please Miss, politeness costs nothing, even when one is in a hurry, and so I yield to courtesy.

ESTELA Goodness me, I'm not in a hurry. I think I'll be around here for years.

DIRECTOR Please, go on, Marquis, I mean, Doctor...

SPANISH READER Well... as I was starting to explain to you: you have in this repository an admirable collection of etchings by the distinguished Piranesi, as accomplished a draughtsman as there ever was and, as you will know, sir, the artist of the aerial perspective. Juan Bautista Piranesi, Venice, 1720 to 1778.

DIRECTOR Yes, I am aware of this... But you were coming...

SPANISH READER You will see, sir... It is extremely interesting... Your admirable collection consists of, amongst other pieces of outstanding value, an etching of exceptional value in itself and in particular for me, although more than for me personally, for my household, understanding by household — although it is not necessary to specify — the entire lineage, speaking genealogically, it is sufficient to say: for those who share my name and my blood.

DIRECTOR Of course, I understand. But you want...

SPANISH READER It is very amusing although, obviously, I must provide some of the historical details. It was the year 1653 when in a backwater hamlet in Siena, a young girl of around 17 years of age married a young army captain. She was gracious, charming and serene. As for him, a sturdy, strapping young man and...

DIRECTOR I'm sorry to interrupt you but I'm in such a hurry! I mean, I'm so pressed for time! I don't know if you know, today... in a few moments, the foundation stone will be laid, for the new... (*he goes towards the door*). Please excuse me (*shouting*) Mrs de Luppi: what time is it?

SPANISH READER For heaven's sake man! It's only twenty to six!

DIRECTOR If you could be brief, sir, I mean Marquis. I'm sorry, Doctor.

SPANISH READER For crying out loud Director! I came to see you at half past four, that is, over an hour ago. After making me wait so long, the least you could do would be to listen to me, given that I am not demanding that you help me with the material that I came in search of.

DIRECTOR But I do desperately want to help you. But immediately.

SPANISH READER I'm pleased to hear of your kind disposition and I'm very grateful for it... As I stated previously: it was in Siena around the year 1653. She was youthful, gracious, fu...

DIRECTOR Please, sir. Tell me precisely what it is that you want.

SPANISH READER But you're not listening to me at all! When I start to string together my sentences, you interrupt me.

DIRECTOR Please be brief, I beg of you.

SPANISH READER I beg of you, sir, try to follow my thoughts.

DIRECTOR You, sir, want to examine Piranesi's etchings, correct?

SPANISH READER In a way, yes and in a way, no. Moreover, I have witnesses who can vouch for the fact that I told you this. Although you will not allow me to explain the whys and wherefores... I...

DIRECTOR (*To the SECRETARY*) Mrs de Luppi!

SECRETARY Sir... (*entering*)

DIRECTOR Tell Monteiro. No, Monteiro was given permission to leave. Tell Martínez to come here. Quickly, please.

SECRETARY What do I do with the man from the tailors? He's insisting on leaving.

DIRECTOR Make him wait for two minutes. Entertain him.

SECRETARY (*Inside the building*) Martínez! The Director... (*MARTÍNEZ enters*).

DIRECTOR Martínez, this gentleman wants to consult the etchings by Piranesi. Would you mind...

MARTÍNEZ He wants to see them now?

DIRECTOR Yes, Martínez.

MARTÍNEZ The reading room is closed.

DIRECTOR Open it.

MARTÍNEZ Besides, if they're etchings then they're in the basement and it's Monteiro who manages that collection. You gave him permission to leave, didn't you sir?

DIRECTOR You go. Do it as a favour for me.

MARTÍNEZ I don't know if it'll be worth it. I mean, I don't know if I will find them.

DIRECTOR If you are determined, Martínez.

MARTÍNEZ And is it worth me being determined?

DIRECTOR If I tell you to do something, you must do it.

MARTÍNEZ It depends. I don't have to do everything that you tell me to do.

DIRECTOR And what do you think you are going to gain with that attitude?

MARTÍNEZ And with the other one, what would I gain? A better salary? No, because you don't draw up the budget, sir. Nor a promotion, because there isn't a vacancy. Prizes are not permitted. Congratulations, I would gain, from you, and a suit covered in dirt from wandering around in the dusty basement. That I would gain, what do you think?

DIRECTOR Do you want to go or not?

MARTÍNEZ I can try. If it isn't too much of a mess down there... Tell the old chap to come with me.

DIRECTOR If you please, Doctor. This clerk will provide you with the material.

SPANISH READER If you will allow me, I simply must explain that I...

DIRECTOR (*Firmly*) Consult the etchings and tomorrow we will talk. (*MARTÍNEZ and the SPANISH READER leave.*) Oh! I didn't think that I was ever going to get him to leave! You will have to pardon my delay in attending you, Miss Grisel.

ESTELA I liked waiting.

DIRECTOR And why did you like it?

ESTELA I was looking at lots of books. I love books. I have one at home.

DIRECTOR Oh really?

ESTELA So gripping! It's a love story. A crazy, passionate, illegitimate love. But the newspaper serials are better. I follow four of them.

DIRECTOR The card says that you would like to work in the Library.

ESTELA I like 'catalogues'.

DIRECTOR Catalogues.

ESTELA I like culture. I don't know why, but I like you, you are so cultured! I am sure that working alongside you must be delightful.

DIRECTOR (*Worried*) Yes?

ESTELA You're gentle and firm at the same time. I was fascinated the whole time watching how you give orders. You're a man of iron and at the same time, so gentle.

DIRECTOR (*Flattered*) Well... that is what I'm here for.

ESTELA If I worked here, I wouldn't be able to get your orders out of my mind. Day or night.

DIRECTOR (*Worried again*) You're very young to dedicate yourself to a library.

ESTELA (*Moving closer*) And to what should I dedicate myself, if not the library?

SECRETARY (*Interrupting. Forcefully*) What do I do with the man from the tailor's shop?

DIRECTOR Make the man from the tailor's shop wait.

SECRETARY He cannot wait. And if he leaves, Mr. Director, (*viciously*) you are not going to be able to get married... on Saturday.

DIRECTOR But, Mrs de Luppi!

SECRETARY (*Towards the door*) Come in. You! I said come in!

The TAILOR enters, greeting them deferentially. During the course of the following scene he makes the DIRECTOR remove his jacket and puts him in the tailcoat that he brought with him. He then tears both sleeves off the tailcoat. He tugs at the lapels to adjust them for the DIRECTOR. He marks the waist and buttons with chalk, like a painter before a canvas. He lifts and lowers the DIRECTOR's arms, handling him like a doll, placing him in absurd positions. He follows him constantly, dancing around him. Finally, he fits a sleeve and fastens it with pins. The SECRETARY GENERAL makes his entrance when the DIRECTOR is still missing the left sleeve.

DIRECTOR (*Who ignores the tailor at all times*) What were we saying when we were interrupted?

ESTELA I was confessing... that I would like to work with you.

DIRECTOR Of course you would, sweetheart! You're taken aback because I'm young. You thought that you were going to find an old director (*he acts like an old man*) with an old face and an old, trembling voice.

ESTELA I adore you! You're wonderful! (*She laughs and takes him by the arms.*)

SECRETARY (*Interrupting*) There are five minutes left until the Secretary General arrives.

DIRECTOR Please, Mrs de Luppi!

SECRETARY There are five minutes left.

DIRECTOR But, Mrs de Luppi!

SECRETARY Miss, the Director does not have time.
ESTELA Yes, I know. There are five minutes left. You said it twice.
SECRETARY From your point of view, Miss, there is hardly any time left. Just two days. The Director is getting married on Saturday!
DIRECTOR Margarita, you have no right! I mean... Mrs de Luppi!

MARTÍNEZ enters followed by the SPANISH READER.

MARTÍNEZ It's impossible to find anything. (*He brushes himself down.*) Filth. I'm covered in dust.
DIRECTOR What can't you find?
MARTÍNEZ That book.
DIRECTOR Mrs, check if... No, leave it. Look in the catalogues, Martínez.
MARTÍNEZ I've already looked. It's not in the old catalogues, or in the new index cards, or in the classified books, or the pink record cards.
DIRECTOR Well then?
MARTÍNEZ It's in the catalogue devised by the Deputy Director.
DIRECTOR Well, what's the problem then?
MARTÍNEZ Nothing really. Except that he is the only one who understands it. If he actually does understand it.
DIRECTOR It's very simple, Martínez.
MARTÍNEZ Simple for you. (*He takes out a piece of paper.*) I searched under Pee. Pee for Pi, for Piranesi. No problem. Based on my knowledge of the alphabet, I found it. It says 23–4–5–7.
DIRECTOR Well there you have it, Martínez. Room 23, shelf 4, bookcase 5...
MARTÍNEZ Room 23 has been flooded for the last two months.
DIRECTOR Did the book get wet?
MARTÍNEZ The room was moved into 21 until there's a provision for draining floods in the next budget. But underneath it says: to 6A–38–7–7 and then someone's added: to NA 6698–P5.G8, and at the end: to R.
DIRECTOR Well then, Martínez? R.
MARTÍNEZ R! Director! R for re-catalogued so it returned to where it belongs.
DIRECTOR Well there you go, there...
MARTÍNEZ But who knows where it belongs? That's why I consulted the catalogue.
DIRECTOR Bring me the index volume. It's simply not possible. You'll see how I find it.

MARTÍNEZ and the SPANISH READER leave.

ESTELA (*Parodying him cheerfully*) It's simply not possible. You'll see how I find it. (*They laugh.*) (*Playing with his tie*) If I ask you for one little thing, would you do it for me?
DIRECTOR What little thing?
ESTELA It would make me happy if I could hear your poem; the one she was asking you for, that old lady with the feather in her hat. I like culture. So you'll recite it for me, won't you?
DIRECTOR My poem 'The Hero of the Oboe'? I can confess to you, Miss Grisel,

that it has only one verse so far; I have fifteen or twenty left to write, it is lacking a lot.

SECRETARY (*From the doorway*) Your speech is lacking even more.

DIRECTOR What time is it? Yes, I know, it's very late. But it's simply not possible that he'll arrive on time. They're always late. (*They are acting as in a romantic scene although their words do not express it.*) If I recite you my poem, my verse, will you be a good girl and leave? (*The TAILOR moves the DIRECTOR's hand, with which he is stroking ESTELA's hip, to her shoulder.*)

ESTELA I'll go but I'll come back... as an employee, ok?

DIRECTOR Yes, if I can convince the Secretary General. Do you want to hear my poem? (*ESTELA makes faces to show that she does.*) Listen. It goes as follows: (*The TAILOR causes him to make great gestures whilst he measures and adjusts.*)

> Beside the marsh, a trace
> A sign of starry space
> Symphonising acoustic pedestrians
> Exorcising mystical equestrians
> Goes the musical hero of the oboe

ESTELA It's delightful! It's incomprehensible!

DIRECTOR If I could count the syllables of the last line, the verse would be finished: goes-the-mu-si-cal-he-ro-of-the-ob-oe. How many syllables does it have? Nine, ten, eleven, twelve, thirteen? It's missing some. I think it's missing some.

SECRETARY (*Appearing at the door again*) There is one minute and mere seconds until the Secretary General arrives.

MARTÍNEZ and the SPANISH READER enter carrying an enormous book between them.

MARTÍNEZ Here you have the catalogue (*they allow it to drop to the floor with a thud in the middle of the room*).

SPANISH READER It's as heavy as The Catalogue of Ships, and in this heat!

DIRECTOR (*He kneels on the floor and opens the catalogue*) Let's see: pee... pee... pi... Piranesi... here it is, didn't I tell you, Martínez, 23–4–5–7?

MARTÍNEZ Go on...

CLEANER (*Interrupting*) A car has stopped at the gate and the person from the band gave the signal. It's a big, black car.

SECRETARY The Secretary General!

CLEANER The spittoon is on the table!

The DIRECTOR rushes over to his desk and takes the blue spittoon. As he looks for a place to leave it on the floor, the band strikes up a jubilant military march and the double doors on the back wall open revealing the foyer, which is excruciatingly bright. The DIRECTOR runs towards it, opening his arms for a warm embrace. Behind him, like a horsefly, the TAILOR buzzes about. The DIRECTOR's left arm is in shirtsleeves and in his right hand he holds up the blue spittoon.

DIRECTOR (*Heading towards the main door*) Secretary... My dear, Secretary.

Curtain

Act II

Scene I

Ten years later. The scene is the same although some tell-tale signs of the passage of time have appeared. When the curtain rises, MARTÍNEZ *and* MONTEIRO *are together in the middle of the stage, kneeling on all fours with their rears to the audience. They are wearing large overalls. They are making marks and taking measurements on the floor; they crawl around on all fours carrying a tape measure in one hand and chalk in the other. Even after the dialogue has started, they should give the impression of being animals who grunt, sniff at the skirting board, inexplicably join their heads together in a corner, pass underneath pieces of furniture, etc.*

MARTÍNEZ Hmm... hmm... hmm (*he draws a line*).

MONTEIRO (*Pause*) There... There... There-you-have-it.

MARTÍNEZ Hum... hum... and... hum... Hum (*he draws a line*). One... One... and... another one (*he pants*).

DIRECTOR (*Acting in the same way and dressed like the others, the* DIRECTOR *comes crawling out from underneath his desk, from where he could not be seen; he moves forwards taking measurements whilst pushing a chair along with his head.*) One... two... and three. (*To both of them*) Are you sure that there are three on the middle one as well?

MARTÍNEZ Mm-hm.

DIRECTOR The long one is that side then?

MONTEIRO Mm-hm.

MONTEIRO (*Standing up*) Oh! I have stiff legs. I might have torn the cartilage in my knee. (*He starts to measure on the walls.*)

DIRECTOR (*Standing up*) It doesn't look like there's going to be a problem. It fits perfectly; it will be very tall.

MARTÍNEZ (*From beneath the window*) It'd be a good idea to take the window latch off. If you open it, the draught will cut through here like a bullet. (*He stands up and pulls the latch off.*)

DIRECTOR We had better go to help bring things down.

MARTÍNEZ Hang on a tic... In the middle here there should be two rows. And this side still needs marking out (*he draws new lines. Satisfied*) At a push, I could even move the fifth in here. Right, now let's get backing.

DIRECTOR Cracking.

MARTÍNEZ (*As the three men leave*) Let's get backing and cracking. It's going to be tough work. (*Pause*)

DIRECTOR (*Entering*) With the marks we've made it's going to be very simple. (*Behind him enter the* DEPUTY DIRECTOR, MARTÍNEZ, MONTEIRO, *the* SECRETARY, ESTELA, *the* CLEANER, MARCUCIANO PERLUCHINO *and* JOSÉ LUIS.) The shelves from number four are drawn on the floor, do you see? We have to bring the books and packages and put them in here in the same order, just like in there.

CLEANER We bring them in here, just like in there. We bring room four and put it... and... where are the bookcases?

DIRECTOR We put the books and packages on the floor and then on top of each other. It's just for a few months. The important thing is to maintain the correlative order, so that the...

SECRETARY The topography?

DIRECTOR That's right! So that the... that the...correlative order does not change and the catalogue still functions. We must be sure to leave space between the shelves and what we'll be bringing in so that all of the books are still accessible.

DEPUTY DIRECTOR And the window? It is going to become...

DIRECTOR We're certainly not going to need any fresh air in here and there will be plenty of light. Think that this is our future. Do you realise that the Secretary General's idea is brilliant? If we put room four into room three and room two into room one and then we do the same with all of the rooms; twenty-three into twenty-two, number six in number seven, etc., etc., then the library reduces mathematically to half its size. It was ten years ago, girls and boys, that the foundation stone of the new library building was laid. And it took ten years for a new, young and entrepreneurial Secretary General to arrive, full of new ideas and initiatives. For all those years, we all thought that it was impossible to construct the new building here; why? Because where were we going to put the library in the meantime? Where were the books going to go when the foundations were being laid and the walls were being built? Books can't be thrown out. But they couldn't be taken to another place either, because if there was another place with space for them, then that would be the new library. Do you see the problem? Where were the books going to go? Only to another large library. But this old one is the only one that there is. So then, what was the solution?

MARCUCIANO I know. To move inside rather than outside.

DIRECTOR Exactly. Those were the words of the Secretary General: to move inside. You're new, aren't you? I don't think I know you.

MARCUCIANO I came to help José Luis. He's my friend and he started work here the day before yesterday.

DIRECTOR (*Addressing JOSÉ LUIS*) Oh! You are the new one. (*To MARCUCIANO*) And you, what did you say your name was?

MARCUCIANO Marcuciano Perluchino, but they call me Tito. I came to help him because he's my friend and he's a bit shy. (*Everyone laughs.*)

DIRECTOR Today is a day, Mr Perluziano...

MARCUCIANO Marcuciano Perluchino, but they call me Tito.

DIRECTOR Today is a day, Mr Marcuchino, when we are in need of people who are keen to work.

MARTÍNEZ I already said to them that if by the end of the day they bring in more books between them than Monteiro and me, then we'll buy the coffee.

DIRECTOR Splendid. A fine bet. Now boys, let's all get carrying. We need to move the entire room this afternoon.

They all leave. From this moment onwards they all enter very rapidly, either alone or in pairs, continuously bringing in more and more books, parcels and boxes that they leave in order on the floor, according to the outline marked in chalk. The Props Managers take part in the task as well, and in this way actual walls are erected which gradually obstruct the main door, block the window and reduce the Director's Office to two compartments surrounded by a narrow corridor. The people carrying start conversations with each other, irrespective of their incessant transportation of books through both doors and eventually through the window. The movement of the books becomes faster and faster and ends up with the characters creating a supply chain like workmen passing bricks from one person to the next.

MONTEIRO They said that it was madness in '24 as well. We went and... we won. We'll bring it home again this time. How can I not get worried? I'm on the brink of becoming an Olympic athlete, you get me? If someone gets injured, someone else can't go because of their job, another little thing and... they'll take me as reserve. I am on the brink, as they say, do you see?

JOSÉ LUIS I saw you play on Sunday.

MONTEIRO I could perform much better than that. Much better. But I'd have to look after myself. Smoke less, go to bed early.

DEPUTY DIRECTOR I'm going to have little bells put all around it, and swings, and a small fountain on the inside.

SECRETARY (*Sitting down on the large desk chair*) And when are you thinking of retiring, Don Esteban?

DEPUTY DIRECTOR In a month and a half I'll have completed forty-four years of service. I came here at sixteen as an errand boy.

SECRETARY You deserve a rest.

DEPUTY DIRECTOR As a boy I used to go out hunting goldfinches, yellow-finches and even the odd cardinal and so now...

SECRETARY And have you already started the process at the State Pensions Department?

DEPUTY DIRECTOR Of course. Didn't I tell you that I have plans for the aviary? I want it to have everything: swings, nests, water bowls and even a little tree inside... and a fountain, even if it's a small one.

MARTÍNEZ This library is getting better and better all the time.

DIRECTOR We're coming to the main phase. This is going to be extremely important.

MARTÍNEZ Although, I'm telling you, if it hadn't been for the readers who used to come here sometimes, this building was pretty good. If you take out all the readers, this library would be perfect.

DIRECTOR The new building is going to be wonderful. (*Pause*) And speaking of which, that's what they say about my daughter, Ana María; she's wonderful. She's nine years old and plays Chopin on the piano. A genius.

MARTÍNEZ We're going to fetch another load, Director. This exercise does wonders, doesn't it?

DIRECTOR Outstanding, they gave her in the exam; her mother was crying... imagine it: nine years old. She's a tiny little thing and she breaks hearts with Chopin.

JOSÉ LUIS They say they're even going to put pneumatic pipes in.

MARCUCIANO Seriously... And heaters?

JOSÉ LUIS Central heating, man!

MARCUCIANO Wow! You'll have to work in swimsuits in the middle of August!

JOSÉ LUIS Underground fire prevention passages and all of the rooms flood automatically.

MARCUCIANO And why would they flood, eh?

JOSÉ LUIS To prevent thieves. If anyone comes to take a book, the alarm goes off and water starts flowing in immediately. They're going to put the collection at a depth of fifty metres, sunk into living rock.

MARCUCIANO But José Luis, if it floods... you can forget the books, they'll get wet.

JOSÉ LUIS It's all been thought through. They told me that the shelves will have a clockwork mechanism which makes the books rise up to the ceiling whilst the thief drowns below. Have you seen *Dr Mabuse*, the one that's showing in the Doré cinema? It'll be something like that...

MONTEIRO Next year is going to be a fantastic year. You're getting married soon, in September isn't it?

ESTELA No. We had to postpone it.

MONTEIRO Again, Estela?

ESTELA Cacho says that his mother doesn't feel well.

MONTEIRO But we are in March... by September... his mother would have time...

ESTELA We thought it would be better to push it back until the 29th of February.

MONTEIRO The 29th of February!

ESTELA Yes. It was Cacho's bright idea to get married on a day that is not easily repeated.

MONTEIRO You see: you're getting married next year. Didn't I tell you that '28 is going to be a fantastic year? If Vasco Cea got ill and Benítez couldn't go and García wasn't performing as well... I'm all set... I'm going for sure.

ESTELA I'm getting married in white, you know! A long dress and my head all... all...

SECRETARY Sweetie, did you speak to the Secretary General?

DIRECTOR What did you say, Mrs De Luppi?

SECRETARY Old Fattori told me that he is retiring in a month, have you spoken about my promotion?

DIRECTOR You can count on my support. I already told you. Although of course, the positions of responsibility are filled directly by the Commissioner.

SECRETARY But did you mention it?

DIRECTOR The Secretary General told me that he understood that you should be promoted and so it would be arranged.

SECRETARY Thank you! Thank you so much. I knew it.

DIRECTOR Like I said before, I barely intervened at all.

SECRETARY They always listen to you. How is your daughter?

DIRECTOR Wonderful! *The Voice of the Strings* published her photograph and above it they put: the little Mozart of Minas Street.

SECRETARY And your other daughter?

DIRECTOR The youngest? She has measles. Her mother is having to look after her... ugh!

SECRETARY I never thought that I would make it to Deputy Director... I feel free, I could laugh, dance, I could fly away like a little bird. The first thing I'll do will be to regulate out of hours visits. I'm so happy!

CLEANER There'll be major changes. I'm going to put the instructions for staff on duty on the wall: Porters must report to the Porter's office between 13.00 and 13.01. Cleaners must report to the Porter's office between 13.00 and 13.01. Signed; colon: Aquiles Arrieta, Head Porter. They say that my uniform will even have three braids on it, can you believe it? Do you think it will really have three gold braids?

DEPUTY DIRECTOR They say salaries will double.

CLEANER I believe it, of course they will.

DEPUTY DIRECTOR I'm waiting until then to retire. Think about it: with deductions and pension from the State, and the rent guarantee, and the neighbourhood cooperative, and membership of the Club and three months' salary in advance, I'll be left with 14 pesos, 37 cents per month.

CLEANER A fortune!

DEPUTY DIRECTOR When they double my salary, I'll buy my aviary cash in hand. Even though my wife doesn't want me to, I'm going to buy it anyway.

SECRETARY I'm going to have a suit made for the day I'm appointed. Carmucha will be green with envy when she finds out. She's the sort who think that women were not born to work.

ESTELA And... let me tell you, she's not wrong there...

SECRETARY I think that it all depends on how efficient one is. If someone is no use at all...

ESTELA I'm getting married in February, did you know?

SECRETARY Wasn't it August?

ESTELA We had pushed it back until September, but it's because of his mother. Now it's definitely going to be in February, the 29th.

SECRETARY Definitely? That's wonderful, isn't it?

MARCUCIANO I think they're ahead of us, I counted what we were carrying and what they were carrying and they are in the lead by two boxes and one parcel.

JOSÉ LUIS Let's get a move on. We might find there's something left to bring in and then we'll beat them.

MARCUCIANO There's nothing left.

JOSÉ LUIS We'll try. Come on. Come on.

MARTÍNEZ (*Imitating the conductor of a murga*[1]) Attention! Now, for an important topical song... dedicated... to the worthy management of this building... and to the people around it... (*As if playing carnival drums and cymbals*) brrr... chim... pum. (*He sings to the tune of 'A Barbacoa me voy'*[2])

The mother library
The mother library
The mother library
is going to move (*he repeats it*).

Everyone gradually joins in repeating the song.

DIRECTOR (*Interrupting the song, which stops suddenly with an abrupt silence*) Gentlemen!... Congratulations, gentlemen. We have completed this move and I'm delighted to see you all so happy. (*He points to the walls made of parcels, books and boxes.*) We can proudly say that, in a certain way, we have built our Library. (*Exclamations of support are heard: Hear, hear! Bravo!*)

MONTEIRO The Cub enjoys the sound of his own voice more and more.

JOSÉ LUIS Who is the Cub?

MONTEIRO Shh... the Director.

MARTÍNEZ Silence.

DIRECTOR We can say, yes indeed, in a way, this is the new library building and it is the best one there is. This one! Built with our hands and held together with our enthusiasm, which is capable of moving mountains (*clapping and cheering*). Please allow me to finish. Tomorrow gentlemen... at the very latest the day after, the pick will sink its steel tooth into the old rotting carcass of this decrepit building. So friends we wait, full of optimism, for that tomorrow full of promise, and we bid each other farewell today, repeating; tomorrow! (*Cheering and applause.*)

Organised by MARTÍNEZ, *from amongst the cheers and applauding rises the chorus of the murga, 'The mother library' which they repeat. Everyone sings and dances.*

Curtain

Interlude

Ten years have passed. A catacomb serves as the reading room. A curtain depicts a wall covered with shelves which are three or four metres in height. Above these painted bookshelves two or three small, narrow windows open up. From small, narrow, side windows fall two oblique rays of sunlight that do not light up the back wall; these two harsh rays of light are the only illumination. A very long table runs the length of the stage; it is situated one metre from the curtain and runs parallel to it. In fact, it is merely a frame, and the numerous chairs which surround it are seen in silhouette and are flat. Three or four lamps with green conical shades hang from wires and illuminate the table for reading when they are turned on, but they are off.

On the right, a very low door, almost like a mouse hole, exposes the extreme thickness of the walls and is the only access to this basement.

Against the right side of the stage, there is a desk to stand and write at: above it, hanging from a nail, a small paraffin lamp casts a small circle of light onto the white-washed wall. When the action begins, ESTELA*,* MARTÍNEZ*, the* CLEANER *and* DEPUTY DIRECTOR *encircle the* RESEARCHER *who is seated at the head of the table on the left. He is blocked from the view of the audience by the aforementioned employees who form a tight circle around him. When the curtain rises loud guffawing and laughter can be heard.*

MARTÍNEZ (*Between laughter*) How did you say it? Say it. How did you say it?

ESTELA Really, repeat it.

TWO OR THREE Say it; say it.

RESEARCHER (*Who still cannot be seen; in the small voice of a frightened mouse*) Ueber die vierfache Wurzel des Satzes von zureichenden Grunde.

MARTÍNEZ (*Tries to imitate him*) Ueber zurenchenden Grunde (*he laughs*). My belly hurts from laughing!

DEPUTY DIRECTOR And what about me? You don't know how glad I am that I came. It's incredible what he does with his mouth.

CLEANER It's like a circus act, isn't it, Don Esteban?

ESTELA Could you repeat it, please. What book do you want?

RESEARCHER (*The same as before*) Ueber die vierfache Wurzel des Satzes von zureichenden Grunde.

MARTÍNEZ Are you sure that that noise is a book? It wouldn't be an engine that you want? (*Laughter*)

RESEARCHER Isn't there a specialist in philosophy amongst you?

ESTELA But sir!

MARTÍNEZ What's that? Tell me, hey.

RESEARCHER And... A German collection... isn't there one of those either?

CLEANER I think that the poor man is crazy.

DEPUTY DIRECTOR When I see things like this I regret having retired. It's a stroke of good luck that I came.

MARTÍNEZ Hey sonny: if that noise you're making is a joke, I warn you that... (*he threatens him*).

ESTELA Don't take any notice of him sir, he's joking. Explain to me what you want.

RESEARCHER The original work was published in Rudolstadt in 1813.

MARTÍNEZ Oh I see!

RESEARCHER But... but if the first edition, miss, isn't available... I could consult a Spanish translation, although I would prefer...

DEPUTY DIRECTOR Books in Spanish are much easier.

MARTÍNEZ We've got an abundance of them here. Look: books galore! (*Laughter*)

ESTELA Could you tell me how you translate everything you said?

RESEARCHER Ueber die verfache Wurzel...? 'On the Fourfold Root of the Principle of Sufficient Reason.'

ESTELA (*Shocked as if it were a rude word*) On the what?

RESEARCHER It's the doctoral thesis of Schopenhauer.

MARTÍNEZ Schopenhauer? (*Laughter*) But you should have said! Schopenhauer who now did you say?

RESEARCHER (*Sounding more and more withdrawn*) Arthur Schopenhauer.

MARTÍNEZ It's a good thing we've cleared that up. For example, we have the complete works of Schopenhauer Pérez. What's more, we can offer you a much better book than that one you're after. What's it called? Ah yes, 'Memoires of a Cub'. I think you'd prefer this book. It's better.

RESEARCHER That may be. But if it were possible, I would like... if you are able to provide, The Fourfold Root... if you do, in fact, have it.

CLEANER Here, we have everything by the Fox Cub (*there is knocking at the door*).

DEPUTY DIRECTOR It must be the Director. When I told him I was coming down to the basement to say hello to you all, he said that he was coming straight down. (*MARTÍNEZ goes to open the door and the DIRECTOR enters crouching down.*)

MARTÍNEZ It seems that a reader has come.

DIRECTOR You can't be serious.

MARTÍNEZ He's over there, sir. Can't you see him?

DIRECTOR Don Esteban came to visit and see you all.

MARTÍNEZ No. There really is a reader. He's half mad. He asked for a book in Russian.

DIRECTOR (*He walks towards the left side of the stage; at about halfway*) There is a reader, Martínez tells me...

ESTELA Yes, sir. But he's a disgrace. He's asking for a ridiculous book.

DIRECTOR (*He has now caught sight of the RESEARCHER and speaks to him in a sympathetic tone*) And so you, sir... came to read.

RESEARCHER Yes, sir. I'm here for a few days. I study in Mendoza.

DIRECTOR Very well. Someone had to come. And what would you like to consult?

RESEARCHER I am looking for a little-known book. In fact, too little-known. I thought that here... but no. I understand that it's not here.

DIRECTOR What is the subject? We are at your service (*inviting him*). Please...

RESEARCHER I do not wish to offend you, but to be honest... I need to consult... the doctoral thesis of Schopenhauer (*embarrassed*), 'On the Fourfold Root of the Principle of Sufficient Reason'.

DIRECTOR I remember it. Unfortunately, I don't think that it's available in German. But the edition by Sempere is definitely here. Martínez, check the large volumes, in Philosophy: Schopenhauer.

MARTÍNEZ If you say so... (*He leaves.*)

DIRECTOR Take a seat, sir. (*The beams of light have gradually faded and the stage is almost in half-light, the* DIRECTOR *lights a candle next to the* RESEARCHER.) You'll have to work with hardly any light; we've not had electricity since yesterday. They'll bring the book right away. And so you are keeping well, Don Esteban?

DEPUTY DIRECTOR Yes, ticking along. I had an appointment yesterday with the ophthalmologist. He says they still can't operate on me. I see everything blurred but it's still not possible.

DIRECTOR Nonetheless you seem sprightly to me.

DEPUTY DIRECTOR Of course, I'm well. But I wanted to speak to you about my son-in-law. It's why I came. Do you remember him? The one who's married to Chichita, my daughter who took me to live with her. I spoke to you about this before, a few months ago. You couldn't nudge them for me, could you, so they appoint him? Even if it's as an assistant.

DIRECTOR I'm your friend Don Esteban. And what's more (*lying*) I've already spoken to the Commissioner... But in any case, tell me his name again. (*To the* CLEANER) Did you finish stamping the donation from Mr Daniel Ferrére, Aquiles?

CLEANER I'm almost finished sir, but José Luis...

DIRECTOR There should be three stamps in each book, do you remember? (*To the* DEPUTY DIRECTOR) What did you say the name of the young man was? (*They leave.*)

CLEANER He's lucky, Don Esteban. He's already been retired for four years. Although I'm telling you now, I've already told the Director: in January, I said to him, come what may, I'm retiring.

ESTELA You're within your rights, Aquiles.

CLEANER Of course I am. You tell me if it's right that an institution like this has just one member of maintenance staff.

ESTELA You're right. Margarita hasn't called us for tea yet has she?

CLEANER Here everyone gives orders but there is only me to drive the institution forward. Aquiles, over here. Aquiles, over there. What about me? If I say 'So-and-so, hop to it', who will do it? Nobody.

ESTELA Life... is a great injustice.

CLEANER It is. And it's not even my time, either.

MARTÍNEZ (*Entering*) That strange book is in this very room. Can you believe it? (*To the* RESEARCHER *from a distance*) Can you believe it? We're searching all over the place and your old tome was here, on this very wall. Aquiles: go up there and I'll go on the other side. Estela, would you mind helping us with the lamp?

MARTÍNEZ and the CLEANER climb up the shelves using rope ladders which are hidden from the audience; they go up and down and move towards the sides like flies on a wall. ESTELA goes to the desk and takes the lamp. The rays of sunlight which were illuminating the stage have faded entirely and the circle of light that is now cast by ESTELA passes over the bookshelves, clearly illuminating MARTÍNEZ and then the CLEANER in their insect-like poses, giving successive snapshots of the tortured positions that they must adopt.

MARTÍNEZ Over here Estela (*she illuminates him and he searches*). Fantastic! You'll never guess what I've just found? The second volume of The History of the Nation. We haven't seen it for years.

CLEANER (*To ESTELA so that she illuminates him*) Would you mind?... (*He searches.*) When you work in the book industry you suddenly realise just how many books there are. Can you tell me why they keep writing new books? Who's going to have the patience to read all these that already exist? You can turn it off. The one we need isn't here.

MARTÍNEZ On Sunday we're going to have a little barbeque out in the country. I think we'll have music and everything. They invited Sosa; he plays the guitar. (*He is happy and starts to move but he almost falls and gets annoyed.*) Stop messing about and hold the lamp up properly! I'll end up falling off here.

ESTELA I am holding the lamp up, aren't I? I'm just in the mood for bad tempers today (*she is almost in tears*).

MARTÍNEZ (*Conciliatory*) But Estela.

ESTELA (*Crying*) Don't take any notice of me. It's nothing really (*she sobs and lowers the lamp*).

CLEANER Estela! (*After a short pause*) I'm sorry, Martínez, but... what are we were looking for?

MARTÍNEZ The book by Schopenhauer.

CLEANER Here it says... Sha-kes-pea-re. That's not the same is it?

MARTÍNEZ That's a different bloke. You need to look for one that starts Show: ess, o.

CLEANER It's demanding work this cultural business. (*The voice of the SECRETARY can be heard: she says the following words in exactly the same tone as in the next scene. However, the voice is recorded with an echo and sounds ghostly, although it is recognisable as hers.*)

Voice of the SECRETARY Estela... Martínez... come on! The tea's ready, come and have your tea. (*MARTÍNEZ and the CLEANER climb down*).

MARTÍNEZ Shall we go, Estela?

ESTELA Yes, let's go. Perfect timing. I could just do with something warm. (*They leave. The RESEARCHER remains motionless in his seat at the head of the table. At the opposite end, next to the table and barely lit by the lamp, the CLEANER stands like a policeman. There is a short pause. The RESEARCHER sneezes very politely.*)

CLEANER (*Responding without raising his voice*) Bless you, sir.

RESEARCHER Thank you.

Curtain

Act II

Scene 2

A further ten years have passed. The stage is the same but the improvised walls from the last scene, which were created from boxes, parcels and books, have been secured in place, as if they are permanent. The DIRECTOR'S *office, which in the previous scene was reduced to two compartments, is now divided into four by an additional floor which has been installed. The two upper compartments are not tall enough to allow a person to stand without bending over. Even in the lower compartments, you can touch the ceiling with your hand. The stage, which is divided into six cells — four compartments and two side corridors — should create an oppressive feeling like that of being inside a submarine or the belly of a whale. In compartment A the lighting should be so poor that it is uncomfortable.*

Compartments B and D are linked by a ladder and compartment C can be reached from A by sliding down a pole like those often used, for example, in fire stations. In the partition wall on the upper level, near to the audience, there is a small hole which is big enough to crawl through: this is the only connection between compartments A and B. C and D are linked by an opening similar to a narrow door which is cut out of the partition wall and against the back wall.

In compartment A there is a table and a bench with very tall legs which crushes its occupant against the ceiling. A small table lamp makes the actor visible and the rest is in shadow.

In compartment B there are filing cabinets against the walls and no other furniture.

In compartment C is the Director's desk, large chairs and tables, all piled in to the point where it is difficult to move around.

In compartment D, against the back wall, there is a little kitchen table with a stove and other objects for preparing and serving tea. Hanging very close to the table is an oil portrait in a magnificent gold frame: a dignitary in a military uniform looks out proudly and sternly onto the stage.

When the curtain rises compartments C and D and the side corridors are in darkness. In compartment A, José Luis is working whilst leaning back on the edge of his bench, like a cockroach. In compartment B, EMA FONTES *and* MONTEIRO *move, bending over, from one filing cabinet to another.*

EMA Daddy said to him, because they are like brothers, he said to him: it's so the girl has something to keep her entertained. And he was right: at home I used to get bored. Embroidery is boring and so is needlework. I wasn't going to start cleaning the house... can you imagine. And so...

MONTEIRO PQ 8519 R8 A, 1924, is it there?

EMA I believe so...

MONTEIRO But did you check?

EMA I think I checked.

MONTEIRO In which filing cabinet, miss?

EMA In this one, I believe.

MONTEIRO Here, you have to put yourself out: seeing is believing.

EMA You're right. Take a look. As I was saying, embroidery, needlework, cleaning, everything is boring. Listening to the radio makes me tired and when I want to read a book, I fall asleep. In summer there is the beach, of course. But in winter? That's why Daddy told him that I needed to have something to keep me entertained. They're like brothers, of course. If not then I would never have come to work here (*she takes out a bottle of nail polish and starts to paint her nails*). Hold the bottle for me. Careful! You're going to tip it over. (*Pause*) Do you like this shade? Monica Patricia says it's too deathly. It's called Bolshevik Revolution. Can you let me dip the brush?

MONTEIRO PQ 8519 R8 isn't here. This filing cabinet is some kind of animal, it swallows record cards and instead of preserving them, it digests them, dissolves them, makes them disappear. I'm sure that I filed a PQ8519 yesterday. But it's always the same with me.

The SECRETARY enters and turns on the lights in the side corridors, then she goes into compartment D; she turns on the light, the water is already on the stove and she finishes preparing the tea by pumping the stove to heat the water. She hums and acts like a housewife in the kitchen.

SECRETARY (*Leaning out into the side corridor*) Estela... Martínez... Estela, tea's re... call Martínez (*returning to the foot of the ladder*). Monteiro, tea's ready, tell José Luis and come down.

MONTEIRO Did you put the candle away?

EMA I put it in the C drawer. C for candle.

MONTEIRO (*He takes a candle from the filing cabinet and lights it; holding it in his hand he crawls through the hole in the partition wall and stops part way with half of his body in each compartment*) José Luis. Tea's ready.

JOSÉ LUIS I'll be right there. Do you remember the number for the serials by Carolina Invernizio?

MONTEIRO 593, isn't it?

JOSÉ LUIS I'll finish this and I'll be right there. (*MONTEIRO returns to compartment B crawling backwards and then puts the candle away. MARTÍNEZ and ESTELA are already in D.*)

EMA (*From above*) Martínez, would you mind turning away? I'm going to come down. (*MARTÍNEZ turns his back and EMA comes down followed by MONTEIRO. The SECRETARY passes the cups of tea around to everyone and opens a box of cakes.*)

MARTÍNEZ For three days the same bloke has been coming here. He's going on and on insisting on reading a book in Greek.

ESTELA In Greek? He must be mad!

SECRETARY Some people are so annoying!

MARTÍNEZ When I told him for the last time that the room wasn't fitted out, he stood there dumbfounded, muttering away. In the end I had to stop him by telling him that if he carried on, I'd complain to the Director. He got scared and left.

MONTEIRO If he knew the Fox Cub... (*they laugh*).

ESTELA Thank you Margarita. I can't eat anything. I didn't have lunch today.

SECRETARY You were with your husband...
ESTELA No. I haven't seen Cacho for months (*she cries*). It's because of Rafael.
DIRECTOR (*Entering with his friend*) This way. Good afternoon.
MONTEIRO Hello.

The DIRECTOR *and his friend go into compartment C.*

MARTÍNEZ He must be the new Deputy Director.
SECRETARY Yes, he must be. He's looks like an idiot!
ESTELA Margarita, can you believe it's been three days since he called or came by the house? (*She cries.*) Rafael isn't even jealous of me.
DIRECTOR (*Sitting at his desk*) Have a seat, Jorge. Move that table, make yourself comfortable (*short pause*). I needed to speak to you and now I don't know where to start (*short pause*). I'm exhausted! I've been exhausted for years without ever realising it. I don't know if you'll understand. Perhaps a good rest would solve everything. I think that if I could go to Europe, everything would sort itself out (*short pause*). I've been wanting to finish my book for years. I told you about it before, do you remember? During the last war... there were some things about the invasion of Belgium, which we are increasingly certain about. But that's not what I wanted to talk to you about... Jorge! I can't stand Isabel any longer. I swear to you. I can't stand her. Her and the girls. And the headaches and the bills... and this about the Gomez Péndola family and that about the Malvarezes... everything, you have to understand. It's too much. It's too much but yet it's pointless. I'm leading a bitter, meaningless life; I know that I'm wasting my life on one stupid thing after another, after another, after another. I'm 47, my friend. And I have had enough! Enough! When I think about going home, I feel ill, I hate my daughters. I hate my wife. It's true. I hate her, I would like to see her...
JOSÉ LUIS (*Enters sliding down the pole*) Excuse... me... I, I'm going to have my tea, Director. (*He passes through the office catching himself on the furniture, stumbling and turning around.*) Sorry... I, I didn't hear anything; I swear to you that I didn't hear anything (*he goes through into compartment D*).
MONTEIRO I remember that it was the ninth of March. Look at the newspaper cuttings, you see I'm mentioned. Here, you see? Here, where they're talking about Monteiro, that's me. There were three hopefuls. Training was on the twelfth and on the ninth I started sneezing. If it wasn't for that flu, I'd have gone. When they did the parade and the athletes went by on two open-top buses, tears were streaming down my face. I was thinking: if I hadn't come down with that fever... the ninth of March was the exact date I started to sneeze. It's as clear as if it was yesterday! I wish that flu had killed me.
SECRETARY José Luis, the new Deputy Director... is that... him?
JOSÉ LUIS I don't think so. I think that he's a friend of the Director. From what they were saying.
SECRETARY The appointment was announced a week ago. The post has been vacant for four years; after all this time, he would do well to hurry up a bit and get to work. This bloke must be a real swine.

JOSÉ LUIS Yesterday, at the Ministry, they were saying that today they would start the excavations for the new building. Just a little sugar, please.

MARTÍNEZ And you believe that, angel-face?

ESTELA Rafael had told me that they were going to start work on it.

MARTÍNEZ Well of course! Everything that Rafael says is true. He's just so charming and... above all, so youthful! He's very smart is young Rafael.

ESTELA Martínez! (*She cries.*) How could you?

JOSÉ LUIS A porter told me. And they know everything.

MARTÍNEZ Angel-face, we made these walls ourselves in an afternoon because we needed to make space, or have you forgotten? And that was... how long ago? About eight years ago.

MONTEIRO Over ten. It was before Columbes.

MARTÍNEZ It's been ten years since they moved us inside and knocked down half the building. And now what?

SECRETARY Have another cake, José Luis. No one is eating them. My daughter María Inés made them.

DIRECTOR I'm out of my mind, Jorge, and you have to help me. That's why I wanted to speak to you (*short pause*). I understand, it's not the normal sort of thing. I didn't think this sort of thing happened to anyone, but... if you knew her!... (*pause*). What's more, there's something magic... Well, between us we call it magic. It's just those little coincidences that leave you almost spellbound. I go to say something and she says it first. Honestly. You won't believe me. Looking into her eyes I know exactly what she's thinking. I swear. It's happened countless times. She's a girl. Practically an angel. A year younger than my daughter, just imagine! There are nights when I'm walking home alone, when I suddenly understand what my life is and what it all means. I can't explain it to you, but believe me. I sense that I'm somehow approaching something meaningful, something which commands all things. I feel as if God or something similar really does exist and we can know him, share in his omniscience. Do you see, my friend? I, who always laughed at all that. I feel that everything is simple and true, and that it's fine just as it is. I feel that the world is born of God and we must be faithful to the world that God made. I feel that I must give myself over to this thing that draws me to it because it is stronger than I am. Because it's God himself.

MARTÍNEZ I interrupted him: that's enough! In a country like this where red bugs rule, I can't help but scratch myself, can I? (*They all laugh.*) What does it matter to me that his brother is the Chief of Police? I told him so, and that was that. And if he doesn't like it, he can go and find the book himself. He's got legs for a reason! (*Pause.*)

MONTEIRO Yes. For you to be able to be promoted Estela, I would have to be promoted, and for me to be promoted, Martínez would either have to retire or die within the next two years.

MARTÍNEZ I'm not thinking of retiring.

MONTEIRO Well then you would have to die.

ESTELA Or you would have to die, Monteiro.

JOSÉ LUIS I liked the little cakes from your daughter. She's clearly very good with her hands.

SECRETARY What's clear is that you set eyes on her.

JOSÉ LUIS I saw her, yes, the other day when she came to pick you up. Such an adorable girl.

SECRETARY And she's very serious. She's studying engineering.

DIRECTOR Life is wonderful, believe me. Years ago, I thought I was old and now I realise that I am younger than ever. We have only one life, Jorge. If I give up everything now, if I don't do what life demands of me, what am I living for? What's the meaning of it all? (*Pause*) Of course, there's Isabel... but she's had her life. She's another thing altogether. And the girls will get married and make their own way in life, but me? I have my book to write, I have my dreams, I have... I have this love which could take me to the very extreme... Because you can be sure, I am capable of anything... I swear to you, honestly: I mean everything. There are nights when I lie in bed, when I feel that even the sheets are tying me down, tying and shackling my hands to Isabel, there are nights when I have even gone as far as to think the very worst. Yes. The worst. I would rather put an end to it all than have to bear this. Life is so wonderful that I have thought of killing myself. Calling her and (*there is a sudden, deafening noise, enough to shake the whole building. Unaffected, the* DIRECTOR *continues his pathetic monologue and his friend continues to listen unperturbed. In compartment D,* MARTÍNEZ, MONTEIRO *and the others cover their ears and go out to investigate. They walk around the side corridor and then point at something through the window on the left-hand side; they communicate by miming their feelings of surprise, joy, indifference or contempt towards the recent event. Some of them return to compartment D, others leave and just before the* SECRETARY *enters the* DIRECTOR*'s office, the din suddenly stops and the* DIRECTOR*'s words, spoken in a loud voice, resonate clearly*).

DIRECTOR That's why I want a revolver to kill myself and then to kill my wife.

SECRETARY Sir, they have just begun the excavation for the new building. The digger is working in the courtyard.

DIRECTOR Leave me in peace. Get out. I don't want to be disturbed. Get out. (*The Secretary leaves.*) Jorge, I'm so happy. I'm certain that I know exactly what I must do. I know my most sacred duty. First... (*The hammering of the machine erupts again. The* DIRECTOR *continues miming his speech whilst the curtain slowly falls.*)

Curtain

Act III

Five years later. It is winter, an overcast day. The managerial office remains but it is now completely empty. The improvised walls and floor have been taken out and there is no remaining furniture, carpets or light fittings. Similarly, the doors and windows have been removed and the ceiling is missing.

At this stage of the demolition, a vertical blue-green light falls between the tall bare walls which, as sunset approaches, will gradually and imperceptibly become increasingly faint, almost ghostly. There is a white builder's bucket and piles of sand are scattered around.

Two boxes and a plank of white lime-washed wood serve as an improvised bench on which JOSÉ LUIS *sits with his clarinet between his legs but he is not playing it. The din of a military march can be heard but it lasts just a few moments. Once it has finished,* JOSÉ LUIS *begins to practice the scale on his instrument for the first time and he fails at the fourth or fifth note.*

CRITIC (*Entering*) Is this Madungue 1–1–1–0?

JOSÉ LUIS Mm-hm.

CRITIC Are you sure?

JOSÉ LUIS Yes, this is it.

CRITIC But there's a band.

JOSÉ LUIS And you think that a band turning up makes a blind bit of difference to the street name or the door number?

CRITIC You make a good point. You're right. But there's a platform for speakers and it looked to me like they were making preparations to lay a foundation stone.

JOSÉ LUIS Of course. It's not the first one to be laid. Those stones are commonplace around here...

CRITIC And so this is...

JOSÉ LUIS Madungue 11–10.

CRITIC I had better ask out front then. Thanks anyway! (*He leaves.*)

JOSÉ LUIS (*After the* CRITIC *has left*) Bye. (*He begins to play the scale again but fails to make it to the seventh note.* EMA *enters and sits on the plank next to* JOSÉ LUIS *and curls up beside him with her head on his shoulder. A moment passes before* JOSÉ LUIS *speaks to her but without looking at her.*) I think we'll get by, my darling. Don't you think we'll get by? (*She doesn't respond. He turns around and takes her chin in his hand.*) Say yes with those beautiful lips.

EMA Mmm mm.

JOSÉ LUIS After taxes and deductions I'm left with 123.50 and you, my love?

EMA I already told you, sweetheart, I earn 300.

JOSÉ LUIS But your take-home pay, my love, how much do you get?

EMA I think... I don't know... I think, my sweet, that it's 180. What do you say to 180?

JOSÉ LUIS I like it. Between the two of us we make up your salary: 300 pesos. I think we'll get by. If we live with your parents, my darling, I'm sure we can. Can't we?

EMA Honey...

JOSÉ LUIS My love...

Whilst they are kissing the CRITIC *enters.*

CRITIC (*Interrupting them*) Should I ask over by the stage or at the hut?

JOSÉ LUIS Ask at the hut (*the* CRITIC *leaves*).

EMA What does he want?

JOSÉ LUIS How should I know. Just so long as he leaves... give me another one won't you, a little one?

Whilst they are kissing, MONTEIRO *and* ESTELA *enter through the opening that was the main door. They arrive stiff with cold under an open umbrella and completely ignore the lovebirds who, in turn, fail to notice their arrival.*

ESTELA They removed 32 gallstones. All the same size.

MONTEIRO Well, these days, removing your gall bladder is less serious than appendicitis.

ESTELA They gave Julia over 27 stitches. An awful cut. From here to here.

MONTEIRO (*Cheerful and enthusiastically*) They can do fantastic things. Juan Carlos's godfather, do you remember Juan Carlos? That guy who used to come and pick me up on Saturdays... well, they gave his godfather a caesarean.

ESTELA Marvellous.

MONTEIRO It's wonderful: they took out his stomach, they cut back the small intestine, they gave him two grafts in his colon and, I'm not sure, but I think they even gave him a new kidney. Oh yes, that's it, they put in a plastic one. In two years, they'll have to change it for him. Something to do with the plastic softening with the...

ESTELA Really, it's wonderful. I'd rather have that than my headaches. There are days, Monteiro...

MONTEIRO That's the trouble I have with my rheumatism. They can't operate on it. When I get pains in my legs and I can't stand it anymore, the doctor comes and gives me more tablets. It's pointless, useless idiot, he might as well stroke my legs and say 'there, there, let's rub it better'.

ESTELA Monteiro!... (*They both laugh. Short pause.*)

MONTEIRO (*To the lovebirds*) Hey! The ceremony's starting. Are you two going to hear the speeches?

JOSÉ LUIS It's not raining any more, you know. It stopped drizzling a while ago. (MONTEIRO *checks for rain and closes the umbrella.*)

ESTELA As if you two would notice... You mustn't even feel the cold!

EMA Cold? You say it's cold! (*They both laugh.*) Come here so that I can tell you something... I think... (*she speaks into José Luis's ear and they both laugh again*).

MONTEIRO It's unbelievable!... And they say that man is an intelligent creature... Would you look at yourself, José Luis.

JOSÉ LUIS (*Checking himself, worried*) What? What's on me? Do I have?

MONTEIRO Talk about 'a stroke of good luck', you had two. In less than fifteen years you've seen the deputy director retire and Martínez die. You went up two grades. And look at what you're up to now.

JOSÉ LUIS What am I up to? Eh?

EMA Don't take any notice of him. Don't you know what he's like?

JOSÉ LUIS What am I up to? Tell me.

MONTEIRO You got a 40 peso pay rise and... now you're ripe, ripe, ripe. What you'd call, ready!

JOSÉ LUIS Hey!

Monterio You're a ripe old pear, you are. She just puts out her hand and you'll fall well... well and truly headfirst into marriage.

EMA You're a revolting man and a... resentful one! Don't take any notice of him, José Luis.

JOSÉ LUIS Now you're really making me...

EMA Leave it! You know yesterday? Last night... (*She lowers her voice and they start again with their secrets and complicit giggles.* MONTEIRO *and* ESTELA *sit down at the opposite end of the stage. Pause.* JOSÉ LUIS *blows into his clarinet, trying in vain to start a seven-note musical scale. He doesn't get past the fourth or fifth note.*)

MONTEIRO He's achieved in fifteen years what I did in twenty-eight: two grades, forty pesos.

ESTELA Some people are lucky (*pause*).

MONTEIRO My brother's boss once offered me a job as a refrigerator salesman. I told him no, I thought it was a disgrace to go around offering things, door to door.

ESTELA You did well, that's a terrible job. Do you remember Juan Emilio?

MONTEIRO Was he a salesman?

ESTELA Juan Emilio! The one with dark eyes and hair and once, out on the street, you gave him a light... he had a handsome face...

MONTEIRO Yes, I remember.

ESTELA He left me! He was living with me, I don't know if you know; well, he left me. He left three nights ago. And I went door to door looking for him. First at his old lodgings, and then I went to the cafe and then I was standing at the entrance to the club until two in the morning. Standing in front of the club and looking all the while at the entrance to his lodgings, from door to door; and when he arrived, he went up to the third floor and wouldn't let me in. Now that really is terrible!

MONTEIRO Well... nobody is without their problems.

ESTELA For three nights in a row I've been waiting and watching and it's the same every time, he won't let me in. He makes me leave him clean clothes with the porter; is there anything worse than that?

MONTEIRO Oh... I'd like to see you on the 20th of the month without a cent to buy a coffee. Last week I hit rock bottom.

ESTELA Yes, I know, but...

MONTEIRO Some things are just unbelievable, Estela... Since I found out about old José... Well, you wouldn't have even heard of him... that old guy was extraordinary. The best midfielder you've ever seen. He used to dribble forwards, with his whole body, you know what I mean? And it was him who invented the fast through-ball between the backs.

ESTELA Did he play with you?

MONTEIRO No. When I started out, he was already a physio. A relic was old José! And he wasn't missing a single tooth, you know. A smile from one side of his face to the other.

ESTELA Yes...of course, but I, Monteiro... If you knew everything that... I!

MONTEIRO And it's so strange, you know! At that time, I used to feel sorry for him, but only every now and then, when I saw him. Then I'd forget straight away. Whereas now, for the past week, I haven't been able to get him out of my head. Poor old José! He was extraordinary, and they were organising a collection for him in the club to buy him a radio. (*Short pause*) Because old José would want to listen to the games!... And... that's all he's left with, isn't it? (*The* DIRECTOR *enters, frozen to death, his nose is red and he is wearing a minister's black slouch hat. He is wrapped up in a black overcoat and a large scarf. He sneezes and blows his nose repeatedly until the end of the act. He enters and no one pays him any attention. Pause.*)

DIRECTOR They still haven't finished work in the salting shed but the ceremony for the foundation stone is about to start (*pause*). At least it's stopped raining (*pause*). What are you all up to?

MONTEIRO (*Pointing to José Luis and Ema*) Those two are up to the same as usual: the odd bit of clarinet, played badly, followed by a bit of the other, discussed in great detail. We're talking about life, killing time. (*The* DIRECTOR *goes to sit on a pile of sand.* MONTEIRO *turns over the builder's bucket for him.*) Sit here Director, it was where your desk used to be. Do you remember?

DIRECTOR (*Sitting down on the bucket*) I received a letter from my daughter; they're heading on to Brussels.

MONTEIRO That's the honeymoon, is it?

ESTELA Such a lovely girl. Although she's a child really. In church, dressed all in white, she looked like she was about to take her first communion. She looked like the image of the young virgin when she came in.

DIRECTOR All my life I've wanted to go to Europe and now... yesterday I was saying to my wife: reading these letters from Ana María, I'm taking the trip I always dreamed of.

ESTELA They're going through Venice, aren't they? They say it's so romantic!

DIRECTOR They are going to take the exact trip that my wife and I planned. It's such a delight! At night, I read the whole stack of letters to Isabel and each time I finish I can't help but say: what do you think of this trip we're on, my dear? (*He laughs and sneezes.* JOSÉ LUIS *blows into the clarinet. To himself*) What a wonderful trip! (*He stands up and the bucket has left a white circle on his overcoat.*)

ESTELA Oh it's such a horrible day! Is it long now?

DIRECTOR A few minutes, just over a quarter of an hour. We'll do our duty until half past five, no later than.

JOSÉ LUIS But I arranged with Esteban for him to come by at six!

DIRECTOR It's too cold and when it starts to get dark, there won't be any light. It's getting dark early now.

JOSÉ LUIS (*To* EMA) I have to wait for him. It's about the Registry Office, think about it.

ESTELA I'm telling you my feet are frozen.

MONTEIRO I can't understand why it's so cold now. There weren't days like this before. May I? (*He hits the* DIRECTOR *on the backside to dust off the mark.*) The lime left a mark. (*Short pause*)

DIRECTOR Monteiro, I'd like to speak to you. Now or later...

MONTEIRO About work, sir?

DIRECTOR No, what is there to say about work? It's... a personal matter.

CRITIC (*Entering*) They told me at the hut out front that you are all from the Library.

DIRECTOR Yes, sir, that we are.

CRITIC You could have told me before! Is the manager here? Where is he?

DIRECTOR I am the Director.

CRITIC Manuel Jiménez, how do you do.

DIRECTOR Pleased to meet you.

CRITIC I need to consult Bartolomé Hidalgo's manuscripts; are they here?

DIRECTOR Here? You can clearly see...

CRITIC They must be here, sir; are they here?

DIRECTOR In any case, Hidalgo is a published author. The manuscripts are something...

CRITIC I'm looking for much more than you think, are they here?

DIRECTOR Even if they were here, at this moment in time... put yourself in our shoes.

CRITIC Am I to understand that the material was destroyed due to neglect or just stored away carelessly?

DIRECTOR Well, sir. There's no need to behave like that. The books have gone, that is to say, they were put into storage or transferred to The Official Warehouse, Number one, in the salting shed at the Port, because now...

CRITIC Get to it. Are the materials that I'm looking for here or not? And if they are here, where?

DIRECTOR If you would let me explain to you, sir.

CRITIC It just so happens that I don't need explanations. I need Hidalgo's manuscripts. It is vital that I consult them.

MONTEIRO The first guy to bother about the Library in the last six years. Unbelievable, eh Estela?

DIRECTOR If you would just try to follow my thoughts... the warehouse is still not fitted out. The salted hides, as I think that I explained to everyone, I told you about it, didn't I? The salted hides have already come out, but the wool is left (*he smiles*). There isn't even space for us. For the time being there's enough room for the boxes of books and the bales of wool, nothing else. Until the next shipment. It's a matter of days.

CRITIC But I am on the verge of an invaluable discovery. Do you understand?

DIRECTOR Of course I do. I am fully aware of it. Evidently.

MONTEIRO It's been years since someone this annoying has come.

CRITIC This is unbelievable. Your head is still completely in the clouds. Do you remember that folk song which starts: 'the pigs that Vigodet has trapped in his pen'?

DIRECTOR I remember... Yes, sir... 'They dance to the tune of the pipe...'

CRITIC Good, well I have clear evidence that Hidalgo wrote: 'swine that Vigodet has trapped in his pen'.

DIRECTOR Oh! And that is why you need...

CRITIC You understand! I have proposed an article to the 'Alfa and Omega Review of Iowa University'. As you know, I am the only scholar in the country with whom they maintain contact. For fourteen years I have devoted myself to studying Hidalgo's poetry between 1808 and 1813.

DIRECTOR Well, if you have studied those five years for fourteen years, you can wait a few weeks now. The reading room does not exist at this time. I urge you to try to understand.

CRITIC I won't understand that or anything else, sir! Can't you see that I am about to change a line from Hidalgo forever? In Iowa my discovery is going to be a bombshell! They think that our poetry is coarse and illiterate, but if we change the common word 'pigs' for the cultured term 'swine' and, above all, if we prove it!... Oh!... Then we must conclude *a fortiori* that Bartolomé Hidalgo was a learned and brilliant poet and not just a musician who was drunk and outspoken. The exchange of 'pigs' for 'swine' could, in itself, earn me the title of Fellow of Iowa University.

DIRECTOR You can be assured that I have understood you quite clearly, but it would please me greatly if you, in turn, could try to understand our situation...

CRITIC But then, you do not want...

DIRECTOR I should only be too glad, sir, believe me; I ask that...

CRITIC With all due respect, this library is public, is it not? (*Cutting off the* DIRECTOR *who tries to speak*) It is public. Do I have the right to consult the manuscript? Yes or no? Yes, I do. You cannot withhold it from me. Therefore, I do not insist. Let it be known that I do not ask. I demand what is mine.

DIRECTOR Put yourself in my place, sir. Try to understand for a minute that...

CRITIC I warn you, moreover, that I am a contributor to the Free Tribune and there will be a lengthy article about your negative response.

DIRECTOR Listen to my words, sir. It is simply not possible that you don't understand.

CRITIC What! Are you insinuating that I do not...? Oh! But you are completely unbelievable, unrelenting, unbearable, uncommon!

ENGINEER (*Entering*) Uncouth is what he meant.

CRITIC And who are you? The Deputy Director?

ENGINEER I am someone who has a good mind to kick you out of here if you don't leave right away. Where do you think you are?

CRITIC (*Gradually becoming less rude*) Don't get worked up, s'il vous plaît. I assume that this is the Library, isn't it?

ENGINEER You assumed incorrectly. This was the Library. It is now the construction site for the headquarters of the third Intergovernmental Committee of Refugees from the Near East Resident in the Far East: I.C.O.R.N.E.R.F.E

CRITIC But I thought... I was told by the gentleman. Honestly I never thought that...

ENGINEER (*Taking him by his jacket and escorting him to the door*) We have a lot to do. I have to complete the demolition tonight. I cannot waste time. Get out (*he throws him out*).

DIRECTOR Mr Engineer, I would like to apologise for... I tried everything I could to calm him down, but...

ENGINEER Don't worry. Years of managing staff on site means you get used to it. It was a pleasure to frighten off that mosquito.

DIRECTOR I am very grateful to you, Mr Engineer. I am very grateful indeed. And speaking of mosquitoes, I remember once, in this very managerial office, the Deputy Minister said to me: Mr Director, the Council is of the opinion that your report on cleaning and renovation...

ENGINEER Well... the fact is, Mr Director, that I was coming... as you know. You are going to have to leave.

DIRECTOR But we can't.

ENGINEER We are working three shifts; to have staff standing idle because you are here would be...

DIRECTOR We have to put in our hours, engineer.

ENGINEER But, as I told you yesterday, this is not the Library anymore. It is the headquarters for the Intergovernmental Committee.

DIRECTOR I'm sorry, sir. We cannot get into the warehouse because it's packed full of wool. I don't think we can get in until they finish the shipment tomorrow.

ENGINEER Mr Director, this is a demolition site.

DIRECTOR As far as we are concerned, until tomorrow, it is the Library.

ENGINEER But tomorrow these walls will be razed to the ground.

DIRECTOR And so we will go down with the ship.

ENGINEER Don't joke around. And, especially, don't get in the way of my job. What time do you insist on staying until?

DIRECTOR Until half past five.

ENGINEER There are only a few minutes to go. So...

DIRECTOR I'm sorry but working hours are working hours and they exist for a reason.

ENGINEER Well... in the meantime will you allow me to send in a couple of men to start putting up the scaffolding?

DIRECTOR Of course you can, and I am grateful to you, Mr Engineer. There is no way I would object! It's essential to get on with things. (*Very quietly*) Fundamental... things.

ENGINEER (*Going towards the exit*) Anyway, you are going to freeze, sat here, getting wet.

DIRECTOR Don't worry about us, Engineer, one gets used to the cold. (*The ENGINEER leaves.*) I would have liked to tell him about the report on cleaning and renovation. (*To MONTEIRO*) It was in '29, do you remember? (*José Luis plays off key.*)

MONTEIRO (*Impatient*) Will you give it a rest? (*Pause. Warm-up exercises. Clarinet playing. Conciliatory tone*) José Luis, do you want to play 'two's company'?

JOSÉ LUIS (*Furious*) What do you mean by that, you idiot?

MONTEIRO Hey, don't get angry. I was being serious. You thought I said it because of... (*pointing to* EMA). I mean to play at throwing five cent coins against the wall and see who lands closest. We'll play forty throws.

JOSÉ LUIS Oh!... That... Wait a minute. I will play, but wait.

DIRECTOR Monteiro, I wanted to speak to you...

MONTEIRO Yes... what can I do for you, Director? Although that business about 1929, I don't remember it at all. You know, at that time they were taking me out of the game and I was nobody.

DIRECTOR Monteiro, I wanted to ask you a favour, we have known each other for years. Tomorrow is the 24th and...

MONTEIRO Yes, director...

DIRECTOR The day I met my wife...

Two workmen enter. They are chatting and laughing cheerfully.

WORKMAN 1 (*Interrupting the* DIRECTOR) Excuse me... (*He makes those sitting on the bench stand up and with this plank, the trestles and other tools that they bring in, they start to assemble the scaffolding.*)

WORKMAN 2 You could do with that old woman from the apartment block. She has money to burn.

WORKMAN 1 Which old woman?

WORKMAN 2 The one who came to complain, didn't you see her? She's got 32 warts and only one tooth. And what lungs! She was complaining non-stop for quarter of an hour without even stopping for breath.

WORKMAN 1 And what's she complaining about, mate?

WORKMAN 2 About the pests. Something about how she got into the lift and found herself shut in there with a huge rat and it was staring at her.

WORKMAN 1 And what about her? Why on earth was she looking at the rat? (*They both laugh, so do* ESTELA, MONTEIRO *and the* DIRECTOR *but quietly.*)

WORKMAN 2 I'm telling you. This demolition has caused an infestation of pests like you've never seen before. The whole area is crawling.

WORKMAN 1 It's not surprising. There were lots of basements full of dirt.

WORKMAN 2 Huge amount. They're coming from the Council today to get rid of the rats. They hunt them with dogs, you know?

WORKMAN 1 Yeah, I've seen them. Tiny dogs, fox terriers. They train them.

DIRECTOR Monteiro, I was telling you that tomorrow is the anniversary of the day when I met my wife.

MONTEIRO Oh yes, you did mention it.

DIRECTOR Of course. You and I have been friends for a long time.

ESTELA Are you going to celebrate?

DIRECTOR No. It's not that. Monteiro: I need five pesos. Could you lend it to me? As it's the 24th... the date when...

MONTEIRO But mate! But, sir... It's the 24th for me as well. I wanted to bet my money for the bus against José Luis, see if I can beat him and get enough for a coffee. Where am I going to get five pesos from?

DIRECTOR I'm sorry. I shouldn't have asked. I swear it's not important. I'm sorry. I shouldn't have...

ESTELA I can lend it to you, Director.

DIRECTOR No, please, Estela... I wouldn't hear of it.

ESTELA I don't need it now. I'm being serious, I don't need it. (*Starting to cry*) If you only knew how little I need money, now!

DIRECTOR It's just that I don't know if I ought to.

ESTELA You should be happy that you have someone to buy something for (*she gives him a note and blows her nose*).

DIRECTOR Thank you. It's for our anniversary, I wanted to buy dates. We both love dates. I must write a few lines dedicated to your good nature and generosity, Estela.

ESTELA Please...

DIRECTOR Although, perhaps not. Now people laugh at those of us who write poetry. Everything is so materialistic!

MONTEIRO In my day you bet the shirt on your back!

DIRECTOR When I retire and I have time, you can be sure of it: I will finish my book 'The Hero of the Oboe'. I want it to be an ode in praise of the spirit and condemning materialism. If I hadn't given so much to my job then I'd have finished it. I've lived my life between these walls. But when I retire, it's going to be different. I'm sure. Then I will really start to work hard.

ESTELA The first time I came to the Library you recited poetry to me. Despite the fact that this room was full of people. Your poetry was so beautiful!

MONTEIRO Poor Martínez! He loved it too. He could sing hundreds of lines, from any murga. And he even used to invent them. Do you remember? (*He sings in a desultory fashion.*) The mother library. The mother library, is going to move... (*Short pause*)

WORKMAN 1 If you could move over a bit. (*He makes the library staff move again. They move about helplessly, close to the walls, like people condemned to death by firing squad. Barking can be heard in the background.*)

WORKMAN 2 Did you hear? The little dogs have arrived. When they start on the rats, we'll go over. They're amazing those fox terriers. A couple of jumps, they corner them and... whack. (*To the library staff*) Would you mind... moving over a bit further, a bit further, this way (*he corners them*).

JOSÉ LUIS Shall we play then?

MONTEIRO It has to be with 5 cent coins. (*They move away preparing to play against the wall.*) How did you get started with the clarinet?

JOSÉ LUIS It was my grandfather's. Blowing into this, the old man raised seven children and paid for his own house. What do you say to that?

MONTEIRO And you want to blow... your troubles away?

JOSÉ LUIS I'm learning because I'm ambitious. I have an uncle who knows the director of the Municipal Band... So perhaps, in a few years, with a bit of luck...

MONTEIRO More like with a lot of luck...

JOSÉ LUIS Well... you have to seize something if you want to progress, if you have ambition.

MONTEIRO Of course you do. You have to clutch at it, like clutching at straws. And you're right. It looks a bit like a straw. Perhaps like a very big straw.

JOSÉ LUIS What do you expect? Expect me to stay here, like you? This is hell, old man.

MONTEIRO And the band? What do you think that's going to be? The same hell but with more puffing (*he blows a raspberry*). Brrr.

JOSÉ LUIS Do us all a favour and just throw.

EMA Is it long until we can leave?

DIRECTOR No. A few minutes. A few minutes and we'll go home. (*Thinking to himself*) They will have given Isabel her injection. Although the nurse didn't come yesterday. Until today I'd never have thought that I was going to live my life between these four walls. All the days of my life, coming to the same place, seeing the same people. And for what? I think it was all for nothing. Or rather: I think that it was all nothing, absolutely nothing. A game, a way to entertain myself and pass the time until it's all over, although time carries on. We leave today, they'll pull down the walls and there won't be the slightest trace of all those days. That's the way it is. All my years are no good even as rubble; they won't stay here, nor will the debris of my soul. The slightest breeze will carry off the air that I breathed and nothing will remain. I ought to write about this.

ESTELA Poor Martínez. He had a beautiful wake. It was hot so we were in the garden. Do you remember, Ema? I was with Claudio. Such an attentive man! He didn't even know old Martínez but he stayed all night and I think that he even cried to make me happy. It was such a lovely wake!

EMA I should have put my wool socks on. It's absolutely freezing and it's started to drizzle, why don't we go?

DIRECTOR It's not long. (*ESTELA opens the umbrella and the DIRECTOR, ESTELA and EMA shelter beneath it.*) It's not long now. It's nice to work your hours. Before, it used to bother me, but for a few years now it has been a sort of relief. You know that you leave the office at a certain time and that until that time, you don't have to worry about anything.

JOSÉ LUIS Mate, you always win. (*Complaining.*)

MONTEIRO It's because I make an effort when I play and you have your mind on something else.

Barking is heard in the background. The WORKMEN leave.

WORKMAN 2 (*Leaving*) They're starting. Hurry up, you're going to see what a show it is!

EMA José Luis: if you lose, stop playing.

JOSÉ LUIS But Ema!

MONTEIRO Throw!

JOSÉ LUIS (*To EMA*) One more throw and that's it, ok? Just one more.

EMA You always do as you please.

JOSÉ LUIS But honey, one last little go.

EMA Do as you please, pig-headed idiot!

JOSÉ LUIS But love... he's already thrown, you see.

MONTEIRO Go on, mate.

JOSÉ LUIS Just this one, my love. Will you be angry if I throw?

MONTEIRO Go on... don't be miserable.

EMA You're always the same. And you're getting wet as well. Come here.

JOSÉ LUIS (*Throwing any old how*) You won this one as well. I'm not playing any more.

MONTEIRO From now on you're not playing at this, or at anything else.

EMA Speak to him now. Go on. Go on.

JOSÉ LUIS Mr Director, do you know Dr. Sony Terra, from the Registry Office?

DIRECTOR I know him, yes. He's the nephew of Izaguirre, who was Secretary General. It was him who appointed me as Director here. An extraordinary man. When he told me that I was going to be appointed, I almost hugged him. It was the happiest moment of my life.

EMA Would you mind giving Sony Terra's card to José Luis?

DIRECTOR Of course I'll give it to him, but why?

JOSÉ LUIS There is a vacancy in the Registry Office and I was wondering if...

DIRECTOR You want to change?

EMA It's twenty-five pesos more.

JOSÉ LUIS To be honest, it's just for now. I'm quite ambitious. I'd like to become a musician and join the Municipal Band.

DIRECTOR And what about seniority?

JOSÉ LUIS It's just that twenty-five pesos a month makes a real difference, Director. And it's because... I want to get married...

DIRECTOR How long ago did you start at the Library?

JOSÉ LUIS About fourteen or fifteen years, but now...

DIRECTOR Well I never! You have fifteen years of seniority and you're going to exchange it for twenty-five pesos?

ESTELA Is seniority so important?

DIRECTOR You mean seniority? No, no, don't take it like that: I didn't mean to say that you were old, quite the opposite. But it surprises me that you all haven't realised that we public servants are like mummies. Each one of us is valued according to the number of years of service that we have behind us.

EMA But we, Director, with twenty-five pesos more, we'll be able to get married...

MONTEIRO Can't you see that he has the face of a mature pear? I mean, a mature person?

EMA You're obnoxious!

DIRECTOR Seniority is of the utmost importance. A fresh mummy isn't worth anything at all, whereas if a living being gradually wraps themselves in metres and metres of bandages and routine, if for years they have cooked on a slow heat, until boredom and weariness have fully seasoned their flesh, well then it's different, then there is merit for promotion.

JOSÉ LUIS But, sir, it's just for now. I mean, then, playing my clarinet... if I'm lucky...

DIRECTOR Seniority is a fine liqueur which gradually embalms us, because it takes a good while for the weariness of indifference to begin flowing through our veins; and the road to complete rest is longer still, until you reach what I call administrative ecstasy. Of course, there are extraordinary beings who, within a few months of being appointed, have already managed to mummify themselves completely, but it's unusual.

JOSÉ LUIS But I... sir... I want to get married...

DIRECTOR Believe me, young man: man requires a certain seniority to be able to be retired without retiring. The average is five years. Oh! And it's such a beautiful situation. Seniority is so beautiful. You can be at home or at work, and nothing matters anymore; you live your life protected from the world and its complaints. You live wonderfully protected beneath the eighth wonder of the world: the paper pyramids, guarded by the impenetrable sphinx of the regulations. You enjoy life like a pharaoh with a big budget, which keeps you in a sarcophagus, where you will forever rest in peace, although you still have twenty years to go before you retire.

WORKMAN 1 (*Entering with WORKMAN 2*) Didn't I tell you that those little dogs were a sight to be seen? They don't miss a single one, they corner them and... crack... (*To the library staff*) Now, you really will have to leave because there will be falling rubble.

DIRECTOR It's time. Twenty-eight minutes past five. We can go.

JOSÉ LUIS I have to wait for Esteban to see about the Registry Office.

EMA And what about me? I'm frozen to death, José Luis.

JOSÉ LUIS Wait for me at your house. I'll be there right away, darling. I told Esteban to come by at six, ok? (*They hold hands and look at each other for a moment.*)

EMA I'll be waiting for you from the moment I get in, ok?

Barking is heard downstage; this is repeated two or three times.

ESTELA And tomorrow? Do we come here?

DIRECTOR Well... if the warehouse is fitted out then we can do our duties there and if not, then here.

JOSÉ LUIS And how will we know?

DIRECTOR It will be a matter of looking in the newspapers.

MONTEIRO Do you think they are going to be interested in this?

EMA Shall we call you to ask before we leave for work?

DIRECTOR How do you expect me to know? The best thing will be to go to the salting shed at the Port at one on the dot and if they don't let us in, we will come here.

ESTELA I hope it doesn't rain tomorrow; I don't fancy traipsing from one place to another in this weather! (*The DIRECTOR, ESTELA and EMA leave sheltering beneath the umbrella. MONTEIRO follows a little way behind them and lifts up his collar*).

MONTEIRO Aren't you coming?

JOSÉ LUIS Didn't I tell you? I'm waiting for Esteban.
MONTEIRO (*Sarcastic*) You're going to go far! Yes indeed! (*He leaves.*)

José Luis sits on the plank of wood and starts to reattempt his musical scale. Rubble starts to fall onto the piles of sand. Suddenly the band strikes up a very short tune. When it finishes the voice of an orator can be heard in the background; he is invisible.

ORATOR Mr Deputy Secretary and interim weekly inspector. Your Excellency, Ambassador to the Republic of Oslibron, Mr Minister of Calachin and half of the southern swamp, Ladies and Gentlemen: today we lay the foundation stone of the new, temporary and unprecedented Intergovernmental Committee of Refugees from the Near East Resident in the Far East: I.C.O.R.N.E.R. F.E. In this way, this small corner of Montevideo becomes trees of papery branches intertwined, from which we can swing, without defiling or dedressing, but in fact dedriving this old dream for a frequendus floral fusion of common goals.

Ladies and gentlemen, we will fight to become unified and to ride camels. On this path, we will plant the segums, the segums of newlyness. I am firm in this belief. We come here empty; but it is a creaption of emptiness, an emptiness to be filled with this newlyformedness. We will not suffer starvabsene from common goals here! We will become stronger and more unified as we move forward. In this corner of Montevideo we, of the I.C.O.R.N.E.R.F.E., will work to elaborate and achieve these goals! So be it!

When the speech finishes there is a brief applause which quickly dies out. During the speech JOSÉ LUIS *has attempted and reattempted the impossible musical scale and he continues in his efforts. Darkness slowly begins to fall and it starts to rain again.*

Curtain

Notes

1. A murga is a band of musicians and dancers who perform in the street on improvised stages. During carnival in Uruguay there are frequent performances of murgas.
2. Antonio Machín, *A Barbacoa me voy*, online audio recording, YouTube, 8 November 2014 <https://www.youtube.com/watch?v=SZSB2Zhf4qE> [accessed 31 July 2021].

CHAPTER 3

❖

Conceptualising Distance and Proximity in Theatre Translation: Analysing Afterlife in *Pedro y el capitán* and *Bailando sola cada noche*

Points of Contact between Cultures

This chapter focusses on the ways in which the theatre translator creates links between source and target cultures in order to conceptualise how a play might find a place in the target culture, the types of discourses and discussions that it might feed into, and the new types of questions that it could generate in that target context. I argue that the translator applies the cultural and historical knowledge gained through the dramaturgical and contextual analyses to establish points of contact between original and target cultures, which allow the dramatic text to become mobile and move into the target context. Through the study of key examples from two plays, I demonstrate how the concepts of distance and proximity can inform both the way we conceptualise this relationship between two cultures and our approach to the translation process. This approach is underpinned by Jean-Luc Nancy's ideas on how proximity can also function to enable a sense of distance or difference to become apparent.[1] This chapter proposes that proximity to a different culture can be achieved through the translation without completely effacing a sense of distance; what makes the translated play so interesting is that it opens up a space for voices that may seem completely remote to speak here and now. Through the analysis presented, I provide examples of how the translator can develop strategies to enable those voices to speak into the target context.

This chapter examines *Pedro y el capitán* [*Pedro and the Captain*] by Mario Benedetti (1979) and *Bailando sola cada noche* by Raquel Diana (2008) which I translated into English as *Dancing Alone Every Night*.[2] Chapter 4 is the full English translation of the latter play. In both cases, the playwright engages with and writes about a situation occurring elsewhere: Diana takes as a starting point the story of a woman in London and Benedetti wrote from exile in Cuba about human rights violations occurring in his native Uruguay and throughout Latin America. Distance and the ways in which stories travel play an important role in the creative processes of the original authors. I will show how the translator can actively incorporate ideas about distance and proximity into the translation process in order to demonstrate how connections between the creative processes undertaken by authors and translators work in practice. This chapter will explore the significance of distances in the original text, the types of audience engagement that they might provoke, and how the dramaturgical analysis can help us to understand the types of connections that the text creates. Distance and proximity in terms of cultural reference points, experiences and discourses exist in the plays in the original language whilst still making connections to the source cultural context. This chapter draws on the analysis of the original plays in order to propose that the translation can also function to communicate multiplicity and provide insights into close and distant cultural realities.

Pedro y el capitán is set in the interrogation room of an unnamed detention centre where Pedro is questioned by the Captain who seeks to obtain information about four of the prisoner's comrades. As Pedro faces and accepts his own death, the play explores to what extent a dialogue can be established between two men who are ideologically opposed to one another. I acted as a Script Consultant for the 2016 production of the play in London and aspects of this work will be discussed in the analysis that follows. *Bailando sola cada noche* takes as a starting point the true story of a woman in London, Joyce Vincent, who was found dead in her flat, slumped in front of her TV, having remained there for approximately two and a half years. Diana dramatises Joyce's death by ascribing actions, gestures, words and songs to the period of time about which it is practically impossible to ascertain any details: the period of time between her death and the discovery of her corpse. Both plays are set in enclosed spaces and the playwrights use the artifice of the private to provide an insight into the experience of the protagonist which centres on how they occupy a space between life and death. This artifice serves to establish proximity between audience and actors, which involves the audience in the action of the play and incites them to interact with the characters on stage and the discourses presented through the dramatic narrative. This intimate insight also produces a sense that these in-between spaces might be used to create, disrupt and challenge our expectations and existing ideas, therefore revealing something new. In this chapter I expand upon Roger Mirza's idea of *Pedro y el capitán* as the portrayal of 'un ritual de la muerte' [a ritual of death] by arguing that in both plays we can identify types of death rituals that take place in the in-between space to prepare the respective protagonists for their death.[3] The analysis specifies the significance of these rituals and the ways in which they also serve to provoke challenging questions about the protagonists' experiences in life. In both plays, the sense that these works explore a possible dialogue to which the audience are privy is heightened through the performance because what the audience witness in the theatre is immediate, transient and unique.

This chapter demonstrates how the translator can make links between the thematic and the theoretical in order to develop a creative translation strategy. For these two plays the thematic–theoretical link centres on the concept of afterlife. I will demonstrate how I made connections between the theme of afterlife within the plays and theories in Translation Studies relating to the idea of the translation of a work as its afterlife. I argue that the protagonists share qualities with Derrida's concepts of spectres.[4] Colin Davis explains that 'Derrida's spectre is a deconstructive figure hovering between life and death, presence and absence, and making established certainties vacillate'.[5] Therefore, in challenging what we think we know, and what we think is certain, what might the spectre reveal and uncover? For Derrida, 'the spectre's secret is a productive opening of meaning rather than a determinate content to be uncovered'.[6] By adopting an approach to these plays as 'productive opening[s] of meaning', we can understand the dramatic space as a constructive and creative one through which meanings continue to be generated. This chapter expands Benjamin's ideas of the translation as an extension of the life of the original to identify the techniques employed by Benedetti and Diana to provoke and sustain a dialogue with the audience, which will continue to resonate in the future and create the possibility of retellings through translation and future performances.[7] This allows the questions posed by and through the original dramatic text to be transformed for the target context, generate new meanings and interact with specific discourses in the UK. Through outlining this process, this chapter shows how the close scholarly reading of the text, as discussed in Chapter 1, underpins the translation strategy chosen for each play, enables the translator to make connections to the target context and equips them to find solutions posed by translation challenges.

Pedro y el capitán: Disruptive Dialogues in the Interrogation Room

Pedro y el capitán was first performed in Mexico in 1979 by El Galpón, a Uruguayan theatre company in exile there during the civic-military dictatorship, and directed by Atahualpa del Cioppo. The text was published by Editorial Nueva Imagen in Mexico the same year.[8] According to Uruguayan theatre scholar Roger Mirza, the two characters are depicted 'en una situación límite' [in an extreme situation] as they engage in an intense conflict with each other through the dialogue.[9] Theresa Mackey suggests that Pedro's exact political stance is never specified in order to critique a broader range of Latin American political conflicts.[10] The play is split into four parts and each one ends with a resolute 'no' from Pedro upon which he is returned to the torture rooms located off stage. Consequently, his conversations with the Captain are punctuated by the physical abuse to his body carried out by officers whom the Captain nicknames 'los muchachos eléctricos' [the electricians] (*Pedro*, p. 27).[11] *Pedro and the Captain* translated by Adrianne Aron was produced in London at the Vaults Festival in 2016 by Blackboard Theatre and directed by Miguel Hernando Torres Umba.[12] In our roles as Script Consultants, Catherine Boyle (from King's College London) and I focussed on supporting the director in adapting some aspects of the language of the text for a London audience (with the permission of the translator); we provided information to enable the actors to understand the cultural context of the play; we participated in a post-show discussion about the relevance of the play today alongside academics, representatives from the Uruguayan Embassy and human rights activists.

In *Pedro y el capitán*, Pedro rejects the offer of life that he is given by the Captain in exchange for disclosing information: 'Usted me ofrece que viva como un muerto. Y antes que eso prefiero morir como un vivo' [You're offering me the chance to live like a dead man. But I'd much rather die as a living being] (*Pedro*, p. 47). Pedro responds to the acts of abuse by seeking to take control of his own death and using this as a technique both to preserve his own integrity and to undermine the Captain's power to extract information from him. Morello-Frosch and Morello-Frosch state that Pedro's death is one which he self-designs.[13] Pedro sets up a distinction between life and death based on the narrative of the regime, voiced by the Captain. He then poses a challenge to the authority of this narrative by blurring the boundaries between life and death and declaring himself as dead at the beginning of Part III. This enables a type of dialogue between interrogator and prisoner to occur, which otherwise would not be possible. In this way, Pedro occupies an in-between space which not only disrupts the life and death dichotomy but also challenges the hierarchy of power through the way in which he confronts the Captain. Pedro affirms three times in quick succession that he is dead at the start of Part III:

> Estoy en la muerte, y chau.
>
> [I'm dead so ciao.]
>
> Estoy muerto. Estamos como quien dice en mi velorio.
>
> [I'm dead. You could even say we're at my wake.]
>
> Estoy muerto. No sabe qué tranquilidad me vino cuando supe que estaba muerto. Por eso no me importa que me apliquen electricidad, o me sumerjan en la mierda, o me tengan de plantón, o me revienten los huevos. No me importa porque estoy muerto y eso da una gran serenidad, y hasta una gran alegría. ¿No ve que estoy contento?
>
> [I'm dead. You don't know how calm I began to feel when I realised I was dead. That's why it doesn't matter to me if you electrocute me, or drown me in shit, or force me to stand in stress positions, or break my balls. It doesn't matter to me because I'm dead and being dead makes you calm, even happy. Can't you see I'm happy?] (*Pedro*, p. 56)

Pedro's assertion and adoption of his own death through using language to narrate it, as shown in the examples above, demonstrates the significance and power attributed to words in the play. Despite the fact that physical torture is not depicted on stage, which was something Benedetti said he did not want to portray (*Pedro*, p. 17), the presence of Pedro's increasingly bruised body, which persists and endures beyond his self-proclaimed death, coupled with the way that he speaks about his experiences at the hands of the torturers, becomes a way to denounce this type of violence. Therefore, whilst the conflict witnessed on stage focusses on the importance of ideology, discourse, language and who has the power to manipulate and control these, the audience are constantly made aware of the significance of the body. Benedetti creates an in-between life and death space in which Pedro is able to take control of the battle for the word and temporarily invert the power balance by asking the Captain questions about why he performs his role in the detention centre and how it affects his relationship with his family (*Pedro*, p. 43). Through manipulating the conversation, Pedro suggests alternatives to the narratives offered and dictated by the Captain that form part of and perpetuate the national narrative, and so this space can be seen as one in which new meanings are opened up. Through their discussions, the audience are given an insight into how weak the boundaries between prisoner and interrogator are and this exposes the possibility for future repetitions and reiterations of this violence which, through the act of translation, can be imagined in new contexts.

The specific location of the detention centre in which the two men meet is never mentioned. However, there are examples of language and references in the play which serve to indicate that it is located in Uruguay. Whilst this does not prevent the play from speaking into a broader context of Latin American dictatorships and political repression, these references are important in identifying the connections and resonances created by the text. For example, there are allusions to the River Plate, which separates Uruguay from Argentina and opens into the Atlantic Ocean. In one of Pedro's monologues about his childhood he states that he likes to go to the sea although, 'Nicolás dice que no es mar [...] dice que es río. Pero en los ríos se ve siempre la otra orilla y aquí no. Y además no son salados. Y éste es salado' [Nicolás says it isn't the sea [...] he says it's the river. But with a river you can always see the other bank and here, you can't. And also they aren't salty. And this is salty] (*Pedro*, pp. 60–61). He refers to the coast again in Part IV and how lovers would often meet there but they can't do this anymore as they are all in prison, hiding or exile (*Pedro*, p. 71). This evokes images of the Rambla in Montevideo, which is a unique aspect of the city: a long promenade beside the River Plate which wraps around the city, separating it from the beach, where people gather to meet or go for walks with friends, family and lovers. There is a reference to Pedro buying a gold pin for his wife in the calle Sarandí, a central street in the Ciudad Vieja [Old City] in Montevideo where there is a crafts and antiques market (*Pedro*, p. 31). One of the ways in which I explored these references with the creative team in my role as Script Consultant for the 2016 production in English was through a discussion of how, by taking them into account in the analysis, we gain a closer insight into Pedro's connection with and love for the city where he lives. We also discussed how they reveal the impact that the dictatorship has had on the experience of young families, like his own. This provided a way for the actors to work creatively with these references and the significance of what they tell us about Pedro's life, and the lives of many people like him, before the onset of the dictatorship.

What is at stake in the play is who will win the battle and how, because the interrogator and prisoner have conflicting objectives. The Captain seeks to extract information from Pedro as a step towards eradicating everyone who opposes the regime, whilst Pedro withholds any information that he has in order to protect and preserve the lives of his comrades so that they can further their political cause. For the Captain, the result is non-negotiable and he spells out how it will be achieved in what Albuquerque refers to as 'threatives' which terrorise and intimidate the person at whom they are aimed and are used to apply non-physical pressure to him or her.[14] By speaking, Pedro is challenging the silence ascribed to him as object by employing the only weapon to which he has recourse: language. However, when he speaks, he does not reveal the required information. Pedro engages in a dialogue which serves to rupture his silent protest maintained throughout Part 1. Unhooded in the second part, Pedro claims his previous silence as a mark of his self-respect; he agrees with the Captain that it is much more difficult to avoid responding when you make eye contact with your interlocutor (*Pedro*, p. 38). We can interpret a self-reflexive dramatic technique through which the words placed in the Captain's mouth by the playwright pose a challenge to the audience: do they dare to look either of the characters on stage in the eye and risk entering into a dialogue with them? Could this implicate them in the violence or attribute responsibility to them for denouncing it?

Pedro's voice challenges the idea that those with power are able to impose a language and narrative which is valid for everyone. This is significant because establishing a new national discourse was central to the aims of the dictatorship. In a study of the Argentine context, Diana Taylor articulates the connections between writing, torture and the creation of a new national discourse.[15] Taylor links torture and writing by proposing that torture becomes an 'act of inscription': firstly, the body is written into the 'nationalist narrative' of identity on which the military discourse and regime of organised terror is founded. She calls this '*writing the body*'. Secondly, torture scars, mutilates and distorts the physical body of the person being tortured thus turning it into a text inscribed with a 'cautionary "message"' to others. She calls this '*writing on the body*'.[16] This was significant because the individual bodies that were tortured were part of the process of reforming the social body. Taylor explains:

> *Writing the body* set up a triangular formulation: it established author-ity (of the military leaders who manipulated the discourse), it cast the torturers as the pen or instrument of inscription (as the midwives in the creation of the new national being), and it turned the victim into the producible/expendable body-text.[17]

According to Taylor's framework, the political prisoner loses control over her or his body as it becomes a text, which is written through the process of torture to explicitly communicate the objectives of the dictatorship and the vision of a new national identity. Therefore, the act of torture and the distortion of the body becomes intrinsically linked to the manipulation of language. Following Taylor's work, I understand that Pedro's body becomes a body-text which narrates several conflicting stories: a national narrative of violence and repression, created by the state, and the story of a corpse, a living dead man, created by Pedro.

The audience witness the impact of torture in the physical deterioration of Pedro throughout the course of the play. This is particularly striking at the start of each part when Pedro is pushed into the interrogation room on stage, following another torture session, and his body is evidently weaker and more distorted than in the previous scene. As Pedro's body is weakened, both through the violence exerted upon it and through the starvation and sleep deprivation that he suffers, he becomes more willing to engage in dialogue and his dialogue becomes more animated. This is referred to explicitly in Part iv when the stage directions state that, 'De todos modos, siempre habrá una contradicción entre la relativa vitalidad que aún muestra su rostro y el derrengado aspecto de su físico' [At all times there will be a contradiction between Pedro's face, which is still relatively lively, and his physical appearance, which is debilitated] (*Pedro*, p. 72). This poses a challenge to the actor to convey the widening gap between Pedro's physical state of deterioration and his ability to engage in dialogue in order to make the audience aware of his weakened physical state and heightened mental state.

At the beginning of Part iii when Pedro begins to speak, his speech is intermingled with laughter as he vividly describes the previous session of torture, which had to be interrupted due to a power cut. At this point in the play, the stage directions begin to refer to Pedro as 'un cuerpo' [a body], for example, 'El cuerpo no responde, pero trata de moverse' [The body does not respond, but tries to move] (*Pedro*, p. 53). This is significant as the specific reference to Pedro as a 'body' demands a shift in action, gesture and interaction on the part of both characters. This shift is also made evident in the stage directions which, at the start of Part iii and Part iv, indicate that the Captain has to assist Pedro to the chair and stabilise him. The change in their interactions is particularly striking in Part iv when the Captain, who is already showing signs of ruin from the experience of his conversations with Pedro, removes his belt in order to strap Pedro to the back of the chair to prevent him from falling off (*Pedro*, p. 72). As Pedro becomes increasingly detached from his own body and begins to view it as a corpse, the Captain begins to interact physically with Pedro's body. As a result, the opposition that the Captain sets up in Part i between those who work with the body (the torturers/electricians) and those who work with the mind or reason (the interrogators) starts to break down as he is obliged to interact physically with Pedro's body in order to be able to carry out the interrogation. These moments also serve to indicate the way in which the plot will develop: Pedro's body will be destroyed by the torturers before his mind is destroyed by the Captain. Stephen Gregory specifies the faltering of the Captain as he begins to look more dishevelled and to address Pedro in the formal *usted* form, which Pedro reciprocates by addressing the Captain using the informal *tú* (*usted* and *tú* both mean 'you' in the registers specified), as important markers of change in signalling both his sympathy towards Pedro and the unravelling of his false identity. The collapse of the Captain's identity, as well as the boundaries that he has sought to establish, are demonstrated symbolically through his appearance at this moment in the play but revealed explicitly later on when Pedro explains that he knows that the Captain is working under a false rank.[18]

The change from the use of the *usted* to the *tú* form is important and can be difficult to capture in the same way in English translation as this explicit way of marking the change of address cannot be easily and directly replicated. However, if, as in this case, the change in forms of address is indicative of a significant change in status and the ways in which two characters interact and treat one another, then this will be present in other ways in the dramatic text. The dramaturgical analysis, as demonstrated in this study, reveals the multiple ways in which this change in the relationship is conveyed. It is present in the language, in the ways in which Pedro takes control of the discussion and in the change in physicality described above. In working with the actors and director for the 2016 production, the dramaturgical analysis underpinned and informed the discussions about the importance of this change and how it is communicated in the original and translated dramatic text. Director Miguel Hernando Torres Umba made a decision to have the two characters swap seats as a way to visually represent the change in their status. This also emphasised the idea of the lengths that the Captain has to go to in order to physically sustain and support Pedro in his attempt to get him to stay alive, as described in the stage directions above. The Captain needs Pedro to disclose the required information in order justify his own purpose in the detention centre, the regime and his own life. This is because whereas 'the body means nothing to Pedro (it's his ideology that he cares about), it certainly means something to his interrogator' because Pedro's refusal to provide information and his consistent 'no' render the Captain useless and expose him as a sadist — by the Captain's own definition — for allowing the torture of Pedro for no real reason (*Pedro*, p. 48). Furthermore, as Di Stefano explains, Pedro's constant refusal to disclose information also undermines the Captain's beliefs: it exposes the extent to which Pedro remains committed to his ideology in a way that the Captain could never be, and this ultimately results in his breakdown at the end of the play. Therefore, the ways in which the characters' physical state and appearance change during the course of the play are representative of the way in which Pedro's commitment to socialist ideology far outstrips the Captain's commitment to bourgeois liberalism.[19]

The change of seats was an effective way to capture this shift in the Captain's attitude and interaction with Pedro. It is significant because whilst the manipulation of discourse, the creation of dialogue and powers of persuasion are significant themes, the transformation of the actor's bodies reminds us that, as Roger Mirza says, 'No se trata, por lo tanto, sólo de lenguaje, sino de dos cuerpos físicamente enfrentados. Estamos ante un ritual de la muerte convocada por los extremos de la violencia' [It is not, therefore, only about language, but also about two bodies confronting each other physically. We are witnessing a ritual of death brought about by extreme violence].[20] The idea that the play, particularly in Parts III and IV, becomes a ritual of preparation for Pedro's ultimate physical death at the end of the play is conveyed through moments such as a monologue addressed to his wife about how she should explain his death to their son (*Pedro*, p. 81). The idea of this in-between space as one where the rituals of preparation for death and burial take place, which evokes the last rites, forms a connection to *Bailando sola cada noche* in which we see the protagonist preparing to leave her flat once her body is discovered.

Nancy J. Gates-Madsen suggests that the fact that Pedro ultimately does not reveal any information would make him more difficult for a Uruguayan or Latin American audience to relate to, particularly because testimonies from during the dictatorships in the Southern Cone indicate that 'such incredible resistance was apparently the exception rather than the rule'.[21] Therefore, despite the fact that many Uruguayans would have undergone a similar experience to that of Pedro in the play, his actions do not mirror those of many political prisoners, which could cause members of the audience to feel distanced from the experience depicted on stage, even within the original context. Gates-Madsen's observation could relate to reasons why the play was less successful in Uruguay than in other countries in which it was performed.[22] The play also received international recognition through a prize awarded by Amnesty International (Golden Flame Award, 1979).[23] Mirza points out that *Pedro y el capitán* has achieved success throughout Europe, North America and Latin America; he gives the example of Mexico where in 1997 one company celebrated four hundred performances.[24] He identifies that as time passes, an increasing number of plays have approached the subjects of torture, repression and state terrorism, such as *Cuentos de hadas* by Raquel Diana (El Galpón, 1998), *Memoria para armar* by Horacio Buscaglia (Teatro Circular, 2002), *Elena Quinteros. Presente* by Gabriela Iribarren and Marianella Morena (Basement, Bar Mincho, 2003), *El Disparo* by Estela Golovchenko (2006).[25] Mirza's observation implies that in the period immediately following the return to democracy in 1985, the theatre was unable to use the dramatic space to expose and denounce the crimes committed in a way with which the audience could identify. This was perhaps because the Uruguayan audience were still searching for a language and a form in which to express the violence committed and the ongoing trauma. This is an important example of how a play might generate a distancing effect within its original context and it raises an important question as to what the different functions of this in-between space created by Benedetti might be.

Whilst it is clear that the play denounces the violence experienced in detention centres during the dictatorship, Pedro's articulation of his own death indicates that something more than a depiction of the experiences in interrogation centres is at stake. Whilst Pedro's refusal to share the names, addresses and details of his comrades may make him difficult to relate to, Beatriz Walker proposes that the process of asking questions about how and why the Captain took up his role in the detention centre functions as an investigation on behalf of members of the audience

> que como partícipe de esa sociedad en la que Pedro vivió debe ineludiblemente tener las mismas inquietudes que tiene el personaje, la misma curiosidad acerca de lo que lleva a un ser humano a ejercer el 'oficio' del Capitán y de los tantos capitanes que ha visto la América Latina toda en un momento u otro de su historia.[26]
>
> [who as members of the society in which Pedro lived must undoubtedly have the same concerns as the character, the same curiosity about what leads a human being to carry out the Captain's 'profession' and that of the many captains that Latin America has seen at one time or another in its history.]

The silencing of the discussion around the civic-military dictatorship has not only prevented Uruguayan citizens from dealing with its aftermath and the resulting trauma but it also denied them the legal right to ask questions, search for answers about how this occurred and why, and pursue legal punishment. There have been restrictions on this type of action due to La Ley de Caducidad de la Pretensión Punitiva del Estado [Law of Expiration of Punitive Claims of the State] which

> dealt with the prosecution of military and police officers, the forced retirement of military personnel in 1974, and the role of civilian political institutions and armed forces in relation to the promotion of military officers. Articles one to four particularly ended the possibility of judicial proceedings for past human rights violations.[27]

Therefore, as Walker suggests, the audience may be drawn into the way in which Pedro asks questions which were yet to be posed in official discourses and narratives. This is crucial because this questioning by Pedro places the audience in a position in which they can gain an insight into how this confrontation with the two men on opposing sides might have come about and how it could be replicated or avoided in the future.

Mackey suggests that in *Pedro y el capitán* a sense of repetition, particularly with regards to political events, stems from the way in which the boundary between the power relations is temporarily altered. Mackey's idea is useful in thinking about how a similar situation, with slightly different powers at play, could be conjured up in the imaginations of the audience of both the original and the translated text. Mackey's analysis focusses on the way in which manipulation allows violence to continue:

> In exposing the fragility of the boundary between oppressed and oppressor and between maintainer and threatener of established order, this play not only elucidates the ease with which political allegiances and political fortunes change such that a new cycle of revolution and authoritarianism repeats — it also suggests a reason that the sociopolitical pendulum cannot cease.[28]

The character of the Captain even seems to suggest that political violence is cyclical when he tries to persuade Pedro to talk and asks him '¿Quién te dice que algún día esta situación se invierta y seas vos quien me interrogue? [Who's to say that someday we might not find ourselves here again but the other way around so that it's you interrogating me?] (*Pedro*, p. 38). Gates-Madsen makes a similar point to Mackey by focussing on the idea of a prescribed role and the concept of the torturer as trained to perform certain duties and to follow instructions, which forces spectators to consider their own potential for violence.[29] We understand this to be the experience of the Captain when he confesses in Part III to a gradual process of instruction in increasingly intense methods of torture (*Pedro*, p. 65). If the state routinely instructs people in torture, and the implication is that these people are chosen more at random than because they possess particular characteristics, then a cycle of military control and violence could begin again; perhaps it never ended but rather has been managed in different ways since the return to democracy. Therefore, the dialogue in the play, particularly the discussion that occurs once Pedro declares himself as dead, creates a productive opening of meaning, following Davis's analysis, through which the audience gain an insight into how these two men came to occupy their opposing roles in the regime. It also indicates ways in which this violence might continue and the audience might be implicated. Are they already implicated by watching the play? Pedro's self-declared afterlife experience therefore serves a dramatic function in opening a dialogue through which the audience gain new insights into the cycle of repression and violence. It also works conceptually to enable us to make a connection between the situation on stage and future manifestations of this type of violence. The perpetual nature of the violence suggested by the action and dialogue in the play creates an opening for future manifestations in a new cultural context through translation. As the play moves into a new context, the cycle of violence is extended so that a link between the target context and the violence of the Uruguayan civic-military dictatorship can be created through the translation. This translation will generate new meanings in the target context by interacting with discourses regarding the use of torture to interrogate political prisoners in democratic contexts today, particularly in relation to combatting terrorism and seeking to tackle radicalisation.

For the 2016 production of *Pedro and the Captain* by Blackboard Theatre Company at the Vaults Festival in London, the company was keen to draw the attention of the audience to human rights abuses and to provoke questions about where torture occurs today and what the role and responsibility of people in the UK might be for this type of violence. Whilst the interrogation room of the play and the characters of Pedro and the Captain seemed familiar both through the language spoken and because they evoked frequent images published by the media relating to recent and ongoing conflicts in places such as Iraq and Syria, the exchange between the two characters on stage served to challenge ideas and stereotypes about what radicalisation might mean and how it might occur. Aspects of the conflict that their discussion brought to light seemed extremely recognisable, particularly in relation to the importance of ideology, yet the names mentioned and the references to communism brought into play a different agenda of repression, from a different time, which challenged the audience to ask where else this violence might be occurring. This may have caused a distancing effect for some audience members but, as discussed above, this may also have occurred in the original context. The sense of raising awareness was heightened through the theatre space, an intimate room in a formerly disused tunnel underneath Waterloo station in the heart of London; did people outside realise what was going on there? How might the audience respond as they leave and re-enter the Vaults festival, which included plays, comedy shows and performance art? There was a specific 'call to action' created through a partnership with Redress, a human rights organisation based in London which seeks to eradicate torture. Therefore, the actions of the play were linked to a response through the actions of the audience.

In this way, the 2016 production created a link from the Uruguayan context depicted in the original play to the target culture and the concerns affecting society at that time without eliminating all references to the source situation. This enabled both a sense of distance and proximity to coexist in the play performed in London. As a result, points of contact were created between two cultures that may initially have seemed different and disconnected. The play simultaneously provokes questions about what happened there and then and what is happening here and now, and, just as in the original, it asks the audience to consider their own role in this cycle of violence. Therefore, the dialogue between Pedro and the Captain in the interrogation room also enables a dialogue between two different cultural contexts once it is transformed through translation.

Gregory has criticised Benedetti for 'mapping large-scale social issues on to the co-ordinates of an almost private struggle between two individuals, [meaning] the political has collapsed into the psychological'.[30] Gregory's approach highlights a key concern for translation regarding how we understand a play in relation to its original context before seeking to move it into a new cultural context. Gregory understands *Pedro y el capitán* as detached from the Uruguayan political context because it focusses on the local and personal, but it is essential to acknowledge that the local and personal interactions that it depicts are rooted within Uruguay at a time of repression which greatly affected the population: at one time Uruguay had more political prisoners per capita than any other country in the world.[31] At the same time, these narratives which demonstrate the political through the personal can also speak into and about other situations. As demonstrated in the examples above from the 2016 production, the personal and interpersonal narratives of individuals can be used to create connections between two cultural contexts which initially seem distant and different.

By placing manipulation at the heart of the play, we understand how the radicalisation of two men might occur and we also understand the limitations imposed by the situation in which they meet. In undermining the Captain's ideas of self-belief, his commitment to his own ideology, and his perception of the way in which the interrogation room should function and his job be performed, Pedro draws attention to the weaknesses in the people who carry out these roles, and weaknesses in the system itself. Nevertheless, whilst articulating his own death grants him a certain freedom, the challenges that Pedro poses do not release him from his actual death; they do give him power beyond the relationship which we witness in the play and they cannot prevent further *writing on his body*, after Taylor, by the military officials. Pedro alters the narrative of the interrogation room by claiming his right as a speaking subject, declaring his own death and questioning the Captain in order to begin a process whereby new meanings and understandings are generated as to how someone might end up in the role of torturer or political prisoner. Pedro's afterlife ultimately creates an in-between space which reveals how a perpetual cycle of violence can exist and it indicates that this will continue into the future. Through translation, we create an afterlife for the play, for the discussions and for the cycle of violence. The fact that Pedro is constantly written back into the narrative of repression when the Captain orders his torture after each part of their discussion accentuates the idea of repeated cycles of violence and also demonstrates that Pedro's power to disrupt these is limited. Therefore, what the audience witness is not a role reversal or triumph. Instead, *Pedro y el capitán* presents a possible exchange between two men cast in opposing roles, despite some common ground, brought together under extreme circumstances. Benedetti's play explores the possibilities and the limitations of this exchange to highlight the fragility of the supposed established order, and in fact to call into question the notion of 'established' by demonstrating that an authority in the process writing itself is not infallible.

Through the dramaturgical and contextual analyses, the translator examines how productive points of contact between source and target cultures can be established so as to create a link between the original and the new text in the target language. Through establishing points of contact, the translator allows a dynamic relationship between two cultures to develop in a way which enables and equips the translator to navigate cultural differences and these points of contact underpin discussions with directors and actors in fruitful ways, as the examples studied in this chapter have shown. By establishing points of contact, this process does not seek to eliminate cultural differences through assimilation but rather to allow for a proximity to the culture of the source text, which can also provide an insight into different cultural contexts. In order to determine how this contact functions, I refer to Jean-Luc Nancy's idea of 'touch' between two singular entities: '[t]here is proximity, but only to the extent that extreme closeness emphasizes the distancing it opens up.' For Nancy, '"to come into contact" is to begin to make sense of one another', but it is not to penetrate or to engulf the other but rather to establish a closeness which recognises an evident difference and distance in between.[32] In this way, we can understand that through translated theatre, plays become mobile and become close to the audience in the target context. The choice of language employed in the translation and the discourses present in society that this evokes establish a sense of proximity, as does the focus on developing the dramatic techniques that invite the audience to feel involved in the dialogue on stage. However, this can occur without effacing all sense of distance between two cultures; it can simultaneously make the audience aware of where this type of violence and repression has occurred before and can provide an insight into aspects of that experience, particularly through representing the connections between the personal and the political. The identification of points of contact allows for a simultaneous acknowledgement of proximity and distance throughout the translation process and the creation of the new dramatic text in the target language for performance in the target context.

It is essential to acknowledge that feelings of distance may also arise from an active will to disconnect from the situation and its violence as a way to avoid any kind of responsibility for it, or there may be feelings of estrangement based on a belief that the situation does not link to any specific experience of the audience members and so seems remote. We cannot predict exactly how an audience will react. However, I want to underline how remoteness and distance plays a crucial role in both *Pedro y el capitán* and *Bailando sola cada noche* but a tendency to view these plays simply as extremes of individual experience can prevent us from engaging with the issues central to the representation. An understanding of the multiplicity in the original text enables the translator to find creative ways to conceptualise and create a new dramatic text which speaks about both the original and the target cultural contexts. In the analysis of *Bailando sola cada noche*, I demonstrate how the focus on rituals and the body throughout Joyce's afterlife draw the audience in and establish a sense of familiarity between the protagonist and the audience. This then serves to create a sense of responsibility at the end of the play when the audience must decide when to leave the theatre as Joyce remains on the sofa.

Bailando sola cada noche: Dramatising Aftermath and Afterlife

Bailando sola cada noche was written by Raquel Diana in 2008. In 2010 the play was awarded the first prize for Theatre (Comedy) in the Premios Anuales de Literatura del Ministerio de Educación y Cultura del Uruguay. In 2013 it was selected for inclusion in the series of rehearsed readings held at the Asociación General de Autores del Uruguay (AGADU) in Montevideo and organised in conjunction with the Escuela Multidisciplinaria de Arte Dramático (EMAD). The text was published by Editorial Yaugurú and this edition was awarded second prize in the drama category in the Premios Anuales de Literatura del Ministerio de Educación y Cultura del Uruguay in 2015.[33] In 2019 it was staged by students of dramatic art working with playwright and director Sandra Massera at the Casa de Cultura de Montevideo.[34] My translation of *Dancing Alone Every Night* is included in Chapter 4 and was performed as a rehearsed reading at the Out of the Wings Festival in 2016 at King's College London and CASA Latin American Theatre Festival in 2017 at Southwark Playhouse, directed by Camila Ymay González on both occasions.[35]

In *Bailando sola cada noche*, Raquel Diana creates an in-between life and death space which the protagonist shares with two other characters, El Tipo [The Bloke] and La Otra [The Woman]. Joyce recalls and retells aspects of her relationship with her former husband who had violently abused her. This is a way in which the experience of the protagonist coincides with the story of the real Joyce Vincent who, according to the information available, had experienced domestic abuse.[36] The dramatic action unfolds in Joyce's flat and the audience become witnesses to the aftermath of Joyce's experience of gender-based violence. This is revealed in her monologues and dialogues, through which she often denounces the violence she suffered, and it is also evidenced through the ways in which Joyce continues to live and experience her afterlife, which reveals the ongoing impact of this type of violence. In *Bailando sola cada noche*, Diana creates a dramatic space in which the period in between life and death occurs in the recognisable domestic setting of Joyce's flat where she carries out familiar tasks and actions rooted in the recognisable reality of her everyday life. The audience are quickly made aware that Joyce does not realise she is dead and, as the action develops, it becomes evident that no one else in her life has realised this either, due to her extreme isolation. The protagonist seems to hover between life and death as she must wait for her corpse to be discovered. In this way, the dead protagonist in *Bailando sola cada noche* poses a challenge to the audience's understanding of death and, as my analysis will demonstrate, provokes questions around security, isolation and vulnerability.

One consequence of Joyce not realising that she is dead is that she continues to live in fear and isolation as a way to protect herself from her violent ex-husband. During the two and a half years that she has to wait to be discovered, the passage of time is frequently referred to in the script, including references to the changing seasons and the fact that the heating remains on throughout (*Bailando*, pp. 8–9; p. 28). As time passes, Joyce seems to distance herself from some of her previous experiences and to make efforts to (re-)establish relationships, which at first seems futile but, in fact, indicate that she is on a journey towards the moment of discovery of her corpse. This is a crucial aspect of what is at stake in the play: how and when will Joyce realise that she is dead and be discovered? The story of Joyce Vincent originates in London, therefore a key challenge in translating it for performance in the UK was not to assume that the task was to somehow bring the play 'back'. It was essential to analyse *Bailando sola cada noche* in the context in which it was produced. It is for this reason that the process detailed in this chapter is crucial to understanding how the play connects to the source culture and context and how the translator works to create specific links between two cultures in order to recognise difference and distance as well as proximity.

For the original audience in Uruguay, *Bailando sola cada noche* provides an insight into a culture which is both distant and close. There are references to aspects of life in London, such as commuting on the underground as well as names and song lyrics in English, which serve to remind the audience of where the story originated and where it is located. At the same time, throughout the play, the playwright constantly interacts with issues which are relevant in Uruguay and brings them to the fore so that the scope of the play is not limited to Joyce's flat but opens up a dialogue between her experience and the reality of Uruguay, which exists beyond the theatre. *Bailando sola cada noche* emerged from a Uruguayan reality in which a woman dies on average every two weeks as a result of domestic violence and the number of reported attacks against women is increasing.[37] Furthermore, by depicting the dead woman on stage, Diana poses a challenge to the notion of death as the end of presence. For the audience of Raquel Diana's original play, the dead protagonist whose body remains undiscovered conjures up the cultural memory of those people who disappeared during the Uruguayan civic-military dictatorship.[38] In this way, there are connections to *Pedro y el capitán* because in the Uruguayan context many people who were taken to detention centres disappeared and were not seen again. It is not known what happened to them and, if they were killed, where their remains are. Taylor insists that people who were abducted in this way are 'always already the object of representation' because of this uncertainty and the absence of a body or grave.[39]Consequently, Diana writes from this social, historical and cultural context in which the concept of a disappeared person is present within society and an awareness of this is essential to understanding her treatment of Joyce's experience of afterlife as corporeal and not merely spiritual. The presence and persistence of Joyce's body, which I will underscore in my analysis, questions and challenges the concept of a forced disappearance by showing how her body endures. The fact that Joyce's body does not disappear and that, throughout the play, emphasis is placed on the fact that it will be discovered suggests that this is necessary as a moment of closure. It also poses a direct challenge to the idea that bodies can just disappear and be forgotten about, which was a narrative perpetuated through the introduction of the aforementioned Ley de Caducidad de la Pretensión Punitiva del Estado.

In *Bailando sola cada noche*, distance and a sense of mobility were fundamental aspects of the creative process of writing the original dramatic text. The prologue to *Bailando sola cada noche* instantly signals this to the audience through the inclusion of articles taken from online media outlets reporting the death of the real Joyce Vincent in 2006, one in English from the BBC and one in Spanish from the website of Spanish broadcaster Telecinco. They underscore the role of the media in disseminating the story internationally and thus enabling it to transcend linguistic and geographic barriers. By including them in the prologue to the play, the playwright acknowledges the interaction and intertextuality with the story of the real Joyce Vincent as the inspiration for the play and alludes to her own creative process by showing how she came into contact with this story through the media. In the English translation I have presented the extract from the Spanish media in the original Spanish accompanied by an English translation (and so not removed the original text in this part). I decided to do this as a way to maintain the emphasis on the dissemination of the story, to signal its movement into Spanish and provide a way for an audience in the UK to interact with the way in which the story was transferred into the Spanish media. In the 2016 rehearsed reading, this report was read in both languages. This placed emphasis on the way that the original story crossed large distances and entered into different languages and provides a way for the audience in the UK to access one form in which the story was communicated outside the country.

Diana also makes references to the news (*Bailando*, p. 29), the headlines (*Bailando*, p. 9) and the Internet (*Bailando*, p. 19) throughout the play. These references underline the important role of the media in the world today, the constant flow of information with which one is faced and how this information enters and disrupts spaces that previously were disconnected and private. In Scene 4, the playwright emphasises the invasive and incessant nature of modern communication when Joyce says:

> Hay tanta gente allí afuera, por todas partes, que es imposible estar solo. Y teléfonos, mensajes de textos, emails, televisión, satélites, internet. (*Bailando*, p. 19)
>
> [There are so many people out there, everywhere, it's impossible to be alone. And phones, texts, emails, television, satellites, Internet.]

However, the irony in this statement is evident as the protagonist is lonely and extremely isolated; despite all the means of communication that she mentions, Joyce's experience of living alone is notably marked by a lack of interaction with others. Joyce has a television, which she explains was the first thing that she bought when she moved into the flat, and she relies on it for company as a way to combat her solitude, but it does not facilitate the exchange and intimacy with another person that she so greatly desires. There is a telephone in her flat which could link her to others but when it rings at the start of Scene 3, her reaction is one of fear and panic and this causes her not to pick it up as she calculates that the risk is too great:

> Cada vez que ese teléfono suena mi corazón se detiene... *(alegre)* ¿Quién será? *(el teléfono sigue sonando)* Cada vez que ese teléfono suena mi corazón se detiene... *(entre alegre y asustada)* A lo mejor es él, me está buscando, me encontró. *(el teléfono deja de sonar)*. (*Bailando*, p. 14)

> [Every time that phone rings my heart stops... (*Happy.*) Who could it be? (*The telephone keeps ringing.*) Every time that phone rings my heart stops (*part happy and part scared*). Perhaps it's him, he's looking for me. He's found me. (*The phone stops ringing.*)]

A link is established between Joyce's isolation and her security: she actively ignores the telephone call in order to protect herself from her ex-husband. Diana draws our attention to Joyce's feelings of anxiety about her husband discovering her, which remain constant throughout the play. The audience are confronted with the aftermath of gender-based violence as an integral part of Joyce Vincent's afterlife, which provokes questions about the repercussions of this type of abuse. Joyce Vincent speaks explicitly about the violent attacks when she is alone in Scene 3. She states that she was hospitalised five times as a result of the injuries that she sustained from the abuse but that she hid it from everyone she knew:

> Lo de los golpes era mi secreto. (*Bailando*, p. 15)
>
> [The blows were my secret.]

The secrecy that she has maintained around the abuse indicates her feelings of shame and embarrassment about the violence and also creates the impression that this is a moment of confession. The fact that the protagonist makes this revelation whilst alone on stage serves to create a sense of intimacy with the audience as she reveals her secret to them.

Diana stated she formed a connection with the story of the real Joyce Vincent through an understanding of her experience of loneliness as pathetic, an idea which is presented in the subtitle to the play, 'comedia más bien negra y patetica' [a black, pathetic comedy]:

> me parece que las mujeres, que la [solitud] vivimos de un modo muy patético, y patético es una expresión, como, interesante porque es una mezcla de tristeza y al mismo tiempo de cosa ridícula.[40]
>
> [I think that as women, we experience it [solitude] in a pathetic way, and pathetic is, well, an interesting expression, because it's a mixture of sadness and at the same time something sort of ridiculous.]

Patética refers to both an intensity of feeling or reaction and a complex mixture of sentiments, as Diana's comment above suggests.[41] In the subtitle, the idea of 'a black, pathetic comedy' indicates the subtle touches of humour which appear throughout the play and arise from the mixture of strange and familiar in Joyce's situation. Diana spoke about how this subtitle gives both actors and audience the permission to laugh and so to recognise the comedy in aspects of Joyce's situation in the play.[42] On two occasions in the play The Woman calls Joyce pathetic, echoing the subtitle and confirming the significance of this idea throughout the play. The first is in Scene 2 after Joyce says that she has been practising to enter a singing contest and the second is in Scene 5 when Joyce writes (by verbalising a message) a gift tag for a present that she had bought for her ex-husband. The singing contest, which seems like an impossible, ridiculous and pathetic ambition, especially because of Joyce's situation, is significant because it links to the end of the play and a moment of celebration when Joyce sings *Knock Three Times* by Tony Orlando and Dawn, a song which is repeated throughout the play and tells the story of two neighbours who never met. (One of the singers in the group Dawn was called Joyce Vincent.) Therefore, this ambition is incorporated into the journey towards the discovery of Joyce's corpse and plays a significant role in the narrative drive of the play. It is also poignant that she is able to live out this dream, albeit in strange circumstances, in her afterlife and so fulfil a dream that she did not have the opportunity to realise in life, which also reinforces the idea that her afterlife opens up opportunities for Joyce that she did not have in life.

In Scene 5, Joyce reveals she bought a gift for her ex-husband and when she considers writing the following message, The Woman calls her pathetic: 'Hijo de mil putas, te mando esta camiseta para que te la pongas en esta navidad. La tela tiene un poderoso veneno que en contacto con tu cuerpo te provocará dolores terribles y finalmente la muerte' [The biggest bastard I ever met. I'm sending you a vest for you to wear this Christmas. The fabric contains a powerful poison. When it comes into contact with your skin it will cause you excruciating pain and eventually, death] (*Bailando*, p. 26). However, the anger that Joyce expresses and the fact that she reveals she never actually intended to give the gift to her ex-partner (because it would be better going to the man who rummages through the bins of her building) are indicative of a gradual change in her self-confidence, as well as in her attitude towards her ex-husband and the violence she suffered. This shift in attitude ultimately leads her to say to The Bloke: 'No quiero que me maltrates. No lo voy a permitir' [I don't want you to abuse me. I won't allow it] (*Bailando*, p. 35). The way in which her attitude seems to change as she asserts herself suggests that she achieves in her afterlife something which she could not do before; in this case we see a resoluteness and a rejection of violence which she did not previously show. The series of gift tags that Joyce writes to her family in Scenes 3 and 5 also seem to be an important part of her journey towards the discovery of her corpse, particularly as The Bloke encourages her to write the two final tags to her parents who have already passed away (*Bailando*, p. 27).

The writing of the gift tags depicts an identifiable ritual of communication and the sense of ritual around the preparations for Christmas is emphasised in *Bailando sola cada noche* through the protagonist's references to curling the ribbons on the gifts (*Bailando*, pp. 5, 14, 25); she also comments that wrapping paper is always the same despite the fact that every Christmas is different and marks change (*Bailando*, p. 6). As Joyce participates in recognisable rituals of preparation for the festive season, which would be identifiable in the cultural contexts of Uruguay and the UK, the playwright creates a way for the audience to identify with the protagonist despite the fact that she is a dead woman. Joyce goes on to remark that at this time of year the shop assistants are too busy to wrap gifts so they provide customers with wrapping paper to prepare their own gift; she adds that this makes it very stressful (*Bailando*, p. 6). This description is an example of a cultural signifier that places the play in the context of Uruguay where most shops offer gift-wrapping services. Therefore, the familiarity of this experience would be stronger for the Uruguayan audience and in the translation into English, a sense of distance could be created around this action. However, the significance of wrapping gifts as part of the preparations for Christmas and the feelings of stress around the preparations would be familiar in both the source and target languages and cultures.

The characters of The Bloke and The Woman seem fluid and to change at different moments, for example, sometimes The Woman's lack of sympathy evokes Joyce's sister as described by Joyce, whilst, following a description of her upstairs neighbour in Scene 6, The Bloke seems to act like him and to fulfil Joyce's fantasy of sharing an intimate moment with her neighbour. Whilst these characters change throughout the play, their function seems to be to guide Joyce to the moment where her body can be discovered, as seen in the example of the gift tags, even though the audience do not witness this moment of discovery on stage. The lack of a final moment of closure provokes questions and challenges the audience to consider if this really is the end of the period of waiting. In my interview with Diana, she spoke of how she saw the two other characters as angel-like figures who came to guide the protagonist towards this moment, but perhaps not in the ways we might expect. She suggested that contradictions are particularly present in the character of The Bloke who even flirts and dances with Joyce, demonstrating both affection and cruelty at different moments. Perhaps The Bloke and The Woman possess qualities of both devils and angels, good and evil, which they use as a way to manipulate the character of Joyce to ultimately get her ready to leave.[43] The intersection between love and death in an in-between life and death space is a concern in Diana's work and is also explored in *Los ojos abiertos de ella* [*Her Open Eyes*] which I translated into English in 2018–19 and which premiered as a rehearsed reading at the Out of the Wings Festival at Omnibus Theatre on 1 August 2019, directed by Fran Olivares.[44]

The insights from my dramaturgical analysis and from Diana had an impact on my translation choices for the names of these other characters in *Bailando sola cada noche*: 'The Bloke' and 'The Woman'. The names would primarily be indicators to the actors and director (or a reader) rather than the audience as the names are never spoken on stage. In my translation of the names, I sought to create a sense of them as recognisable, familiar and human because these are important aspects of the ways in which they relate to Joyce and each other. Through the choice of names, I also wanted to create a sense of them as encapsulating a broad range of characteristics in order to indicate the ways in which the two characters shift and take on different qualities described by Joyce. I decided against 'The Other Woman' for La Otra because the connotations of the mistress of a married man would dominate the interpretation of this character. In rehearsals for rehearsed readings in 2016 and 2017, I discussed with the actors ideas about the way in which the characters change and try many different tactics to get Joyce to prepare to leave. We discussed the way in which this created possibilities for different types of playfulness, manipulation, humour and frustration as they adopted shades of people described by Joyce and tried to persuade her to get ready to be discovered.

Joyce's presence in her flat and her experience of afterlife are marked by their corporality and the audience's attention is drawn to her body, particularly through the references to the decomposition of the corpse. Joyce is constantly engaged in familiar rituals of preparation, which intensify the feeling that she is getting ready to leave and evoke the rituals of preparation for death and the last rites. The centrality of her body to her afterlife is reinforced by the ending of the play where the stage directions specify: 'Joyce Vincent se queda frente al televisor hasta que el último espectador haya dejado la sala' [Joyce Vincent remains in front of the television until the last member of the audience has left the theatre] (p. 39). The ending not only serves as a reminder of the length of time that Joyce had to wait to be discovered but it also forces the audience to actively participate in an act of abandonment of the protagonist. Prior to the end of the play, there is knocking at the door, which creates the impression that the moment of discovery has arrived. The Bloke's comment increases the expectation that the audience are about to witness the discovery of the body:

> Es el problema con los cadáveres. Se empeñan en ser encontrados. (*Bailando*, p. 35)
>
> [That's the problem with cadavers. They insist on being found.]

These comments reinforce the idea that the protagonist, Joyce Vincent, has not disappeared completely, her cadaver remains and it is imperative that it is discovered. This interacts with the discourse around the *desaparecidos* in Uruguay, meaning it is crucial that Joyce remains present; the endurance of her body into and through death serves a key function in displaying disappearance as a fallacy, thus undermining aspects of this practice employed during the civic-military dictatorship whilst also acknowledging its repercussions in the present day. At the end of the play an uncomfortable tension is established between the permanence of Joyce's isolated body on stage, which indicates an ongoing experience of disappearance, and the final moments of dramatic action, including the knocking from outside, which seem to indicate the moment of discovery presented in the newspaper articles in the prologue. Joyce Vincent's body is an essential part of the afterlife depicted in *Bailando sola cada noche* and so the permanence of her corpse indicates that this experience is not concluded.

Joyce Vincent's afterlife does not serve to communicate a specific message but to provoke and sustain a dialogue with the audience, which will continue to resonate in the future, beyond the theatre. In this way, her function as a protagonist shares characteristics with Derrida's concept of the spectre, particularly in the sense of a link to the future:

> There are several times of the specter. It is a proper characteristic of the specter, if there is any, that no one can be sure if by returning it testifies to a living past or to a living future, for the *revenant* may already mark the promised return of the specter of living being.[45]

Returning is inherent to the behaviour of the spectre and is explicit in the word 'revenant' from the French *revenir*. Derrida's focus on temporality forces us to recognise that the spectre is necessarily and absolutely linked to the future. For the spectre that enters an afterlife, which we might refer to as returning or coming back from the dead, does not go back at all. The spectre remains and participates in the future, precisely by coming into their afterlife and prolonging their presence. In a similar way, if we interpret spectres as possible manifestations of the future then they signal something yet to occur and through their presence, they function to open up new meanings by which they indicate aspects of this future reality. In both cases the spectre, through their continued presence, is necessarily linked to the future. It is also crucial to note that Derrida states that we may not be able to distinguish between these two possible functions and so we are required, in all cases, to examine the spectre as living past and living future. This conceptualisation of the spectre ascribes function rather than meaning to the afterlife: it is characterised as productive and provocative.

One way in which the experience of afterlife depicted on stage continues to be manifest in the future is through translation. In translation for the audience in the UK, the depiction of the aftermath of domestic violence would evidently interact with this issue in the UK and the portrayal of Joyce's experience serves to highlight both similarities and differences in how the issue is treated in Uruguay and the UK.[46] Furthermore, in London in 2016, when the reading was first performed in English, the references in the play to social assistance and isolation were evocative of recurring discourses about a welfare system which cannot sustain the welfare of all members of society and in which some people are treated like a persistent burden and constantly moved around. This causes them to disappear within the system itself, whilst others remain isolated from it altogether and struggle to find any kind of support and security. These discourses represent ongoing issues which remain unresolved. A link can therefore be established between these issues and the unending nature of Joyce's situation. These links established with current discourses in the UK allow the play to enter into a discussion of issues and topics beyond those immediately presented in the play. This is an essential step in the process of finding a language which speaks in the target culture. The references to violence are present, they evoke aspects of the situation in Uruguay and the UK, but they are also able to resonate in a different way by forming points of contact with current issues affecting society in the target context. A link between the severity of the issue of domestic violence in Uruguay and the welfare of vulnerable people in the UK is created but this proximity is achieved without effacing difference and distance. Through Raquel Diana's depiction of Joyce's afterlife, the audience confront familiar and remote experiences. The constant interplay between the recognisable and unfamiliar enables and invites the audience to relate to the protagonist whilst forcing them to engage with the wider questions provoked by the play. In this way, the translated play maintains an essential movement between familiar and remote, as the audience are able to gain an insight into a close and distant cultural context. Raquel Diana opens up a private space in which to portray a protagonist who, whilst obliging the audience to confront key themes of domestic violence, isolation and disappearance, also serves as a 'productive opening of meaning' so that the play is able to interact with specific discourses in the UK.[47]

I understand both Pedro and Joyce Vincent to demonstrate qualities of the spectre as they hover between life and death in the dramatic space created by the two playwrights studied in this chapter. Both playwrights use the dramatic space to portray experiences of afterlife which challenge the audience's expectations by emphasising the centrality of the body, denouncing violence and provoking questions about how the encounters that they witness might have come about. By incorporating ideas about the spectre into the dramaturgical analysis (and not just the analysis of the characters), we understand that the dramatic space becomes an explorative and provocative one.

Conclusion

In *Bailando sola cada noche* and *Pedro y el capitán* the dramatic space becomes one in which to explore and challenge perceptions about extreme situations resulting from extreme violence. Both plays create ways for the audience to engage with the protagonists as they experience a type of afterlife which constitutes the aftermath of this violence. The dialogues that these dramatic texts open up indicate how the aftermath of violence affects the characters on stage but they also serve to provoke questions about responsibility and agency in order to highlight the impact upon society. In this way, the discourses of the play are able to extend beyond the characters on stage to resonate with the audience through which we are challenged to confront the questions: how did this happen? What role and responsibility might we have?

In *Pedro y el capitán*, we are presented with the fragility of the boundary between interrogator and prisoner. In *Bailando sola cada noche*, we witness the fragility of the state system when it comes to protecting a person who has suffered gender-based violence. In both cases the characters have disappeared in some way and the plays themselves indicate wider narratives of disappearance, neglect by the state, and violence, which link to the cultural context to Uruguay. The afterlife portrayed is multiple, depicting characters in complex ways and allowing their experiences and dialogues to serve as productive openings of meaning through which we can make connections to the target context where new questions will be generated. My analysis has shown that the dramatic structure of each of the plays provokes questions as to whether the protagonists' experiences have ended and the ways in which these experiences might be repeated and continue to exist. Drawing on Walter Benjamin's ideas of the translation as an extension of the life of the original, I have demonstrated how this informed my dramaturgical analysis of the structure of the plays which open up the possibilities of future manifestations through translation. This allows for new possibilities of depicting how the forms of violence present in these plays continue to shape and have an impact on societies, thus extending their resonance whilst maintaining contact with the original context. The dramatic space created by the playwrights allows for a dialogue to occur and the protagonist serves a dramatic and spectral function in provoking questions and indicating a wider reality beyond the boundaries of their own life and death. The link to the future opens up a space for retelling and recreation through translation which allows a new manifestation of this prolonged afterlife in a new cultural context.

Notes to Chapter 3

1. Jean-Luc Nancy, *Being Singular Plural*, trans. by Robert D. Richardson and Anne E. O'Byrne (Stanford, CA: Stanford University Press, 2000).
2. Mario Benedetti, *Pedro y el capitán* (Montevideo: Editorial Planeta S.A. / Seix Barral, 2011). This edition will be referenced throughout as *Pedro* after quotations in the text. Raquel Diana, *Bailando sola cada noche, Dramaturgia Uruguaya*, (2008) <http://www.dramaturgiauruguaya.uy/obras/bailando-sola-toda-la-noche/> [accessed 17 September 2020]. This edition will be referenced throughout as *Bailando* after quotations in the text. (See p. 19 n. 2 regarding the title.) All translations are my own unless otherwise stated. Some of the research for this chapter was published at an earlier stage in Sophie Stevens, 'Distance and Proximity in Analysing and Translating *Bailando sola cada noche* [Dancing Alone Every Night] into English', *The Mercurian: A Theatrical Translation Review*, 6 (2016), 81–99, available online at <https://the-mercurian.com/2016/11/16/distance-and-proximity-in-analysing-and-translating-bailando-sola-cada-noche-dancing-alone-every-night/>.
3. Roger Mirza, 'Escenificaciones de la memoria en el teatro de la postdictadura: *Pedro y el capitán, Elena Quinteros. Presente* y *Las cartas que no llegaron*', in *La dictadura contra las tablas: teatro uruguayo e historia reciente*, ed. by. Roger Mirza and Gustavo Remedi (Montevideo: Biblioteca Nacional, 2009), pp. 37–81 (p. 58).
4. Jacques Derrida, *Specters of Marx: The State of the Debt, the Work of Mourning and the New International*, trans. by Peggy Kamuf (New York: Routledge Classics, 2006). Proquest Ebook Central.
5. Colin Davis, *Haunted Subjects: Deconstruction, Psychoanalysis and the Return of the Dead* (Basingstoke: Palgrave Macmillan, 2007), p. 11.
6. Ibid.
7. Walter Benjamin, 'The Task of the Translator: An Introduction to the Translation of Baudelaire's *Tableaux Parisiens*', trans. by Harry Zohn, in *The Translation Studies Reader*, ed. by Lawrence Venuti, 2nd edn (New York: Routledge, 2004), pp. 75–85.
8. Beatriz Walker, *Benedetti, Rosencof, Varela: el teatro como guardián de la memoria colectiva* (Buenos Aires: Ediciones Corregidor, 2007), pp. 55–56; Mario Benedetti, *Pedro y el Capitán (Pieza en cuatro partes)* (Mexico City: Editorial Nueva Imagen, 1979).
9. Mirza, 'Escenificaciones' in *La dictadura*, ed. by. Mirza and Remedi, p. 53.
10. Theresa. M. Mackey, 'Reverse Stockholm Syndrome in *Pedro y el capitán*: Paradigm for the Cycle of Authoritarianism in Latin America', *Literature and Psychology: A Journal of Psychoanalytic and Cultural Criticism*, 43.4 (1997), 1–15 (p. 3).
11. There are two English translations of *Pedro y el capitán* and both of them use the term electricians for the 'muchachos eléctricos'. I have also used this to translate this term because I think it captures the sense of their role in the detention centre as a job. The two translations are: Mario Benedetti, 'Pedro and the Captain (translation from Spanish)', trans. by Freda Beberfall, *Modern International*, 19.1 (1985–87), 33–52 and Mario Benedetti, *Pedro and the Captain: A Play in Four Parts*, trans. and intro. by Adrianne Aron (San Francisco, CA: Cadmus Editions, 2009).
12. Mario Benedetti, *Pedro and the Captain*, trans. by Adrianne Aron, The Vaults Festival, London, 3–6 March 2016.
13. Marta Morello-Frosch and Martha Morello-Frosch, 'El diálogo de la violencia en "Pedro y el capitán" de Mario Benedetti', *Revista de Crítica Literaria Latinoamericana*, 18 (1983), 87–96, p. 92.
14. Severino João Medeiros Albuquerque, *Violent Acts: A Study of Contemporary Latin American Theatre* (Detroit, MI: Wayne State University Press, 1991), pp. 39–41.
15. Diana Taylor, *Disappearing Acts: Spectacles of Gender and Nationalism in Argentina's 'Dirty War'* (Durham, NC: Duke University Press, 1997), pp. 151–52. Taylor's argument develops to explore how this rewriting also, in many cases, entailed a (re-)gendering of the tortured body as feminine thus 'bring[ing] together a whole constellation of gendered images that appear in the military's rhetoric' (pp. 154–55) and thus intersecting with the military's discourses about the new social and political body in Argentina. See pp. 151–57.
16. Ibid., p. 152.
17. Ibid.

18. Stephen W. G. Gregory, 'Humanist Ethics or Realist Aesthetics? Torture, Interrogation and Psychotherapy in Mario Benedetti', *La Trobe University — Institute of Latin American Studies, Occasional Paper*, 12 (1991), 1–43 (p. 20).
19. Eugenio Claudio Di Stefano, *The Vanishing Frame: Latin American Culture and Theory in the Postdictatorial Era* (Austin: University of Texas Press, 2018), p. 34. The argument presented by Di Stefano centres on the importance of ideology in the play; even when the Captain focusses on the body, this is both brought about by and reminds us of the opposing ideologies of the two men. However, Di Stefano argues that human rights narratives, particularly on an international level, often focus on the injustice of torture itself and thus abstract the tortured bodies from the ideologies that they represent. (See Chapter 1: 'From Revolution to Human Rights' pp. 25–41).
20. Mirza, 'Escenificaciones', in *La dictadura*, ed. by. Mirza and Remedi, p. 58.
21. Nancy J. Gates-Madsen, 'Tortured Silence and Silenced Torture in Mario Benedetti's *Pedro y el capitán*, Ariel Dorfman's *La muerte y la doncella* and Eduardo Pavlovsky's *Paso de dos*', *Latin American Theatre Review*, 42.1 (2008–09), 5–31 (p. 18).
22. Walker, p. 65.
23. Di Stefano, p. 35.
24. Mirza, 'Escenificaciones', in *La dictadura*, ed. by. Mirza and Remedi, p. 55.
25. Ibid., pp. 42–43. Mirza provides an extensive list of plays dating from 1985 to 2009 which deal with this topic.
26. Walker, p. 61.
27. Francesca Lessa, *Memory and Transitional Justice in Argentina and Uruguay: Against Impunity* (New York: Palgrave Macmillan, 2013), p. 137, referring to the Text of the Ley de Caducidad N.15.848.
28. Mackey, p. 1.
29. Gates-Madsen, p. 19.
30. Gregory, p. 26.
31. Walker, p. 38.
32. Nancy, p. 5.
33. Raquel Diana, *Bailando sola cada noche: comedia más bien negra y patética* (Montevideo: Yaugurú, 2013).
34. Performances: 5 October 2019 (Día del Patrimonio), Casa de Cultura Anexo; 5 November 2019, El Galpón, as part of the Festival de la Movida Joven organised by Intendencia de Montevideo; 11 December 2019, Casa de Cultura Central.
35. Cast CASA 2017: Joyce Vincent: Rachel Summers; The Woman: Leanne Shorley; The Bloke: William Gregory. Cast Out of the Wings 2016: Joyce Vincent: Rochenda Sandall; The Woman: Roanna Lewis; The Bloke: Graeme McKnight. Full details: 'Dancing Alone Every Night', *Out of the Wings Festival*, <https://ootwweb.wordpress.com/dancing-alone-every-night/> [accessed 27 October 2020].
36. The documentary film *Dreams of a Life* (dir. Carol Morley, Dogwoof, 2011) postdates the play and seeks to provide an insight into the type of woman the real Joyce Vincent was and to explore how she became so disconnected from those around her, even those who loved her. The extensive work carried out by Carol Morley to investigate Joyce's life and death has provided an important point of reference when researching this play. However, it is important to underline that much of this information was unavailable when Diana was writing the play but, as the newspaper articles included in the prologue show, there were indications that Joyce Vincent had been in an abusive relationship. At the time of writing the play, Diana was aware that Morley was carrying out research and in Scene 4 of the play La Otra says to Joyce that someone called Carol is looking for her (*Bailando*, p. 19). This is used by the playwright to draw attention to Joyce's fear and isolation as the protagonist's first reaction is to assume that her ex-husband has been trying to track her down.
37. 'Violencia doméstica: una mujer murió cada 15 días', *El País*, 24 November 2014, <http://www.elpais.com.uy/informacion/violencia-domestica-mueren-mensualmente.html> [accessed 31 March 2015] (paragraphs 4, 5). This article, consulted at the time of research, is now archived. For more recent information about the number of deaths resulting from gender-based violence, see Soledad Gago, 'Muertas no sueñan', *El País*, <https://servicios.elpais.com.uy/especiales/

digital/2018/muertas-no-suenan/> [accessed 31 July 2021]. In 2017 Uruguay introduced the Ley de Violencia hacia las Mujeres basada en Género [Law on Gender-based Violence against Women] (Ley 19.580): 'Normativa y Avisos Legales del Uruguay, Ley N° 19580', *IMPO: Centro de Información Oficial*, 9 January 2018, <www.impo.com.uy/bases/leyes/19580-2017> [accessed 31 July 2021].

38. Francesca Lessa gives an account of key aspects of the dictatorships in Uruguay (1973–85) and Argentina (1976–83) in her chapter, 'The Downward Spiral toward Dictatorship', including a definition of *desaparecidos* as 'persons apprehended at home, work, or on public thoroughfares; after abduction, seized persons disappeared: never to be heard from again'. *Memory and Transitional Justice*, pp. 31–47 (p. 40). The chapter on 'Pacification or Impunity? The Ley de Caducidad and the Interweaving of Memory and Transitional Justice in Uruguay' (pp. 163–213) discusses the ongoing impact of dictatorship crimes and unresolved cases.
39. Taylor, p. 140.
40. Raquel Diana, Interview conducted in Spanish, Montevideo, 30 October 2013.
41. I consulted *Diccionario de la lengua española*, 21st edn (Madrid: Real Academia Española, 1992) and María Moliner, *Diccionario de uso del español*, 2nd edn (Madrid: Gredos, 1998) for the definition of 'patética'.
42. Diana, Interview.
43. Diana, Interview.
44. Cast: Her: Jilly Bond; Him: Richard Glaves; with Music by Haylin Cai. The translation was published in 2020: 'Her Open Eyes', trans. by Sophie Stevens, *The Mercurian: A Theatrical Translation Review*, 8.2 (2020), 186–206 <https://themercurian.files.wordpress.com/2020/11/the-mercurian_8.2_fall-2020_final-1.pdf> [accessed 12 July 2021].
45. Derrida, p. 123.
46. Domestic violence is a serious issue in the UK with one in four women suffering abuse from their partner. 'In the year ending March 2019, an estimated 2.4 million adults aged 16 to 74 years experienced domestic abuse in the last year (1.6 million women and 786,000 men).' *ONS*, <https://www.ons.gov.uk/peoplepopulationandcommunity/crimeandjustice/bulletins/domesticabuseinenglandandwalesoverview/november2019> [accessed 10 October 2020].
47. Davis, p. 11.

CHAPTER 4

Dancing Alone Every Night by Raquel Diana

A black, pathetic comedy

Information about rehearsed readings can be found on p. 104. Information about casts is included in Chapter 3, n. 35 (p. 114). For details of the original text in Spanish see p. 113 n. 2.

The notes that preface the play were selected by Raquel Diana and included in the text published in Spanish. The BBC story was in English; elsewhere I have translated from the Spanish, though I provide the original of the article from Telecinco.com as well.

Characters

JOYCE VINCENT
THE WOMAN
THE BLOKE

Preface (by Raquel Diana)

This play takes as a starting point the death of a woman in England. Following the discovery of her body, the circumstances surrounding her death not only made headlines and attracted attention from the press for many weeks but also sparked numerous studies by sociologists, psychologists and philosophers.

I include below two news reports, one from the Spanish media and one from the British media.

(i) INFORMATIVOSTELECINCO.COM — 16 de abril de 2006

El esqueleto de una mujer inglesa fue descubierto en su casa de Londres frente a un televisor encendido y, según los expertos, más de dos años tras su muerte. Según el *Telegraph* inglés, Joyce Vincent estaba rodeada de regalos navideños. La televisión y la calefacción de su casa todavía estaban encendidas cuando la encontraron.

El esqueleto, de una mujer de unos 40 años, estaba descompuesto y la única forma de identificarla fue comparar varios expedientes dentales con una fotografía. La Policía británica cree que murió por causas naturales a principios de 2003 y que fue encontrada en enero de este año cuando oficiales de la asociación de alquileres entraron en su casa de Wood Green, al este de Londres y encontraron el cadáver tumbado boca arriba en el salón.

Esperaban recuperar los millares de libras en retrasos de alquiler que se habían acumulado tras su muerte. Un portavoz de la investigación asegura que la mujer estaba alojada en un refugio para mujeres, escapando de un problema de violencia doméstica. El doctor Simon Poole, patólogo, afirma que no ha podido establecer la causa de la muerte porque los restos son 'en gran parte esqueléticos'. De todas formas, la policía descarta cualquier crimen.

[**The skeleton of an English woman has been found at her flat in London in front of her television which was still playing. According to experts, she had been dead for two years.** The English newspaper *The Telegraph* reported that Joyce Vincent was surrounded by Christmas presents. Both the television and the central heating in her flat were on when her body was found.

The skeleton of the woman, aged around 40, was decomposed and could only be identified by comparing dental records with a photograph. British police believe Ms Vincent died of natural causes at the start of 2003 and was found in January of this year when officers from a Housing Trust entered her flat in Wood Green, north-east London, and found her body lying face up in the lounge.

They were hoping to recover thousands of pounds in rent arrears that had accumulated since her death. A spokesperson for the investigation confirmed that the woman was housed in a women's refuge as a result of domestic violence. Pathologist Dr. Simon Poole stated that he was unable to ascertain the cause of death because the remains were 'largely skeletal'. Police are not treating the death as suspicious.

(ii) BBC News, 14 April 2006 <http://bbc.co.uk/news>

Woman's body in bedsit for years

A woman's remains were found surrounded by unopened Christmas presents in a London bedsit two years after she is thought to have died,

an inquest heard. The TV and heating were still on when housing officers discovered the body of Joyce Vincent, 40, in her living room. They had gone to the flat — a refuge for victims of domestic violence — to investigate thousands in rent arrears. Police believe she died of natural causes probably in December 2003 and an inquest recorded an open verdict. [...]

Dental records

Ms Vincent's body, found in January this year at the flat in Wood Green, north London, was so decomposed that the only way to identify her was to compare dental records with a holiday photograph. A spokesman for the coroner said she had apparently been placed in the women's refuge accommodation as a victim of domestic violence. When staff from the Metropolitan Housing Trust (MHT) arrived at the flat on 25 January they drilled the door open and discovered piles of mail — some marked February 2003 — plus medication and food with February 2003 expiry dates, the spokesman said.

Pathologist Dr Simon Poole told the inquest he had been unable to establish the cause of death because the remains were 'largely skeletal', but police did not regard the circumstances as suspicious. MHT issued a statement which read: 'Ms Vincent moved into the property, which is general needs rented accommodation, in February 2003. Housing benefit was in part paying Ms Vincent's rent, therefore, given her age, there was no reason to suspect anything unusual had happened. During this period our records show MHT were not contacted by neighbours or family to raise any concerns and so we were only alerted when significant arrears built up and we tried to gain access.' The flat is part of a complex build above a shopping complex in Wood Green. Neighbours told the *Guardian* newspaper whenever they knocked at the door, no-one answered, so they assumed it was unoccupied.

No family shock

Michael Dobbs, who moved in summer 2004 said: 'I always thought it was an empty house. It's a shock to think that she had family and nobody came. It's also a puzzle how her electricity was not cut off because her TV was on all this time.' He told the paper it was a noisy building frequented by drug addicts, which could explain why no-one noticed the noise from the TV. He said he had discovered someone dead, clutching a bottle of drink, in the lift weeks ago. 'I did notice a kind of rotten smell but the bins downstairs are strong and the stairwells smell with junkies. I did get a few bugs coming into my house so I had to keep the windows closed.'

Joyce Vincent was the name of the English woman who inspired this play. She shared her name with one of the singers from the group Dawn who accompanied Tony Orlando. They are famous for the pop song 'Knock Three Times', which was a success worldwide in 1971 and is sometimes still played at parties today. The song is about a romance that could have flourished between two neighbours, but they don't know each other despite living in the same building.

At present no further information about Joyce and her life is known.

As a result, this play only comprises facts imagined by its author.

With unending love, respect and solidarity for all women who are alone.

With fear and dread of being alone.

Dancing Alone Every Night

Inside the flat of the dead woman, JOYCE VINCENT*.*
The set design should include a television.

I.

JOYCE The last I remember is a headache... an overwhelming, staggering pain. Strange because it was so sudden, like, bam! I turned around to try to see who hit me. What an idiot! I was alone, of course... It sounded something like, boom! Or more like, whack! I thought: God is striking me down. If only, at least he'd be showing some interest in me. But why now, and like this? No, no it wasn't God... I did a quick comparison with the blows I used to get from my husband. No. This hurt more. My husband always faced me when he hit me, like a man. This blow came as if from behind, treacherously... It was like a knitting needle nailed into my skull with a hammer. Or as if my demented brain had grown teeth and started to chew away at itself, driven by my own cannibalistic dementia. Or as if the drill my upstairs neighbour loves to use, especially on Sundays, bank holidays and whenever I have a nap, penetrated me. The drill, I mean, not my neighbour, in the back of my neck. Or as if the blades from the blender had come flying out of the kitchen and gone straight into my ear. I've always been a bit scared of electrical appliances. There are so many of them everywhere and you never know. The last I remember is a headache that felt bigger than my own head. Calm... focus... breathe deeply and try to remember something else. Something before the pain. What was I doing before?... No. There's nothing... I need to distract myself so the memories come back on their own. (*She sings softly.*)

> Oh my darlin'
> Knock three times on the ceiling if you want me
> Twice on the pipe if the answer is no
> Oh my sweetness

I've got it! I had a knife in my hand and I was curling ribbons on the presents. Green ribbon for girls. Red for boys. There was some red ribbon left over. I spent ages doing that. It seemed like the most important thing in the world. A perfect curl to add a touch of beauty and love. If I could make something myself; that would be a real gift. But I'm no good at anything really. Besides, people like the stuff you get in the shops. It's quicker and easier. And the supermarket is right here, next to the building. I don't have to think about what to buy: I let the trolley take the lead and the stuff chooses me. I just have to take it off the shelf. It's simple... But those little curls... In this supermarket here they give you the ribbon as it comes: pressed flat, plain as anything, apart from the shine. I was curling ribbons. I'm doing well. Focus on what I was doing before the curling... Of course! I wrapped the presents. Because it's Christmas, the staff can't cope so they don't offer to gift-wrap your presents. They give you a sheet of paper that's the right size but you have to do the job yourself. It's very stressful. I couldn't get the wrapping paper to stay flat so I ended up with some huge gaps. I hid them by gluing pieces of the same paper over the top, making sure the pictures matched up. The years go by and Christmas paper is always the same, or almost the same. They ought to put a bit of effort in, be creative and change the designs. Every Christmas is different. Everything changes, moves on... I feel better. I feel like I'm getting back to my usual self... Was I lost?... Is it the mid-life crisis? Of course! I did my make-up. Before I wrapped the presents, and because I'm 40, I put my make-up on. Poly-filler, plaster and wall paint! I put on some plum lipstick, which is what everyone wears now. I drew a red line around my mouth to make it look the opposite of what it actually is, so because my mouth is too big, the line has to go on the inside so that from a distance it looks smaller. I remember! I put some powder on so that my face looked smooth, pale, almost deathly. And rouge on my cheeks, to put a bit of life back into them. Before that, I put on a base coat to cover my blemishes: wrinkles, moles, dark spots, wrinkles, pimples, redness, wrinkles. And underneath the base coat, what would we do without it: concealer. A wonderful invention to recoup a couple of years and a bit of hope. At some point I put on some green eye shadow, which is what everyone's wearing now. And I must have spent ten minutes with my mouth open, putting black mascara on my lashes... Yes! The memories are flooding back. Before that I did my hair. Hours with the hairdryer, it was far too hot. I remember the smell of burnt hair. I don't really have the patience for all that and the salon was full of women desperate to be at their Christmassy best... Why isn't there a little Christmas tree in here? And before that, I got dressed, and before that I was trying to decide what to wear, I spent ages deciding. Where was I going? And before that, I had a bath to rid myself of the supermarket and the tube and the people on the tube and the office and the computer and the telephone and my boss and the clients. And 'Good afternoon, Water and Closet Partners, how the hell can I help you?' The bath is a place for purification. I always buy the best products for cleaning furniture, floors, walls and the human body. Products with disinfectant, perfume, anti-stress oils, energisers, stimulants, purifiers, antioxidants, neutral pH and natural extracts. Before that I turned on the television. Yes! The television was the first thing I bought when I moved in here. I didn't have anything, just a mattress from the Housing Trust... I hope it's good and lasts a while; the television that is, the mattress will last because it isn't used intensively. Did I finish paying the instalments on the TV? Yes! Good! I'm starting to have more distant memories; this is getting better and better! I turned it on when I arrived, weighed down by the presents, the tube, the people on the tube, the office and my boss, because I felt the silence of my flat... I even missed the noise from my upstairs neighbour's drill, which is strange because usually it drives me mad and all I can think to do is hit the broom handle against the ceiling (*pointing upwards*). There you can see I'm breaking the plaster, stupid woman... I was saying that I felt the silence like it was a huge mouth about to swallow me up... So I turned it on for the sake of it. I didn't pay any attention to it. I didn't watch it. I didn't listen to it... Then? Nothing... nothing... I've got it: the last I remember is closing the door and leaving the key in the lock. How odd. Why did I do that? I never leave the key in the door, in case something happens to me. My husband used to have a habit of doing it. And I used to tell him not to, that if he had an accident or felt unwell, how was I going to get in to help him?... That was when I still felt like helping him. You shouldn't leave the key in the lock in case... What an idiot. Nobody except me has a key to that door.

Light from the television. The scenes or moments in the play are not separated by lights out but rather by the flickering and unnerving light produced by the TV when it is playing. Always playing.

2.

The WOMAN *is in an armchair opposite the television.*

WOMAN When the world is facing an energy crisis surely it's a sin to have the heating on in the middle of summer.

JOYCE Is it on?

WOMAN Yes.

JOYCE I don't feel hot.

WOMAN You don't feel anything.

JOYCE Is it summer?

WOMAN Sweltering. And you're contributing to global warming.

JOYCE Is that what they're saying on the news?

WOMAN Yes.

JOYCE That I'm contributing to global warming?

WOMAN No. They don't talk about you on the news.

JOYCE One day I'm going to be on TV.

WOMAN How do you know?

JOYCE One day I am going to do something important. Something that makes the headlines.

WOMAN Important for who?

JOYCE For people.

WOMAN Is the news important to people?

JOYCE It's what matters to people.

WOMAN That's not the same.

JOYCE I've been practising so maybe I'll enter a singing contest.

WOMAN (*Bursts out laughing*) Sorry... that's pathetic.

JOYCE Really?

WOMAN Absolutely.

Silence. Both women watch the television.

JOYCE Is there long left?

WOMAN Yes.

JOYCE I can't remember what it is we're waiting for... To be honest, the only thing I can remember is a headache. I'm going to wash the dishes.

WOMAN No! You can't! The dishes must be washed as soon as you've finished with them. It's too late now.

JOYCE Can't I do something as simple as that? Something you do every day? All your life? Because it was always my turn, from being a little girl. Mum would cook, I washed up and my sister did nothing. It was an unfair distribution of labour but I never complained. I always put a lot of effort in and I felt really proud of myself for making the plates shine and the glasses sparkle. But what fascinated me was the drain. Everything goes down that hole. Whirling, whirling. Where does it go? My dad told me there was a network of tubes to carry all the waste far away, to the sea, perhaps. Grains of rice, bits of fat, meat and soap, from my humble drain to the infinite, mysterious sea. Once I thought: everything drains away. Including me. Too much rubbish. My life is draining away through a hole that gets bigger every day from all this rubbish. I'm a colander. So much water. I'm always building dikes, dams, filling in the gaps. I get tired. I can't stop it. It all goes too fast. The drain... Tiny grains of rice, bits of fat, meat and soap... I always wanted to have hands like a princess but my nails keep breaking. I need to change washing-up liquid... It whirls, whirls, then goes. I scrub the pan, the same old pan. I brush myself down, make myself look beautiful, study singing. I chop an onion, find a job, iron ties. I get married. I stop singing, hang out the clothes to air. It's fine. Everything's fine... But it whirls, whirls, then goes. The drain. I do everything that I have to, I do it well, with love. It's fine. Everything's fine. The drain. Tiny grains of rice, bits of fat, meat and soap. It whirls, whirls, then goes. Why can't I do something as simple as washing the dishes?

WOMAN You should celebrate. You've escaped a chore detested by the vast majority of the human race. Or at least by people who've had food on their plates. And people who don't have a dishwasher.

JOYCE Lately it's been so easy that my nails stopped breaking. A glass, a plate, two pieces of cutlery. I don't even have wine glasses. But I always make sure I put a tablecloth on the table. Even when I was tired, I took time to set the table. It's the little details that count. It's a sign of self-respect.

WOMAN Don't lie. Most nights you sat in front of the TV eating biscuits for dinner.

JOYCE That wasn't very often... Only when I was depressed and I couldn't be bothered...

WOMAN How many times a week were you depressed?

JOYCE I have an idea. How about I cook a delicious dinner and we toast with the tumblers, but we pretend they're wine glasses, and put out a beautiful plastic tablecloth that I bought when... well, I don't remember when, but not very long ago. A God Market special.

WOMAN The God Market doesn't exist anymore. It closed down. The locals weren't buying enough.

JOYCE How strange! The stuff in there was always good. And it was the only one in the area. What am I going to do now? It was always full of customers.

WOMAN Everything comes and goes and one day shuts down.

JOYCE What would you like for dinner? This is really exciting for me. I haven't cooked for anyone since I moved to this flat. I haven't had dinner with anyone since...

WOMAN That's very kind but I don't have an appetite. And neither do you.

JOYCE You're right. But we still have to celebrate that you're here with me. It's an important day for me.

WOMAN There's nothing whatsoever to celebrate about me being here.

JOYCE Yes. Of course there is. I'm happy just talking to you and watching the TV together and...

The telephone rings. Both women listen but don't answer.

Light from the television.

3.

The telephone continues ringing. The WOMAN *has left.*

JOYCE Every time that phone rings my heart stops... (*Happy.*) Who could it be? (*The telephone keeps ringing.*) Every time that phone rings my heart stops (*part happy and part scared*). Perhaps it's him, he's looking for me. He's found me. (*The phone stops ringing.*) It's a shame the ribbons on the presents are all flat. It must be because of the dust or the central heating or the damp. The heat and damp spoil everything. It's awful. Why are the windows closed? I can't remember now who each present was for. I should have written a little card with their name on it, and a few words. Something to say to them. You never say what you ought to in time. And then life becomes burdened with all the things you never said. Take this one: it's a scarf for a woman called Mary. She was always hoarse, I suppose it must be because she spends so much time fighting with feminists who keep talking over each other. Dear Mary, I wish you a happy Christmas. I'm sending you a gift, even though I'm not really sure you'll remember me, given that you deal with so many women. It's a sign of my immense gratitude for all the help the Trust gave me in finding me this flat where I can feel safe. I feel comfortable and secure here... Should I have sent a present to the Council as well? They're paying the rent. I pay all my taxes on time, as I ought to, because I'm grateful. I don't think I'd know who to send it to. Surely the Mayor doesn't know me. Do I have a number? Am I female victim of domestic violence number 36,583? Should I know my number, if I've got one? Is there a file about me? They protect me. The Mayor protects me.

The city protects me and I, being ungrateful, didn't buy a present. I should have opened the window and shouted out through the cold and snow: Merry Christmas! To, to everyone. But I didn't. The Housing Trust is on the other side of the city so I'm not sure I'd have been able to deliver the scarf. But it's the thought that counts... This one is for Peter and Shirley. An adorable little dog with batteries so it moves its tail, raises its little paw and even pees. My darling niece and nephew, you must have grown so much that I'll hardly recognise you. I'm your aunty, do you remember me? Of course you do. We must see each other more often. We could go to the zoo or for ice cream. No, not ice cream now. Next summer. But now we could go for hot chocolate or to the cinema. The cinema. You two would be doing me a big favour. I never go. I know lots of stories and fairy tales as well. We could all sit together in the park or at my house and I'll tell them. I'll buy plastic cups with little pictures of people from the TV on them and colourful biscuits and Coke. I could even make you a cake, if I can remember any recipes. I love you lots. Signed, aunty. Yes. I was going somewhere, I don't remember where, but first I was going to stop by my sister's house. She hadn't invited me to have dinner with them and so I thought I'd pop in mid-afternoon, say hello and leave. She has her family, her responsibilities, the house is small, and all the rest. And I've had my problems. When I first got married I went years without hardly ever seeing her because I was so busy with my own life: the house, the decorating, the two jobs so I could pay the rent, three if you count the housework as well. And love. Because we really were in love. I only had time for him and the house. My sister always thought that I'd chosen the wrong man. I'll never forgive her for that. For working it out before I did, I'll never forgive her for it. Or for telling me. He had started drinking a bit too much and I would join him sometimes. I didn't want them to see each other so that she wouldn't keep on criticising him. The blows were my secret. The first time I had to go to hospital, I didn't call her. Anyway, he was there at my side crying and begging me for forgiveness. The second, third and fourth times I didn't want her there either. And then there was the last time, when the police wouldn't let him into the hospital. They had no right. I wanted him at my side because I knew he was going to cry and beg me to forgive him. That's much better than being alone with broken ribs and a bruised face. When I left him, I got the feeling my little sister was pleased and that bothered me. I called her and all she could say was 'At last!' Nothing else. She came to see me just once and brought me single sheets, towels and a tea set that belonged to Mum. Dearest sister, I bought this fine perfume that I know you like, because you always were a princess, to wish you a Merry Christmas with your family. I want you to know that... I need you. Signed: your ugly sister.

She cries and watches the television.

Light from the television.

4.

The WOMAN is sitting next to JOYCE VINCENT.

WOMAN There's no point crying. You've already cried enough in your life. Now you should feel free. Enjoy this.

JOYCE What is 'this'?

The WOMAN doesn't respond.

JOYCE Will you hug me?

WOMAN No.

JOYCE Just for a moment?

WOMAN No.

JOYCE Hold my hand?

The WOMAN takes her hand.

JOYCE You're freezing.

WOMAN So are you.

JOYCE Is it winter?

WOMAN Yes.

JOYCE It's a good job the heating's on.

WOMAN It was never turned off.

JOYCE I can't remember what we're waiting for.

The WOMAN doesn't respond.

JOYCE Will you tell me?

WOMAN You don't want to know. Besides, you ought to be happy. You've just stopped crying because you realised it's unnecessary, pointless, useless. And it ruins your make-up.

JOYCE I want to know.

WOMAN We are waiting to go.

JOYCE Where to?

WOMAN For God's sake. I'm not putting up with all these questions. I've no idea how long this will take. It's unbelievable. We should have already left. You are so scared of solitude that you don't want to leave until...

JOYCE I'm not scared of solitude.

WOMAN Ok. Whatever you say.

JOYCE There are so many people out there, everywhere, it's impossible to be alone. And phones, texts, emails, television, satellites, Internet.

WOMAN That reminds me, someone posted something about you on the Internet.

JOYCE About me? That's fantastic. What was it? What did it say?

WOMAN They were looking for you.

JOYCE It was him.

WOMAN No. Someone called Carol.

JOYCE I don't remember anyone called Carol.

WOMAN It looks like she's an artist who wants to make something about you.

JOYCE You're lying to me. Or you're being nice to me to cheer me up. What artist would be interested in me!

WOMAN She makes films.

JOYCE VINCENT laughs loudly.

WOMAN She wants to make a film about you but she doesn't have very much information. She's trying to find out if anyone knows you. It says: her parents were from the Caribbean. Please contact Carol.

JOYCE Does it say my full name?

WOMAN Yes.

JOYCE Do you know why my parents gave me that name?

WOMAN It's the kind of name that makes you believe you could win a singing contest.

JOYCE My mum used to adore a singer who was all the rage when I was born. She was black, like her, and she used to sway and sing these choruses, like, 'whoa, whoa, whoa'. This country was always too cold for Mum.

WOMAN And you?

JOYCE I'm alright.

Both women remain silent.

Light from the television.

5.

JOYCE I'm not really practising for a singing contest but I do sing sometimes.

WOMAN Don't the neighbours complain?

JOYCE I don't know any of them. I mean, I haven't had any complaints. Besides, I hardly ever open the windows. The corridor always reeks of drunken vomit.

WOMAN (*Screwing up her face, annoyed*) This is a nightmare! The smell won't give us away. We aren't ever going to get out of here.

JOYCE What?

WOMAN Nothing.

Silence

JOYCE Do you want me to sing you my namesake's most famous song?

WOMAN Yes, of course.

The WOMAN makes herself comfortable in the armchair, as if she's preparing to listen, but she immediately falls asleep and starts to snore loudly.

JOYCE *Sings 'Knock Three Times'.*

Hey girl, whatcha doin' down there?
Dancin' alone every night while I live right above you

I can hear your music playin'
I can feel your body swayin'
One floor below me, you don't even know me
I love you
Oh my darlin'
Knock three times on the ceilin' if you want me
Twice on the pipe if the answer is no
Oh, my sweetness, knock, knock, knock
means you'll meet me in the hallway
Twice on the pipe, knock, knock
means you ain't gonna show

The loud noise of an electric drill interrupts her and wakes the WOMAN.

WOMAN What's happening? Is it over? Are they here?

JOYCE It's my stupid upstairs neighbour who spends the entire day making holes with his drill. He's obsessed with D.I.Y.

WOMAN Do you know him?

JOYCE No. I've never seen him.

WOMAN (*As if scolding her*) You've lived here for years and you've never seen him. You've never knocked on his door to tell him that the noise bothers you. You haven't spoken to anyone else about him. Does he only bother you?

JOYCE Well, I... sometimes I hit the broom handle against the ceiling and he quiets down for a bit.

WOMAN I see. The only way you can communicate with men is by hitting. How do you know it's a man?

Suddenly, the BLOKE *appears.*

BLOKE Merry Christmas!

WOMAN That's all we need. (*To* JOYCE VINCENT) Don't listen to him. Tell him to leave.

JOYCE Is it Christmas? Is it still Christmas?

BLOKE Still Christmas. Another Christmas. What does it matter?

JOYCE The presents are all dingy, covered in dust.

WOMAN (*To the* BLOKE) Would you please just leave us in peace.

BLOKE (*Singing*) Silent night. Holy night. All is calm. All is bright.

WOMAN (*To the* BLOKE) What do you want?

BLOKE She called me.

JOYCE Did I?

BLOKE You knocked three times on the ceiling.

JOYCE No I didn't. I mean, I've done it before, loads of times, but not today.

BLOKE Before? Today? What's this woman talking about?

WOMAN She's not thinking straight.

JOYCE Well, if it's still Christmas, I've still got time. I'm going to my sister's house and then, where was I going afterwards?

The WOMAN *and the* BLOKE *sit and watch the television. There is a funny programme on and they laugh every so often.*

JOYCE It's a shame the curls have come out of the ribbons. Maybe I could do them again with the scissors.

WOMAN No. You can't.

BLOKE (*Pointing to a parcel*) And who was that present for?

WOMAN Just leave it, will you.

JOYCE For him.

WOMAN That's unbelievable. How did you have it in you to buy something for him?

JOYCE It's a thermal vest.

BLOKE (*To the* WOMAN) You don't know the slightest thing about love.

JOYCE It's a thermal vest. He feels the cold a lot.

BLOKE I don't think he's in need of anyone to keep him warm.

WOMAN Would you shut up!

JOYCE I never wrote the tag. What was I going to put? My darling... No... My ex-husband... No, not that either... John... No... The biggest bastard I ever met. I'm sending you a vest for you to wear this Christmas. The fabric contains a powerful poison. When it comes into contact with your skin it will cause you excruciating pain and eventually, death.

WOMAN Pathetic.

BLOKE Were you really going to give him the present?

JOYCE When I bought it I thought I needed to forgive him because by forgiving him, I'd stop hating him and hate binds us together. I thought that if I forgave him, I would feel more at peace. But more alone. Hating him every day was a sort of reason for living. I'm a monster, aren't I? Other times, I convinced myself that I should love him. At the end of the day, the only thing you can change is the past. The present is happening right now, too quickly. The future isn't here yet and you never know. But the past, where is it? Mine is in my memory: it belongs to me. Why shouldn't I alter it? Who's stopping me? I can decide to forget and create a new memory of only the good things. He was handsome, caring...

BLOKE Like me?

JOYCE He promised the life that every woman longs for: home, children, holidays, calm.

WOMAN You should put backing music to that. And you have to sing the chorus, maybe like, 'whoa, whoa, whoa'.

JOYCE I wasn't going to give him the present. I didn't want to risk him finding out where I was living.

BLOKE That's the only reason?

JOYCE When I get home from work there's always an old man rummaging through the bins from the flats. The vest would suit him better.

WOMAN (*To the* BLOKE) She's a charitable soul. You needn't have come.

BLOKE She called me. And this business is long overdue. Darling, you have two presents left.

JOYCE Dear Mum, I bought you the music that you love so much. I miss you, you're always with me. Dear Dad, this book tells a tale of the sea, just like you, it's the story of an old whale and a man and fate. I know you've never liked reading anything except newspapers but this book is wonderful. Your big girl loves you. I'll never forget you... I've just remembered where I had to go: to the cemetery to take them their presents.

Light from the TV.

6.

The BLOKE and JOYCE are watching television.

BLOKE Your contribution to global warming is most kind. Having the heating on at the height of summer is a modest but welcome gesture.

JOYCE Is it summer?

BLOKE Sweltering. Beyond sweltering. Why did you call me?

JOYCE I called you? I don't know. I never call anyone. I ought to. I'm not that old, yet, am I?

BLOKE Forty is a wonderful age. All earthly desires are known, you can start afresh, with wisdom and freedom. You still have your energy and beauty.

JOYCE Yes. I ought to touch up my make-up.

BLOKE There's no need.

JOYCE The bloke upstairs.

BLOKE Who?

JOYCE My neighbour in the flat above... What must he be like? Once I dreamt that I'd been hitting the ceiling so hard with the broom handle, I made a hole and the bloke fell through onto my armchair. I apologised, I brushed the dust and bits of plaster off him. I offered to call him a doctor and he said that there was no need. Well, please accept a bowl of soup, a cup of tea, a glass of wine, something to make up for this mishap of having broken his floor, or my ceiling, and him falling onto my armchair, good thing that it was onto the armchair. Of course, I was lucky, he said, I'll accept a glass of wine. Does it matter if it's in a tumbler? I said. Not at all, as long you'll have one too, he said. It's odd that we've never met in the hallway, we said, strange, stranger still to meet like this, out of the blue. We laughed, we made a toast, we talked about the weather, the news on TV, about his favourite programme, about mine. I told him that I was a widow and he felt sorry for me and wanted to protect me, and that I was a retired singer, and he was impressed and asked me to sing something for him. I sang a sweet bolero and he asked me to dance, here in my tiny living room. There's nothing in the world more wonderful than dancing on a stone cold floor, he said, and so it was...

The BLOKE takes her in his arms and they dance whilst he sings.

BLOKE If you look out your window tonight
Pull in the string with the note that's attached to my heart
Read how many times I saw you
and how in my silence I adore you
And only in my dreams did that wall between us come apart
Oh my darlin'
Knock three times on the ceilin' if you want me

Loud knocking is heard, it seems to be coming from the door. They carry on dancing in silence. The WOMAN *appears.*

JOYCE Were you knocking at the door?

WOMAN Of course not.

JOYCE They were knocking a lot, what must they want?

WOMAN For you to open the door. What else could they want? For you to pay the service charges for the building. For you to pay the electricity company, for you to explain why those little black bugs and that nauseating smell are creeping out from underneath the door, for you to turn down the TV. But the most important thing is that you pay the service charges for the building because it isn't fair that all the other neighbours pay and not you.

BLOKE Would you please stop bothering us? Can't you see we're dancing?

WOMAN (*To the* BLOKE) Let go of her!

JOYCE No. It's alright. I feel happy here. I'm cold but I'm alright.

BLOKE It's only natural. It's one of the coldest winters of the century.

JOYCE Is it winter?

WOMAN How can you possibly feel cold? (*Pause*) Don't let him hold you.

JOYCE I can't remember the last time that someone held me. You didn't want to.

WOMAN He's deceiving you.

BLOKE Am I deceiving you?

JOYCE No. It's all I want; a bit of music, a man to hold me, love me and maybe even a few plans for the future together.

The BLOKE *starts laughing raucously. The* WOMAN *struggles to separate him from* JOYCE VINCENT. *Knocking at the door.*

JOYCE Why can't I open the door? Someone's looking for me.

WOMAN Quick. We need a photo.

JOYCE What?

WOMAN A photo of you. An old one, it doesn't matter.

BLOKE You have to be smiling in it.

JOYCE Happy?

BLOKE That doesn't matter, you just have to be smiling.

JOYCE I think there's a shoebox of photos in the wardrobe. I haven't looked at them for a long time. I must have smiled once.

WOMAN Good. There isn't long to go now.

Knocking at the door.

JOYCE Why can't I open the door?

Pause.

WOMAN Because you're dead.

Light from the television.

7.

JOYCE, motionless, watches the television.

BLOKE ¡Feliz navidad!
(*Sings*) Last Christmas, I gave you my heart
But the very next day
You gave it away
This year, to save me from tears...

WOMAN Leave her in peace.
JOYCE How long have I been dead?
BLOKE It's your third Christmas.
JOYCE The headache.
BLOKE A brain haemorrhage, perhaps. They might have been able to operate on you or something.
WOMAN Don't torture her.
BLOKE Torturing a corpse is, if nothing else, paradoxical.
JOYCE I was alone.
WOMAN Bad luck. It could have happened to you at work or on the tube or in the street.
JOYCE Someone would have helped.
BLOKE Maybe, but you are rather an 'invisible' sort. Besides, you would have missed out on our company.
JOYCE I'm a little pile of bones. And grey dust.
BLOKE Yes, but don't you worry. They're going to identify you from the photograph of your smile. Teeth don't rot.
WOMAN That's enough now.
JOYCE And why am I here?
BLOKE That's the problem with cadavers. They insist on being found.
JOYCE Nobody found me... What could be worse than dying alone without anyone knowing?
BLOKE Surely nothing... But death throes can be awful to endure.
WOMAN Don't treat her like that. She doesn't deserve it.
BLOKE Who knows what anyone deserves?
JOYCE I don't want this.
BLOKE What? To have died? There's nothing you can do about that.
JOYCE No. I don't want you to abuse me. I won't allow it.

WOMAN (*Clapping*) Very well said.

Knocking at the door.

JOYCE They're coming for me.

WOMAN Yes.

JOYCE The television has been on all these years.

BLOKE I'm going to tell them to put your name on this model. It'll be a best-seller.

JOYCE It's funny that televisions outlive us. There'll be a world full of televisions and cockroaches... They're going to find me here, amongst all this dust and dirt, how embarrassing. Well, they're going to find me, at last. I'm sure that lots of people were worried about me. I bet they thought I'd gone travelling. Or run away with a mystery lover... Who knows what the Mayor must have thought, or the women from the Housing Trust. You see, at the end of the day, individual liberty is the highest good. Not the police, not my sister, not even my boss has any reason to meddle in my life, or my death... Besides, everyone is very busy. I never took any notice of my upstairs neighbour...

WOMAN That's enough rubbish. Now's not the time. Perhaps something more spiritual would be appropriate.

JOYCE (*Tries to think*) Nothing comes to mind.

Knocking at the door.

WOMAN Look. You're on TV!

JOYCE Are they announcing they've found my body?

WOMAN No. It's a singing contest. You're beautiful.

There is a noise as if someone has broken down the door. Simultaneously show lights come on and all three characters sing the song, with backing music, as if they are doing karaoke. The song is interrupted by sounds and voices coming from the television.

VOICE OF SHOW HOST OFF STAGE Let's welcome our next contestant with a big round of applause.

JOYCE, WOMAN AND BLOKE

Hey girl, whatcha doin' down there?
Dancin' alone every night while I live right above you
I can hear your music playin'
I can feel your body swayin'
One floor below me, you don't even know me
I love you
Oh my darlin'
Knock three times on the ceilin' if you want me
Twice on the pipe if the answer is no
Oh, my sweetness, knock, knock, knock
Means you'll meet me in the hallway
Twice on the pipe, knock, knock
Means you ain't gonna show

VOICE OF SHOW HOST OFF STAGE Well done sweetheart! To die for.

JOYCE, WOMAN AND BLOKE

If you look out your window tonight
Pull in the string with the note that's attached to my heart
Read how many times I saw you
And how in my silence I adore you
And only in my dreams did that wall between us come apart
Oh my darlin'

VOICE OF A REPORTER The body of a forty-year-old woman, who lay dead in her flat for two years, has been found by the building manager investigating missed rent payments. A television, which was still playing, and bags containing Christmas presents were also found in the flat. The woman from London died in complete solitude, watching the television. Nobody has missed her in the last two years.

JOYCE, WOMAN AND BLOKE

Knock three times
On the ceilin' if you want me
Twice on the pipe if the answer is no
Oh, my sweetness, knock, knock, knock
Means you'll meet me in the hallway
Twice on the pipe, knock, knock
Means you ain't gonna show

Towards the end of the song the BLOKE *and the* WOMAN *start to move away individually, as if inviting* JOYCE *to go with them.* JOYCE VINCENT *sits in front of the television and remains motionless, watching.*

Light from the television.

The play has finished. The actors who played the BLOKE *and the* WOMAN *take a bow, now out of character.* JOYCE VINCENT *remains in front of the television until the last member of the audience has left the theatre.*

CHAPTER 5

Form and Theatre Translation: Analysing the Folkloric in *El Herrero y la Muerte* and Flashbacks in *Punto y coma*

The Folkloric and the Flashback

This chapter explores two distinct styles of theatre narrative: the folkloric and the flashback. Through a detailed analysis of two plays, *El Herrero y la Muerte* [*Death and the Blacksmith*] by Mercedes Rein and Jorge Curi (1979) and *Punto y coma* [*Ready or Not*] by Estela Golovchenko (2003), it specifies how engaging creatively with these forms can underpin a robust translation strategy.[1] Both plays centre on an encounter which is the starting point for the dramatic narrative. Through the encounters portrayed, the protagonists grow in their understanding of their own role, agency and responsibility, both in society and in their relationships with others. The audience gain an insight into a process whereby the protagonist becomes increasingly aware of how they relate to the social and political context depicted in the play. This chapter will argue that the encounters presented in these plays use the theatre as a site of resistance where everyday life reaches a 'crisis point'.[2] It demonstrates how these texts use the dramatic space to examine and critique established discourses and to enable their protagonists to question the accepted norms of the society in which they live. At the same time, the dramatic action provokes the audience to consider their own relationship to their current context. My analysis will illustrate how a critical engagement with the theatrical forms of the folkloric and flashbacks create ways of conceptualising and applying translation strategies which enable the potency of this crisis to be communicated to new audiences in a new cultural context. I discuss how the theatre translator can approach a dramaturgical understanding of forms of theatre which draw on a particular cultural, historical and literary heritage, and how these theatre narratives can be creative tools to reach new audiences and make new connections to the target culture. Through the translation, the audience in the target culture are able to access aspects of Uruguayan culture and literary heritage. I demonstrate how the translator can view the translation as playing a part in continuing that tradition whilst also transforming it for the new target audience.

Throughout this book, I have demonstrated how the dramaturgical and contextual analysis enables a rich engagement with the play which informs and underpins the translation strategy chosen by the translator. This chapter will show how attention to form, rather than limiting the possibilities, can enhance the translation process and enable the translator to make creative choices.

El Herrero y la Muerte by Mercedes Rein and Jorge Curi begins with an encounter between Jesus, St Peter and a humble blacksmith. After the blacksmith helps them, Jesus and St Peter grant him three wishes to thank him for his generosity towards them. The play is narrated by the character Peralta who also plays the role of the blacksmith Miseria [Misery], which we later learn is his nickname. Rather than wishing for eternal life, the blacksmith makes a series of wishes which enable him to outsmart his neighbours, the local authorities and ultimately Death himself. Thanks to Miseria's astuteness and his ability to manipulate his simple wishes to his advantage, Death ends up stuck up the tree in the middle of the blacksmith's ranch where he is ridiculed by the local residents and unable to fulfil his fatal role. The play is an adaptation of Chapter 21 of *Don Segundo Sombra* (1926) by the Argentine author Ricardo Güiraldes in which Don Segundo Sombra tells the story of a blacksmith called Miseria who, without realising their identities, assists Jesus and Saint Peter.[3] *El Herrero y la Muerte* was staged during the period of the dictatorship in Uruguay and the play uses allegory to tell a story of resistance to inspire those experiencing the crisis caused by state repression, as well as future generations. It was translated into English by Raúl Moncada as *Ballad of the Blacksmith* and performed at the Old Globe Theatre in San Diego in 1993, directed by René Buch. The theatre ran a workshop around the play under the title *Death and the Blacksmith* as part of the research and development process in 1989, and the literary department shared photos, scripts and programmes from their archive with me.

Punto y coma depicts a meeting between a young woman and her father, whom she has not seen (in person) for many years since they were separated during the civic-military dictatorship. We learn that he left her with her mother in order to try to create a way for the whole family to escape to Argentina but the plan never came to fruition and the Mother disappeared during the widespread repression. The play is set in the present day when the Father is in the role of Senator in the Uruguayan parliament and so is in the public eye. We also learn that he has been diagnosed with terminal cancer and intends to transfer ownership of two properties and a bank account to his daughter.[4] The play portrays the difficulty of reconciliation both with an estranged relative and also with a different version of the past. The influence of the past on the present situation is emphasised through the use of a series of flashbacks to the Daughter's childhood which disrupt the meeting taking place in the present day. I translated *Punto y coma* into English as *Ready or Not*; it was presented as a rehearsed reading at the Out of the Wings Festival at the Cervantes Theatre in 2017, directed by Camila Ymay González, and I participated in rehearsals. In this chapter I will reflect on some of the decisions made in the translation and rehearsal process in relation to the flashbacks present in the dramatic narrative and I will discuss how my analysis informed my translation of the title. A full translation of *Ready or Not* is included in Chapter 6.

El Herrero y la Muerte: Transforming Tradition through Translation

Mercedes Rein and Jorge Curi had already collaborated on projects to create plays, many of which were adaptations of existing texts, before working together on *El Herrero y la Muerte*; they also continued to work together after its success.[5] The play premiered, directed by Curi, at the Teatro Circular in Montevideo in 1981 and received the *Florencio* award (Uruguayan Theatre Critics' Award) for best show of the year. It had a run of over four years, totalling more than 500 performances, and also went on to tour other Latin American cities and theatre festivals.[6] *El Herrero y la Muerte* is included in several anthologies of Uruguayan theatre: *50 años de teatro uruguayo: antología*; *Teatro uruguayo contemporáneo: antología* (1992); *Teatro uruguayo contemporáneo: antología* (1993).[7] The last of these is aimed at secondary school students studying Uruguayan theatre and includes notes, activities and historical information to help contextualise the play and the two others included in the anthology, *Doña Ramona* by Víctor Manuel Leites (1982, Teatro Circular) and *Y nuestros caballos serán blancos* by Mauricio Rosencof (written in 1967). The fact that it is printed in several anthologies, including this anthology for students, demonstrates the recognised importance of the play in Uruguay.

Argentine dramatist Juan Carlos Gené had already created an adaptation of Chapter 21 of Güiraldes's novel for the stage in 1954.[8] Gené's version, *El herrero y el diablo*, also shares some characteristics of the novel by Colombian author Tomás Carrasquilla, *En la diestra de Dios Padre* (1897). These texts share the same premise as Rein and Curi's version: the encounter between the blacksmith, Jesus and St Peter, which results in the granting of wishes. However, the blacksmith's wishes and the way in which the narrative unfolds differ in each of the cases. Rein and Curi stated that in modifying the wishes, the dramatic action was able to progress in a different way to the previous versions so as to 'llegar a un desenlace que busca una nueva salida a la situación a la vez picaresca y dolorosa, fantástica y verdadera, absurda y coherente, que plantea la obra' [to arrive at an ending which seeks to create a new way out of the situation depicted in the play, which is picaresque and painful, fantastic and truthful, absurd and coherent all at once].[9] My analysis will demonstrate how the authors created a protagonist who is able to respond with resilience, humour and ingenuity to challenges he faces and the consequences of his wishes.

Jorge Abbondanza in his introduction to *El Herrero y la Muerte* in *Teatro uruguayo contemporáneo* and Roger Mirza in his study on the performance of the text both refer to the interplay between the play and the texts by Carasquilla, Güiraldes and Gené.[10] They also establish links to other texts from Latin America in order to demonstrate how the play forms part of a wider tradition of the legend of the blacksmith. In fact, in his own introduction to *Teatro*, Gené states that there are very few cultures in the world that do not include a tale of the blacksmith who tricks or takes advantage of the Devil or Death.[11] These connections to a Latin American narrative tradition enable us to consider this play as part of a folkloric tradition in which the tale is adapted and retold for new audiences. The ideas of storytelling and adaptation for new audiences are central to my analysis and my thinking about how this play is able to travel and make connections with audiences in a new time and place. These concepts intersect with key questions about theatre translation and so, I argue, allow for a productive reflection on the translator's work. Rein and Curi acknowledge that they draw on existing traditions and mention the texts by Carrasquilla and Gené in their introductory note to the play-text published by the Teatro Circular; they also state that the play and staging by the creative team at the Teatro Circular have echoes of the circus performance of the Podestá brothers.[12] In this way, they form a link to both a broader Latin American literary and theatre heritage and also specifically to the theatre of the River Plate region. This demonstrates how texts continued to move between Uruguay and Argentina, thus evoking the idea of the shared tradition of *Teatro rioplatense* (theatre from the River Plate region) presented in Chapter 1.

The dramatic narrative of the play is that one day Jesus and St Peter are travelling through Tierra Santa [Holy Land] and seek refreshment and a place to rest. They enquire at Miseria's ranch and do not reveal their identities. Miseria is generous and hospitable and refuses to take any money from them, saying that they seem to be poorer than he and his sister. St Peter and Jesus reveal their identities and to thank him, they offer to grant him three wishes. Although at first he does not believe them, Miseria eventually makes the following requests because, as his sister points out, he has nothing to lose: anyone who goes up the fork in the tree at the centre of his ranch cannot come down until he gives them permission; Miseria will always win at cards when he wants to; and when Death comes he will give Miseria an extra hour of life to have a drink and say his goodbyes. What is at stake in the play is how the blacksmith will use these wishes in practice. The wisdom of the blacksmith will be tested as the consequences of these requests are played out and he develops self-awareness of his role in society. Mirza refers to the quality of the play as a moral tale in his write up of the production in *La Semana de El Día*; he suggests that the experience of the blacksmith warns the audience against aspiring to be wealthy and powerful and instead shows them how, within society, a humble blacksmith can bring about change.[13]

Miseria uses his ability to win at cards to gain a small fortune which attracts constant attention and requests for help, leading him eventually to see his wealth as a burden. One day Miseria's opponent at cards is a cheat who always wins; the cheat is so enraged when he loses to Miseria, in accordance with the latter's wish, that he accuses him of cheating and stabs him in fury. When Death appears to take Miseria away, he must wait an hour. Miseria persuades Death to pass the time that he has to wait by admiring the view from the top of the tree fork and, once he climbs the tree, Death is obliged to remain there until Miseria gives him permission to descend. In this way, Miseria's ranch constitutes the centre of the dramatic action and, in trapping Death up the tree, it becomes the centre of the world.[14] This reinforces Miseria's connection to his home and also shows how a humble man takes control over life and death; this ultimately requires the intervention of earthly and heavenly authorities, who all come to visit Miseria at his ranch, to resolve the situation. At the end of the play, Miseria climbs the tree and is unwilling to come down; this makes it evident that the blacksmith's ultimate objective is to remain there as long as possible. This is important because during the civic-military dictatorship, life at home, privacy and a sense of national identity were disrupted and recast by the regime's leaders. Therefore, for the audience of the original play, it is significant that Miseria's steadfastness, his attachment to home and his sense of integrity are strongly conveyed at the end of the play. Miseria's qualities and the ways in which he resolves the situation communicated important ideas about resistance and resilience in the face of challenges.

The play begins with the opening line from Miseria: 'Les viá a contar una historia pa'que se la cuenten a un amigo cuando ande en la mala', [I'm going to tell you a story for you to pass on to a friend when he is down on his luck] (*El Herrero*, Scene 1, p. 435). This opening signals intertextuality with Chapter 21 of *Don Segundo Sombra* which begins in a similar way.[15] Mirza points out that the staging of the play in Montevideo, which was in a round performance space, created the impression that the audience were gathered around a fire to hear the tale and served to evoke *Don Segundo Sombra* because in the novel Don Segundo tells the story to his companion when they stop to camp for the night.[16] This opening is significant because it instantly alludes to an oral storytelling tradition, and it invites the audience to be part of that tradition by passing the story on. The audience of the translated play might not identify the precise connection to Don Segundo Sombra but the emphasis on storytelling, and the past and future re-telling of this narrative, is clear.

Miseria continues his opening speech by setting up the story: he states that it concerns a blacksmith who lives in poverty with his sister on a ranch in a place called Tierra Santa [Holy Land]. The blacksmith is good natured and generous and constantly criticised by his sister, called Peraltona but known as Pobreza [Poverty], for putting the needs of others first whilst she and he barely have food to eat. He states that the name of the young *criollo* (native of Uruguay) blacksmith is Peralta, but he is usually known as Miseria. As Miseria tries to continue with his story, his sister Peraltona interjects to complain about the poverty in which they live (*El Herrero*, Scene 1, pp. 435–36). The similarities between the story that the narrator sets up and the situation in which the audience encounter him are evident. Through this opening, the audience are made aware of the fact that the narrator is also the protagonist of the story, Miseria. Miseria will continue to switch between the roles of narrator and protagonist throughout the play. At the time when the play was written and performed, the message that this story should be re-told to anyone experiencing a difficult time was poignant because Uruguay was experiencing a repressive civic-military dictatorship. Therefore, as Riccetto points out, the whole country was like a friend going through a bad time and so the story of the humble blacksmith became an inspiring one:

> la alegoría dramática del Herrero pobre y generoso, protegido por Dios y vencedor de la Muerte, era un mensaje de esperanza, un guiño cómplice que alentaba a resistir la opresión y el horror de una dictadura que afectaba en mayor o menor grado a toda la familia uruguaya.[17]

> [the dramatic allegory of the poor and generous Blacksmith, protected by God and victorious over Death, was a message of hope, a sly wink to encourage people to resist the oppression and horror of a dictatorship which affected to a greater or lesser extent the whole Uruguayan family.]

This perhaps goes some way to explaining why Rein and Curi chose to create a new play based on this folkloric legend during the dictatorship: the use of allegory enabled them to avoid censorship whilst creating a play to reassure the audience that they could stand up to the challenges they faced, as others had done before them. The experience of the powerless and poor blacksmith conveys a message about the importance of wisdom and integrity in one's beliefs and actions. The significance of this message of hope communicated to the audience in the shared theatre space is also underscored by Mirza: whilst many theatres and companies were forced to close down or go into exile, those that remained became a space for community within a context in which public gatherings and protest were illegal and, as a result, theatres became sites of resistance.[18]

The ways in which this opening line functions as an invitation to the audience to connect with Miseria's story and to play an active role in sharing it is also related to the theatrical form. In *A Theory of Adaptation*, Linda Hutcheon proposes that we analyse and understand adaptation as transforming narratives between modes of telling, showing and interaction, rather than focussing on the medium, such as a book or film.[19] Following this, we can understand that the authors adapt the legend of the blacksmith into a dramatic representation which is a 'mode of showing'. However, by presenting Miseria as a narrator and storyteller, Rein and Curi also incorporate into this 'mode of showing' a technique that is more prominent in a 'telling mode' such as literature.[20] This is particularly important for this play because it evokes the literary origins of the legend. In this way, Miseria's role as narrator captures and represents the way in which the story has moved across oral and written forms by incorporating features we normally associate with literature into the dramatic action. At the same time, it places emphasis on storytelling, re-telling and sharing. As Miseria moves between the roles of protagonist and narrator, the audience are invited into his story, which he is sharing with them, and this creates a sense of intimacy and complicity. Attention to the way in which Miseria invites us into the narrative and the ways in which the dialogue facilitates his movement between the roles of narrator and protagonist enable the translator to situate Miseria within the context of the play and the context of a folkloric tradition of storytelling. The figure of the narrator is particularly interesting precisely because he can be seen to guide the audience through the story, signal key changes in the plot and critique what is happening. For the audience of the translated play, this can provide a route into the story and the folkloric tradition to which it belongs.

One of the ways in which the dramatic action progresses is through a series of negotiations, exchanges and deals. This begins with the wishes granted to Miseria by Jesus, who despite his all-powerful status refuses to go back on their deal, even when Miseria traps Death, leading St Peter to complain about the fact that people have stopped dying whilst Death is trapped: '¡Ni una almita asoma las narices por estos pagos!' [Not a single soul has poked its head in here for days!] (*El Herrero*, Scene 15, p. 455). Miseria donates the money that he has amassed through winning at card games to the Governor and they make a deal as to how it will be used to benefit the local community, but the Governor does not keep his word and so is shown to be corrupt. These deals are structurally important to the dramatic core of the play but they also demonstrate the way in which all of the characters negotiate through these exchanges to seek to achieve their goals. The way in which Miseria and the Governor make deals and pacts displays a recognisable human quality of seeking to protect one's interests. At every stage there are gains and losses: it is Miseria's ability to make decisions based on an awareness of the power that he possesses and how to use it that enables him to release Death and then escape up the tree himself and protect and extend his life (whilst we must assume that this leads to the death of others now that Death is released). The humble blacksmith is able to use heavenly powers to his advantage and he does not choose to secure eternal life for himself, but rather to secure his existence in the world in which he enjoys living.

During the civic-military dictatorship in Uruguay, the government made pacts to preserve and maintain the status and control of the regime. Members of society were also constantly required to renegotiate their position to try to ensure their security and maintain some autonomy within the context of the regime; in all of these pacts there were gains and losses. Francesca Lessa identifies the enduring importance of 'negotiations, pacts, concern with stability and governability, and slow and conciliatory attitudes' after the dictatorship period throughout the process of transition and as Uruguay negotiated its route to Transitional Justice.[21] The pacts made in *El Herrero y la Muerte* can be seen to be representative of this moment in Uruguayan history, which could be one of the reasons why Rein and Curi chose to recreate the tale of the blacksmith at this time. The play brings to light different types of pacts, calls them into question and depicts a pact made by an everyday citizen as able to challenge those made by the Establishment.

In order to expand our understanding of the message conveyed by the play and its function, it is productive to reflect on it in dialogue with Vitez's idea of the theatre laboratory as a space where alternatives to accepted discourses and ways of behaving can be tested, tried and exposed. Vitez's idea enables us to specify the significance of Miseria's choices to wisely apply the small amount of power that he has as a way to disrupt the norm and bring about changes which benefit him. He uses his power to preserve his interests and his life; the repercussions of his actions are played out both in heaven and on earth as he disrupts the established order and hierarchies of authority. He acts against corruption, against greed and against death to preserve his humble life on his ranch and, in doing so, he exposes others as dishonest and manipulative. This message of resistance, resilience and hope is crystallised in the final scene of the play. Miseria releases Death from the tree but then quickly climbs up the tree himself. Death demands that he comes down and tries to reason with him by saying that it is uncomfortable and he has no reason to hang around infecting the earth. But Miseria responds: 'Mientras hay vida hay esperanza. Vos seguí haciendo daño por el mundo, que yo de aquí no me abajo' [Whilst there is life there is hope. You can get on with causing harm to the world but I'm not getting down from here] (*El Herrero*, Scene 19, p. 464). Miseria takes control and these small acts of defiance indicate the potential of the average man to reclaim some sense of control over his life and alter the expected course of action. Thus the play becomes a laboratory in which alternative narratives, actions and power structures are explored. The play is allegorical because the wishes granted are not replicable in one's everyday life; instead Miseria's honesty, steadfastness, astuteness and challenge to Death are replicable. The play can therefore inspire the audience to remain hopeful, even in the face of challenges, by reflecting on their agency and ability to bring about change.

El Herrero y la Muerte is a retelling which conjures up and adapts Latin American literary traditions and uses them to tell a story for the present, in this case, the context of the dictatorship. As Mirza identifies, in addition to the links established through the existing legend of the blacksmith, the play interacts with other situations of repression and inequality in Latin America and the world: 'el espectáculo es sobre todo una invitación a la irreverencia y a la libertad frente a todo sistema opresor' [the play is above all an invitation to act with irreverence and freedom in the face of any kind of oppressive system].[22] The dramatic text takes as a starting point a story that exists in other parts of Latin America and the playwrights rework it to create a version specifically for a Uruguayan audience. They ultimately use this to convey a message of resilience to encourage others to pose a challenge to established authority and this serves to communicate the idea that alternatives to repression could be brought about through small acts of defiance. The narrative is able to serve a function as a moral and folkloric tale in which there is a final explicit message to the audience. This prompts the audience to consider their own small acts of resistance in the face of oppression.

Analysis of the play, its retellings and adaptations helps us to understand how narratives can become mobile and connect with new audiences. This play adapts the legend of the blacksmith which exists throughout Latin America. However, it is important to recognise that the audience of the original might connect and identify with this in different ways: the folkloric form can seem both remote and familiar for audiences of the original. An audience in Uruguay might not make all the literary connections identified in this chapter and they may make new ones. This is especially true as the play continues to be performed for contemporary audiences in Uruguay and other parts of Latin America, meaning the play becomes more distanced from the context in which it was created. From the point of view of the translator, it is both valuable and productive to consider the idea that for audience members of the original play, the folkloric legend might cause distancing effects. I argue that this would not necessarily cause them to disconnect from the dramatic narrative, what is at stake in the play and the messages conveyed through the play. This is because the robust way in which the dramatic narrative is constructed, incorporating techniques identified in this analysis, enables the dilemmas, questions and challenges posed by the play to speak forcefully to the audience. One of the ways in which the audience are drawn into this situation is through the character of the narrator who involves them in and guides them through the action. The inclusion of a narrator character who tells part of the story demonstrates and provides insights into how this story is a legend which has passed down over time. The translated play becomes another retelling which serves to continue the tradition but is also another step removed from it. However, it is essential to recognise that the translated play can still provide an insight into aspects of the literary traditions from which the play emerged whilst also speaking into the new context and asserting relevance for a new audience. Whilst Sirkku Aaltonen points out that '[t]he aim of a translated theatre text is very seldom, or never entirely, to provide an introduction to the Other or to mediate the Foreign', therefore suggesting that greater emphasis is placed on the relationship to the new site of production, it is nevertheless important to remember that the translated text still *can* provide an insight into the culture from which it emerged.[23]

Sarah Maitland underlines the way in which translation plays an important role in alerting us to the fact 'that others exist and that they construct the world differently' and this poses a challenge to the idea that these other ways of worldmaking can simply be 'subsumed' into the world of the target audience.[24] Through the performance of the translated text, the audience are able to develop an awareness of the fact that there are different worlds, experiences and ways of worldmaking; this can enhance our understanding of others and ourselves. In establishing a relationship to the target culture, which will render aspects of the source text familiar to the target audience, the translated dramatic text can reveal and display aspects of the culture of the original. This book demonstrates that the translator can develop strategies throughout their translation practice in order to establish a dynamic relationship between original and target cultures which can indicate both familiar and remote cultural realities.

David Johnston proposes the idea of the 'blend' to suggest different types of engagement opened up through the performance that can allow for an insight into otherness at particular moments, whilst creating a play which speaks into the current situation. His comments below can be used to understand audience reactions to the folkloric in both the original and the target contexts (after translation). The way that Johnston specifies what the blend means in practice for the audience supports the idea that the dramatic text in translation can retain references to the original culture and historical context, which indicate how the text has travelled from a different time and space, whilst still speaking with relevance and force into the target context:

> the more intensely the spectator experiences the play in the *blend*, the more he or she engages with the lived world of the play itself. The spectator exists most forcefully within the blend, is drawn back into it, when it is enriched through the importing of perceptions, for example, from the interplay between reality and fiction (when we stand back to admire aspects of the performance) or, in this case, between a sense of being in the presence of a voice that speaks compellingly from elsewhere or elsewhen, and the awareness that the cultural work of that voice is still alive, that it still involves us today.[25]

By focussing on different types of spectator engagement in this way, Johnston signals how the translated play does not merely have to be a reflection of the audience. The translation into English does not eliminate or close down the possibility of seeing something other than oneself or only the universal aspects of the text. He demonstrates how the performance of the translated text can include a sense of multiplicity, which can speak about familiar and remote cultural contexts whilst also allowing for multiple types of audience engagement with the play. I propose that the idea of the blend enables translators to conceptualise the different ways in which an audience might experience a play and how this experience can change and vary throughout the course of one given play as the audience move between stepping back and feeling deeply involved. The idea of the blend creates a useful framework in which to think about how references to the original situation and political context do not necessarily have to be removed or explained because, whilst one aspect of the play may cause a distancing effect, this does not mean that the audience will disconnect from it completely, especially as another aspect of the play may draw the audience in. It is also through this process of being drawn in, involved and implicated that the audience gain an insight into the potency of the crisis and the challenges affecting the characters, and how these are linked to the political situation. By conceptualising a bold blend, the translator can move away from ideas of foreignising and domesticating which are often posited as opposite extremes. Instead, they can think of the play as multiple and embrace multiplicity as a way to creatively explore the different possibilities of the original dramatic text through translation.

The translation into English of *El Herrero y la Muerte* for a contemporary UK audience would need to take into account and convey the interplay between the folkloric aspects, which communicate the history of the legend of the blacksmith, the more universal messages, and the culturally specific references. In order to do this, one strategy for the translation process would be to develop an oral style of language, like that present in the original, to maintain the texture of the story as one that has been passed from one person to another, and from one country to another (within Latin America and, through the translation, to the UK) through different voices at different moments in time. The opening scene, which takes place on the ranch and highlights aspects of Miseria's life and work there, would serve to help the audience in the UK to locate the play in Uruguay. Then, as Miseria enters into the negotiations and pacts with those around him, the translation process can open up the possibility to show the relevance and urgency of these types of negotiations for the political situation of the UK today. Through developing the language of the character of Miseria for performance in the UK so that the key messages identified in this analysis are communicated to the audience as calls to action, which suggest alternatives to established discourses, the play can function as a laboratory in which new ideas are trialled in ways that can have an impact in the target context of the UK.

Whenever a play is translated, it undergoes a process of interpretation and transformation as it moves into the target language. Often in theatre translation, a discussion surfaces about how a play can be inserted into the target culture and this sparks questions about whether this leads to a disconnection from the culture of the original. I propose that the translator adopts an approach whereby they think creatively about inserting themselves into an existing literary and dramatic tradition. In this way, they become part of that tradition but they also shape it for a new audience and think creatively about how it can be recreated for them. In order to be able to insert themselves into the text in this way, translators draw on the type of scholarly and dramaturgical researches illustrated in this book. This approach is particularly relevant for the folkloric form in which an emphasis is placed on the links to literary heritage as well as the passing on of the narrative and message. By thinking about how, as translators, we retell the story for a new audience by becoming part of the text, we can move away from ideas of cultural appropriation and instead place emphasis on the translation as an extension of the original in an 'ever-renewed latest and most abundant' afterlife.[26] To conceptualise this process, I refer to Aaltonen's ideas about the tenancy of translators and creative teams:

> Translators, and through them entire theatrical systems or sub-systems, move into texts which have been found suitable for a particular purpose. These texts have had other tenants, who have left in them sediments of their histories, and there will be new tenants who continue to do so.[27]

The process of occupying a text described by Aaltonen underlines the way in which the theatre translator moves into the text as they study, research and ask questions of the text in order to begin the process of crafting the translation for the target culture. The focus of the translator is to construct the text for the target culture so the actors and directors can then begin to occupy it to develop it for performance. However, as the text moves into the target context, the idea of the remainder, of the traces left behind by previous occupants, is useful in conceptualising the way in which aspects of the source culture and context can continue to exist in the new dramatic text. Aaltonen's comments are also important because they remind us that the translation process is the first step of the process to creating the mise-en-scène and the translator is part of the creative team who will enable the staging of the new dramatic text.

Punto y coma: Staging and Translating Transitions

The idea of sediment, a residue or remainder left over from those who have previously occupied the text, is particularly powerful and relevant when analysing and translating the play *Punto y coma*. This play deals with the topic of memory both formally and thematically whilst also portraying the impact of the political on the personal. Playwright Estela Golovchenko depicts the experience of a family during the civic-military dictatorship and its aftermath. A series of flashbacks presents snapshots of the Daughter's experience as a young girl in hiding with her mother. The character list indicates that the same actor plays the Daughter in the scenes set in the present and the flashbacks; this has informed my analysis of the transitions because the character and actor move between two times and spaces.[28] The dramatic narrative alternates scene-by-scene between the flashbacks in the past and the present in the Senator's (her father's) office. This means that the flashbacks interrupt the narrative of the present-day meeting and demonstrate how the young woman's present and past realities are interlinked. The flashbacks also serve as a dramatic device to demonstrate the disruption suffered by the young woman. This is because her family was distorted by the dictatorship through the estrangement from her father and the disappearance of her mother, leaving the young woman as an abandoned child to live with her grandmother. Despite the fact that they emphasise disruption by revealing the effects of the dictatorships in Uruguay and Argentina across generations and altering the narrative of the encounter in the Senator's office, the flashbacks are integrated into the dramatic narrative of the play and are an essential aspect of the dramatic core. They also shed light on the context in which the estrangement between Father and Daughter occurred and this dramatic technique, through which the details are gradually revealed, serves to heighten the significance of and tension surrounding the reunion between Father and Daughter. I will demonstrate how an analysis of the significance of the flashbacks and the ways in which they are integrated into the dramatic narrative informed and enhanced my translation process. The play demonstrates the ongoing impact of the past on the present and in doing so, raises questions about the process of transitioning to democracy in Uruguay. Golovchenko portrays a difficult and complex reunion in order to problematise ideas about individual, societal and institutionalised forms of remembering and forgetting. Ultimately the audience are left to make the decision as to whether the meeting between Father and Daughter in the Senator's office is a moment of reconciliation or not.

Punto y coma was written by Golovchenko in 2003. It was performed at Teatro Sin Fogón in Fray Bentos in 2004 and directed by Roberto Buschiazzo. In 2003 the play was awarded first prize in the Segundo Concurso de Obras de Teatro de la Comisión del Fondo Nacional de Teatro (COFONTE).[29] The Teatro Sin Fogón company is the only one to date to have performed the play and is referred to as a 'grupo referente del movimiento teatral del interior' [a significant group from the movement of theatres in the interior].[30] *Punto y coma* instantly sparked my curiosity because, despite the seriousness of the topic, there is a playfulness at the heart of the play, both structurally and thematically. I'll return to the theme of play shortly but I want to underline the fact that a key reason for including Golovchenko's work in this study, in terms of its scope as an investigation into theatre in Uruguay, was because she is one of a small number of Uruguayan playwrights (and one of just two female playwrights) not based in Montevideo.[31] Golovchenko's plays have been performed in the capital, most notably, *Vacas gordas* was performed at El Galpón (2004).

I first met Golovchenko at the 2013 Festival Internacional de Artes Escénicas de Uruguay in Montevideo where the Teatro Sin Fogón company were presenting Federico García Lorca's *Bodas de Sangre*. During our second meeting in Uruguay, which took place in Fray Bentos, Golovchenko read a paper to me entitled *Teatro Interior* [Interior Theatre] that she had presented at the Coloquio de Teatro. In it she calls for more exchange between theatre companies located inside and outside Montevideo so that they can learn from one another and collaborate, which would also lead to greater recognition of theatre from the interior in competitions administered by organisations in Montevideo.[32] The prizes that she has been awarded, both for her writing and for her theatre company, indicate that this is changing, as does the increasing profile of the Bienal de Teatros del interior, as well as increased attention to *Teatro del interior* from research groups at the Universidad de la República.

Punto y coma demonstrates how the military repression disrupted the national narrative of a country which had previously been democratic and liberal, as well as the personal narratives of families who were forced to separate, go into hiding or whose members disappeared. The play also provokes questions about how memories are constructed and transmitted from one generation to the next and what role an active choice to forget might have to play in dealing with experiences of repression. Susana Kaiser, in her study of how young Argentineans of the post-dictatorship generation remember the period, points out that, 'since we cannot remember everything, memory is highly selective' and an individual's memory is influenced by 'mechanisms of historical memory and amnesia' shaped by the state, official reports, historians, the media, community groups and local oral narratives.[33] An individual decides how and what to remember within a complex framework of influences, pressures, political discourses and family histories. And, as Ana Elena Puga points out: 'Both dictatorships and dissidents engage in competing ceremonies and practices that build and rebuild memory.'[34] The idea of an active construction of memory is evidenced through the Daughter's questioning of her father and her accusation that he has sought to erase their family history through not acknowledging it or her: 'Nunca me molestaste, todo bien. Pero que borres la historia, nuestra historia, vos que fuiste protagonista, eso sí que no lo puedo entender' [You never bothered me. Fine. But for you to erase history, our history, you who were the protagonist. That I can't understand] (*Punto*, p. 14). This is a criticism of his active choice about what to remember and how to do it, which is in conflict with her own active choice and desire to keep the memory of her mother, and the injustice she suffered, alive. It is also important to recognise that as well as representing forms of memory by depicting flashbacks on stage, the play itself becomes a creative tool to activate and challenge the audience's own processes of memory construction amongst all of the pressures detailed above. Therefore, as an artistic and cultural product, it also plays a role in questioning, critiquing and provoking the creation of memories.

A key aspect of the Daughter's time in hiding with her mother is that the Mother frames their experience as a game of hide-and-seek. The Mother uses this as a way to explain why the Father is hiding, why they cannot hide with him (because they would be more obvious in a group) and why she herself must leave at the end of the play. This enables the Daughter to understand the experience and her role in it because she relates it to the game played at school:

> LA HIJA Igual que Santiago. Se vino a esconder conmigo atrás del árbol y nos descubrieron a los dos. Se hubiera quedado donde estaba. Lo descubrían a él solo y yo después lo libraba. (LA MADRE SONRÍE)
> LA MADRE ¿Quién es Santiago?
> LA HIJA (EN SECRETO) Santiago es mi novio.

> [DAUGHTER Just like Santiago. He came to hide with me behind the tree and they found us both. He should have stayed where he was. They would have only found him and then I would have freed him. (*MOTHER smiles.*)
> MOTHER Who's Santiago?
> DAUGHTER (*Secretly*) Santiago is my boyfriend.]

This is one of the games that links the Daughter to Santiago; her childhood companion is now her father's assistant. This connection serves as a strategy to reinforce the link between past and present. It also calls into question the topic of memory because Santiago also seems to have forgotten his past (and her), whilst simultaneously demonstrating the multiplicity of experiences and memories arising from the dictatorship period. In the final scene of the play, the game of hide-and-seek becomes prominent and poignant: the Daughter counts as her mother hides, although the stage directions specify that the Mother disappears (*Punto*, p. 31). The Mother explains that the Daughter should not search for her but that she will always accompany her. After the Daughter has finished counting, she calls out: 'Punto y raya, el que se escondió se calla; punto y coma, el que no se escondió se embroma' (*Punto*, p. 31), which warns those who have successfully hidden to keep quiet and those who haven't that they are in trouble because she is looking for them. In British English, the phrase 'ready or not, here I come' would be used in this situation. Part of this phrase is used in the title for the play, *Punto y coma*, and it is for this reason that I have chosen to translate the title as *Ready or Not*. 'Punto y coma' also means semicolon and this suggests a link between two ideas, a relationship between two clauses and a hesitation in the continuation of the idea. This is indicative of the link between past and present in the play. However, I chose *Ready or Not* because of the significance of the hide-and-seek game to the Daughter's understanding of the separation from her family. This title also emphasises the significance of childhood and play in *Punto y coma* and how this affects the language employed. I also decided that, as a title for the play, it has a greater potential to spark an audience's interest. Whilst the duality of 'punto y coma' is lost in the English 'ready or not', the connection between the past and present is evidenced in other aspects of the dramatic text, and in the next section I will demonstrate how I worked to develop the transitions between the flashbacks and the scenes in the present day.

Through replaying scenes from the Daughter's past, the playwright is able to present a developed character whose present is infused with her past. At times, this strong connection to the past creates what Golovchenko alluded to as the Daughter's childlike approach when she encounters her father in his office.[35] This is presented primarily through her expectations because the Daughter has fixed her father's identity in her mind as the image of the man who she adored but who selfishly abandoned his family. An important aspect of the translation process of this play was to create a language for the target context to encapsulate the childlike attitude without reducing the discussion to complete child speak. This is an essential aspect of the texture of the language employed by the playwright. It is the Daughter's essential connection to her past and her ability to vividly re-live and voice aspects of this past that allow her comments surrounding memory to emerge with such force in the present situation of the Senator's office. The childlike attitude infuses her reasoning and utterances whilst allowing her to raise important questions about the characters' relationship with the past. A key way in which this is demonstrated is in the transitions between scenes because Golovchenko crafts a dialogue which spans across the flashbacks and the Senator's office. This means that transitions between scenes in the past and present are mediated through the dialogue, usually by the repetition of a question or idea. This technique weaves the two narrative strands together and serves to sustain the continuity of the dramatic action, despite the fact that the expected narrative order is disrupted. For example, at the end of Scene 4 the Father asks his daughter if she wished him dead and her response is: 'Si supieras cuántas veces lo deseé' [You don't know how many times I wished you were] (*Punto*, p. 15). The next scene, which is a flashback which takes place in the refuge, begins with her as a child asking her mother if her father is dead.

The transitions, which are facilitated through the dialogue, are a fundamental aspect of the experience of the character of the Daughter as she moves between the two times and spaces. Identifying the links and the overlaps in the conversations was an essential part of the dramaturgical analysis and these shifts are an important formal aspect of the play. An awareness of these connections informed my choice of the language so as to ensure that the link was maintained and the sense of the play as a dialogue with the past remained. By creating and sustaining the dialogue across the two time periods present in the original, the translated play offers creative options to the actors. Whilst the scenes are clearly defined, the continuity of the dialogue means that there are a range of choices open to the actors because the end of a scene does not rupture or end each exchange. These choices made by actors and the director were illustrated in rehearsals for the dramatised reading of *Ready or Not* (2017) directed by Chilean theatre practitioner and scholar, Camila Ymay González. On stage, the hiding place, located in the past where the flashbacks occurred, was located upstage whilst the present-day encounter took place downstage to create two distinct and constant spaces without imposing a divide. During the rehearsal process, the creative team worked on how the Daughter would deal with the moments of transition and where she would be located when speaking the lines at the end of one scene which formed a link to the next. Sometimes the director played creatively with this by having the actor say the first line of a scene set in the present day whilst she was still in the hiding place, and then the Daughter would move into the Senator's office. In this way, the traces of the Daughter's discussion with her mother then echoed throughout her discussion with the Father in the present day.[36] These links in the dialogue show how the Daughter's memories form an integral part of her way of reasoning and understanding in the current situation.

The use of flashbacks as a dramatic technique demonstrates the significance of family narratives within the context of a national crisis. As the Daughter moves between the present and the past, the dramatic narrative creates a strong sense of the Daughter as the protagonist of the flashbacks which provide an insight into her experience. In this way, they can help to explain some of the contextual details that the audience of the translated play might need to understand the dramatic action. The Father is largely absent from the flashbacks because he left to go into hiding (he appears in two flashback scenes). Therefore, as well as filling in certain gaps in the narrative, the use of the flashbacks simultaneously generates a sense of incompleteness, of gaps in the narrative, and they function to spark questions about the dangers of one-sided narratives. Many of these ideas are also present in the discussions between the Father and Daughter which create a link between the thematic and the structural elements of the dramatic core of the play. Throughout the dramaturgical analysis, I was aware that these flashbacks do not provide all of the answers or fill in all of the gaps in the narrative. They serve to spark questions, particularly about the Father's experience, relationships across generations, and the way in which this family's experience relates to the national context.

The national context in which the play was written was the aftermath of the civic-military dictatorship. Following the end of the military rule, what was at stake in the Uruguay was how to navigate the transition to democracy. The end of the dictatorship and the transition to democracy was agreed following a long period of negotiations and discussions between political leaders, which were overseen by the military at all stages, and which culminated in the Pacto del Club Naval in 1984, with elections scheduled for November that year. During these negotiations and in the democratic period that immediately followed, the military held 'residual power'.[37] The elected centre-right Colorado president, Julio María Sanguinetti, sought to create a peaceful transition ('cambio en paz') which looked to a democratic future, rather than allowing for a reappraisal of the recent past.[38]

The efforts by the government to create a peaceful transition were solidified by two amnesty laws introduced soon after the return to democracy. The first (law 15737, introduced on 8 March 1985) related to the release of the majority of political prisoners (some others had sentences adjusted and reduced).[39] This was significant because the dictatorship enforced many long prison sentences, and often prolonged solitary confinement. A significant consequence of this law and the efforts to create a smooth transition to democracy was that people had to work very quickly to reintegrate and find a new place in society, both politically and professionally, and for many the transition was problematic; this is explored in the play particularly through the character of the Father who refers to some of the difficult decisions that he had to make. The following year, in response to the fact that a growing number of accusations of human rights violations committed by the military were presented to the courts, the Ley de Caducidad de la Pretensión Punitiva del Estado [Law of Expiration of Punitive Claims of the State] was introduced on 22 December 1986. This law effectively granted amnesty for human rights violations committed by the military during the dictatorship and prohibited investigations into these crimes. As a result, the scope for accountability for human rights violations, particularly relating to disappeared people, was extremely limited. This was the case both in formal judicial settings and in less formal ways in civil society discussions. Therefore, a consequence of the Ley de Caducidad was that it imposed silence surrounding cases of torture and imprisonment. It is sometimes referred to as 'Ley del Impunidad' because '[a]rticles one to four particularly ended the possibility of judicial proceedings for past human rights violations'.[40] This prevented the public and legal examination and criminalisation of aspects of the recent past (there were two failed referendums to revoke it, in 1989 and 2009; the second one took place after this play was written). In *Punto y coma*, there are two references to an upcoming vote on a new law; one at the beginning and a second at the end of the play (p. 3, p. 30). These can be seen to allude to the Ley de Caducidad but the Father never explicitly states how he will vote and so it is left to the audience to decide if the conversation with his daughter and, through her, a reconnection to the past might have an influence upon his decision.

Golovchenko explained that *Punto y coma* was inspired by the story of a woman who was forced to flee Uruguay during the dictatorship, leaving her two children behind. They were reunited four years later in Spain and Golovchenko imagined this moment of reunion as the starting point for the play. This initial story then took on other shades to do with the return to democracy 'cuando mucha gente [que] estuvo en la resistencia pasa a ser oficialista y hay ahí como una contradicción' [when many people who were part of the resistance movement became part of the Establishment and there is a sort of contradiction in that].[41] She linked this specifically to the leader of the left-wing Frente Amplio government at the time, José Mujica (President of Uruguay 2010–15), who was previously one of the leaders of the left-wing guerrilla group Movimiento de Liberación Nacional — Tupamaros and was imprisoned during the civic-military dictatorship (when the Frente Amplio was also rendered illegal). She was intrigued by the idea that someone might suddenly find themselves in a role that they would never have imagined taking up and this involves rethinking their stance.[42] In this way, a link can be established to the series of negotiations that came to light in the analysis of *El Herrero y la Muerte*, because what Golovchenko is alluding to is the way in which members of society who had opposed and had been victims of violence committed during the dictatorship had to attempt to negotiate this transition in order to reformulate their ideas and find their role in this new, unanticipated political context. They also had to negotiate within new power structures to find ways of operating to achieve and protect their interests. In many cases, this was facilitated through a type of 'collective amnesia' in which members of society were expected to act as if relatively little had changed during the dictatorship.[43] This then enabled people to occupy roles within the new democracy. However, Mujica's presidency did open up ways for the past to be discussed and explored in ways that challenged institutionalised practices of forgetting.

The end of the twentieth and start of the twenty-first centuries saw increased demands from civil society for the prosecution of crimes committed during this period and proper investigation into the cases of disappeared persons. Tabaré Vázquez (2005–10 and 2015–20) was the first president from the Frente Amplio centre-left coalition party. He enabled some investigations into human rights violations to occur and, primarily through reinterpreting aspects of the existing law, paved the way for people being brought to trial:

> The unprecedented stand on accountability adopted by left-wing presidents Vázquez and Mujica signaled a rupture with past governments' lack of interest in — if not a blatant obstruction of — accountability; the sustained activism of human rights groups who strategically tackled impunity from different angles, combined with international pressures regarding the Gelman case and the unprecedented discovery of the human remains of Uruguayans who had disappeared, forced the government to provide long-awaited answers regarding past crimes.[44]

Therefore, written in 2003, Golovchenko's play can be seen against a backdrop of changing attitudes towards memory and accountability. These are key themes in the play which uses the dramatic space to open up a dialogue on these issues across generations with differing experiences of the dictatorship. In doing this, the play poses a challenge to state discourses and societal practices of 'collective amnesia' but also questions how individuals construct, preserve and transmit memories.[45] In opening up a dialogue between a father and daughter who seem to hold opposing views on what should be remembered, Golovchenko underlines the need for greater dialogue and understanding between the state and members of society. Golovchenko's play is crafted in such a way as to reveal the different layers and the complex nature of reconciliation. The play depicts reconciliation with family, with the past and with a political situation that people must confront and decide how to respond to, both as individuals and as a society. In *Punto y coma* accountability is central to the play, both at a personal and political level, and these two aspects are shown to be intertwined. The young woman seeks explanations as to how her father could abandon his political beliefs and, in doing so, undermine the integrity of the family, particularly in relation to the disappearance of the mother, and then go on to take up a role in parliament.

Accountability is evident in the discussions between the Father and Daughter which reveal that they have both spent time searching for answers, for explanations and for justifications for their own and others' behaviours. Alongside the need for explanations, the tense reunion of the Father and Daughter demonstrates the need for accounts so that there are not gaps in history. The fact that he has become '[u]n político de cuarta que vota en contra de los intereses por los que una vez arriesgó el pellejo' [a second-rate politician who votes against the very things that he once risked his life for] (*Punto*, p. 15) creates such a disconnection with the father that she knew that it is interpreted by his daughter as an act of betrayal. The lack of respect that the Daughter shows towards her father in her discussion with his assistant whilst she waits for their meeting demonstrates the bitterness that arises from a lack of contact with one's own personal history. This culminates with her describing her father as a corrupt traitor who must be living off dirty money (*Punto*, p. 8). In this way, the play depicts accountability as central to familial, personal narratives and to political, national discourses to show how the personal and political are intertwined. Scene 9 explores ideas around accountability when the Daughter poses the following questions:

> LA HIJA ¿Por qué cambiaste tanto?
> EL PADRE No encontré otra manera de sobrevivir.
> ...
> LA HIJA (AL PADRE) ¿Y vos cómo llegaste a este sillón?
> EL PADRE Me fueron a buscar a mi casa. A esa altura yo ya me había peleado con todo el mundo. No lo pensé mucho. Necesitaba creer en otra cosa. (*Punto*, p. 22)

> [DAUGHTER Why did you change so much?
> FATHER It's the only way I found to survive.
> ...

DAUGHTER (To the FATHER) And how did you end up in that seat?
FATHER They came for me at home. By that stage I had fought with everyone in the world. I didn't give it much thought. I needed to believe in something else.]

This alludes to the threat to his life but also emphasises the need to justify one's choices and actions. As they interrogate one another (and I use interrogate here aware of the connotations with police investigations, which the play sometimes evokes) in order to seek clues to explain the choices of the other and to piece together what has occurred during the period of absence, questions are continually provoked about how a person behaves, how they justify their behaviour and what role accountability has to play. The Daughter says that she admires the way in which her father resolved everything by cutting all ties whilst he says that he admires her passion to go on fighting and her thirst for justice (*Punto*, p. 23). Golovchenko brings to light opposing possibilities for dealing with the memory of the loss of a loved one and managing the moment of transition. Through the discussions in the play, Golovchenko highlights contrasting strategies for dealing with this experience and the incompleteness that they have caused for both Father and Daughter. The emphasis on incompleteness and accountability calls into question established discourses on these topics and the smooth transition to democracy in order to underline the need for a greater understanding of the past.

For *Punto y coma* and the period of national history to which it relates, the idea that sediment remains from the period of military repression and that it continues to affect the present-day experiences of both the Daughter and the Father is pertinent. The memory is not one which can easily be washed away and comes to the forefront in their dreams and in their intimate moments because there is not a space in society to explore it. The tension of the political transition, the burden of memories and a sense of urgency and a displacement within the new democratic structure infuse the play, and when allowed to infuse the translation can alert the audience to a situation elsewhere that has gone before. Through the translation, the play is able to provide insights into the complexity of the transition process on an individual and societal level in a way that allows the questions posed through the dramatic action to speak with impact into the target context of the UK. In the play, the details of the political conflict in Uruguay are not called into question; the kernel is how one might deal with the aftermath, particularly in a context where reconciliation and reintegration might be possible.

In *Punto y coma* in translation into English, the sediment of the history of the previous tenants remains a part of the play as it goes through the processes of translation. This can rise to the surface in a new context and in a new language as an indicator that the voices in the play tell a story that has been told before, in a different historical and cultural context. When the play is moved into English, there are indications of the fact that it has come from a different time and place: the specific references to disappearances, the use of a dramatic language in the flashbacks which conveys the constant threat from and fear of soldiers, and the shift between two spaces and times which reminds the audience that the Daughter was in hiding with her mother when key exchanges occurred. The references to the Mother's death as a disappearance evoke the methods of kidnap, torture and imprisonment employed during the Uruguayan civic-military dictatorship to repress subversives and so indicate the reality from which the text emerged. Therefore, the voices continue to speak of that time and place. At the same time, the relevance of the exchanges between the family members when dealing with fear and loss, the anxiety and anger which arises from the complex family reunion, and the destabilising experience of seeking to find a place and a new role in a society undergoing a moment of change are also able to speak of the here and now.

The tensions and issues surrounding the family reconciliation extend beyond the context of Uruguay and are relevant to audiences in the UK today. I was translating this play in 2016 and rehearsing in 2017; at that time, the play's representation of the generational clash over political ideologies, the impact of the memory of institutional structures and the changing shape of society evoked discourses which emerged in 2016 surrounding the referendum on the UK's membership of the European Union. The centrality of the family as part of the dramatic core in *Punto y coma* and the present-day struggle of the Father and Daughter to understand and reconcile their own family narrative in the context of a national one means that the dialogue created by Golovchenko is also able to speak about situations beyond the Uruguayan context. It is through the personal that the political can be depicted on stage and consequently provide an insight into the reality to which it refers to the audience in the UK. The target audience in the UK can gain an understanding of an unfamiliar political situation through the stories of individual characters to whose concerns they can relate.

Throughout the translation process I worked to create a dramatic language for the target audience which exposes them to and involves them in the shifts between past and present through developing the dialogue which links the scenes. Through the choice of lexis to render into English the accusatory tone of the Daughter when she meets her Father, I sought to render visible the anxiety caused by the absence of a dialogue about the past and the challenges that this poses for reconciliation. By analysing in detail the exchanges between characters, as demonstrated in this chapter, I worked to produce dialogue in English which creates a sense of immediacy in relation to the situation depicted on stage and enables the audience to engage with what is at stake for the characters.

The Out of the Wings Festival of play readings from Spain, Portugal and Latin America created an important space for the UK premiere of the play at the Cervantes Theatre in London and also opened up a space for informal discussions with audience members after the show. The response to the play was overwhelmingly positive and many audience members expressed empathy for the difficulty and complexity of the Daughter's situation, which was then compounded by the ending of the play where she is left alone. The sense of empathy coupled with the dramatic ending then challenges the audience to ask what they might have done in her situation or how they might have reacted. The language employed in *Ready or Not* was familiar to the audience and enabled them to gain a clear insight into and to connect with the complexity of a family situation marked by the political context in Uruguay.

The link between the personal and the political was evident and whilst aspects of the political situation may have been unfamiliar and unknown, the impact upon the personal family relationships was constantly clear and the way in which the tensions played out was recognisable.

Conclusion

Both plays studied in this chapter deal with aspects of the impact on society of the civic-military dictatorship in Uruguay, which was ongoing at the time of writing of *El Herrero y la Muerte* and the effects of which were still being felt when *Punto y coma* was written. Miseria in *El Herrero y la Muerte* and the Daughter in *Punto y coma* both develop a sense of self-awareness: for Miseria, his wishes grant him a small amount of power which he uses to disrupt established structures of authority whilst protecting and preserving his own life. In *Punto y coma*, the protagonist escapes the museum of her past and meets her father after years of estrangement. This meeting enables her to develop an awareness of the incompleteness of her methods of coping with the death of her mother, which have prevented her from moving on. Through the encounter between Father and Daughter, reconciliation with the past and with a person from the past is explored as a complex process. Each play begins by establishing a crisis to be explored and investigated; each one emphasises the connection between and the intensity of what is at stake on a personal and political level. Through translation, the theatre space becomes a laboratory which allows these crises to engage new audiences who get an opportunity to learn about them and to learn from them. This allows discussions in the plays surrounding national histories to enter into dialogue with concerns, ideas and discourses in the target context. Both *El Herrero y la Muerte* and *Punto y coma* serve to pose questions, to communicate messages that might challenge an accepted discourse and also to encourage the audience to continue posing questions and learning. Neither of the plays creates an ending in which the situation is fully resolved. In translation for an audience in the UK, sediment from the original which indicates the previous voices that have told the story or asked the questions can rise to the surface. This is achieved by maintaining aspects of the play which refer to the Uruguayan context to create echoes of previous stories in the target context.

I have shown that focussing on form can be a creative and critical tool for engaging with plays and underscoring how, as translators, we can retell stories for a new audience. For both of the plays analysed in this chapter, the idea that we inhabit the text in order to then retell the dramatic narrative and enliven the voices present in the original for a new audience can instigate translation strategies which enable the familiar and unfamiliar to exist in the translation. By referring to the translator as a tenant who occupies the dramatic text in order to recreate the stories and voices present in the original for a new audience, we are able to conceptualise the role of the translator as writer for the stage. At the same time, viewing the translator as a tenant provides a different perspective on the idea of moving the text towards or into the target culture. Whilst this movement into the target language and situation is part of the process of theatre translation, the idea of the translator and creative team as first moving into the dramatic text emphasises their role as part of a team of creators who revitalise the voices in the dramatic text and allow the sediment of those who have previously occupied it to rise to the surface at key moments. An awareness of the previous occupants can enable us to create a play which is a bold blend, alerting us to stories from 'elsewhere or elsewhen', involving us in those stories and demonstrating their relevance for the target audience.[46] An awareness of form, in this case the significance of the folkloric legend and the integration of flashbacks into the play, constantly informed my choice of language in rendering the text for the target audience. This enables the translated dramatic text to speak within and for the target context and the concerns that exist there whilst providing the audience with an insight into a time, place and space where those concerns have existed (and may continue to exist). Attention to form can help us to conceptualise how translators become part of the dramatic text and navigate the shifts between familiar and remote references in the text. I argue that references to the culture and situation of the original dramatic text do not need to be eliminated in order to allow for only the universal concerns to take precedence. The audience are able to engage with the text in multiple ways. Universal questions and concerns can be brought to light and simultaneously enter into dialogue with situations that have occurred in the past, and with present-day discourses in the target culture. In this way, we can create the sense of a dialogue which involves those who have gone before, whose voices are part of the translated dramatic text. Through translation, we bring the target audience into the conversation. Therefore, I propose that this process enables translators and audiences to engage productively and creatively in a dialogue across times and cultures.

Notes to Chapter 5

1. Mercedes Rein and Jorge Curi, *El Herrero y la Muerte*, in *50 años de teatro uruguayo: antología*, ed. by Laura Escalante, 2 vols (Montevideo: Ministerio de Educación y Cultura, 1988–90), II, 429–64. This edition will be referred to as *El Herrero* after quotations in the text. Estela Golovchenko, *Punto y coma*, 'Dramática Latinoamericana', *CELCIT*, (2003) <https://www.celcit.org.ar/publicaciones/biblioteca-teatral-dla/?q=golovchenko&f=&m=> [accessed 18 October 2020]. This edition will be referred to as *Punto* after quotations in the text. All translations are my own. Since completing my research on this play, and my translation into English, *Punto y coma* has been published in an anthology of work by Golovchenko: *Estela Golovchenko: teatro*, ed. by A. Rodríguez, intro. by Emilio Irigoyen (Montevideo: Editorial Fin de Siglo, 2021). Some of the analysis presented in this chapter will be published in Sophie Stevens, 'Representations of Transition, Memory and Crisis on Stage in *Punto y coma* [Ready or Not] by Uruguayan Dramatist Estela Golovchenko', in *Theatre, Performance and Commemoration: Staging Crisis, Memory and Nationhood*, ed. by Alinne Balduino P. Fernandes, Miriam Haughton and Pieter Verstraete (London: Bloomsbury, forthcoming).
2. Patrice Pavis, ed., 'The Duty to Translate: An Interview with Antoine Vitez', in *The Intercultural Performance Reader* (London: Routledge, 1996), pp. 121–30 (p. 127).
3. Ricardo Güiraldes, *Don Segundo Sombra*, ed. by Sara Parkinson de Saz, 13th edn (Madrid: Ediciones Cátedra, 2009), pp. 254–66.
4. The characters are referred to in this way in the play and are not given proper names so, when capitalised, Mother, Father and Daughter refer to the character names. Santiago is the only character given a name in the play.

5. They collaborated on: *Operación Masacre* (Teatro Circular, 1971) based on texts by Argentine reporter Rodolfo Walsh; *Los comediantes* based on Spanish Golden Age and Renaissance texts (Teatro Circular, 1977); *Del pobre B.B.* using texts from Bertolt Brecht (1984); *Entre gallos y mediasnoches* (El Galpón, 1987); *El Coronel no tiene quien le escriba*, an adaptation of the novel of the same name by Gabriel García Márquez (Teatro Circular, 1988). Information taken from: Roger Mirza, ed., *Teatro uruguayo contemporáneo: antología* (Madrid: Fondo de Cultura Económica; Centro de documentación teatral, 1992), p. 482 and *50 años*, ed. by Escalante, II, p. 432.
6. Roger Mirza, 'De la desacralización liberadora a la denuncia: I', *La Escena Latinoamericana*, 2 (1989), 52–56 (p. 52).
7. Rein and Curi, *El herrero y la Muerte*, in *50 años*, ed. by Escalante, II, 429–64. Rein and Curi, *El herrero y la Muerte*, in *Teatro uruguayo contemporáneo*, ed. by Mirza, pp. 483–534. Rein and Curi, *El herrero y la Muerte*, in *Teatro uruguayo contemporáneo: antología*, ed. and introd. by María Nélida Riccetto (Buenos Aires: Colihue, 1993), pp. 123–68.
8. Curi had, according to Rein, appeared as an actor in Gené's *El herrero y el diablo* many years before he directed their new adaptation of *El Herrero y la Muerte* in the Teatro Circular in 1981. *Teatro uruguayo*, ed. by Riccetto, p. 126.
9. Extract from the programme of the play cited in *50 años*, ed. by Escalante, II, 432.
10. Jorge Abbondanza, 'Una leyenda criolla', in *Teatro uruguayo contemporáneo*, ed. by Mirza, pp. 477–81 (pp. 478–79). Mirza, 'De la desacralización', p. 52.
11. Juan Carlos Gené, *Teatro* (Buenos Aires: Centro Editor de América Latina, 1983), p. 9.
12. Mercedes Rein and Jorge Curi, 'El Herrero y la Muerte: leyenda criolla de Mercedes Rein y Jorge Curi', *Escenario: Revista Teatro Circular de Montevideo*, Serie Autores Nacionales, 1 (July 1982), 1–43 (p. 1).
13. Roger Mirza, 'El Teatro Como Fiesta Popular', *La Semana de El Día*, 12 September 1981, p. 21.
14. Ibid.
15. Riccetto, p. 131, notes.
16. Mirza, 'De la desacralización', p. 55.
17. Riccetto, p. 131, notes.
18. Roger Mirza, 'El naturalismo y sus transgresiones', in *Teatro uruguayo contemporáneo*, ed. by Mirza, pp. 11–64 (pp. 52–53).
19. Linda Hutcheon with Siobhan O'Flynn, *A Theory of Adaptation*, 2nd edn (Oxford: Routledge, 2013), p. 22.
20. Ibid., p. 23. Note that a 'showing' form can also include film adaptations.
21. Francesca Lessa, *Memory and Transitional Justice in Argentina and Uruguay: Against Impunity* (New York: Palgrave Macmillan, 2013), p. 131.
22. Mirza, 'De la desacralización', p. 52.
23. Sirkku Aaltonen, *Time-Sharing on Stage: Drama Translation in Theatre and Society* (Clevedon: Multilingual Matters Ltd, 2000), p. 48.
24. Sarah Maitland, *What is Cultural Translation?* (London: Bloomsbury Academic, 2017), p. 4.
25. David Johnston, 'Professing Translation: The Acts-in-between', *Target*, 25.3 (2013), 365–84 <doi.org/10.1075/target.25.3.04joh> (p. 381).
26. Walter Benjamin, 'The Task of the Translator: An Introduction to the Translation of Baudelaire's *Tableaux Parisiens*', trans. by Harry Zohn, in *The Translation Studies Reader*, ed. by Lawrence Venuti, 2nd edn (New York: Routledge, 2004), pp. 75–85 (p. 77).
27. Aaltonen, p. 47.
28. The first reference to the Daughter in Scene 1 is to 'LA HIJA PEQUEÑA' [THE LITTLE GIRL]. This is the only time it appears and so I understand that it underscores the fact that she is a child in the flashbacks and the reference to this character as LA HIJA [DAUGHTER] throughout the rest of the play indicates that it is the same character played by the same actor.
29. Estela Golovchenko, *Punto y Coma, Dramaturgia Uruguaya*, (2003) <https://dramaturgiauruguaya.uy/punto-y-coma/> [accessed 17 October 2020].
30. Marcelino Duffau and Gabriela Gómez, eds, *Premio Autor Nacional COFONTE: Dramaturgia 2002–2005–2006* (Montevideo: COFONTE, 2011), p. 13.
31. *Las Hermanas de Shakespeare: perspectivas de género en el teatro* (Montevideo: Intendencia de

Montevideo, 2018), p. 32; available online at <https://montevideo.gub.uy/sites/default/files/biblioteca/publicacionsimposiolashermanasdeshakespeare_0.pdf>.
32. Estela Golovchenko, 'Teatro Interior', in *Dramaturgia interior: proceso de creación de cinco dramaturgos en red*, ed. by Mariana Percovich and Ariel Mastandrea (Montevideo: Ministerio de Educación y Cultura; Dirección Nacional de Cultura, 2009), pp. 17–23. The book also includes *La Murguita* by Golovchenko, pp. 65–77.
33. Susana Kaiser, *Postmemories of Terror* (New York: Palgrave Macmillan, 2005), p. 10.
34. Ana Elena Puga, *Memory, Allegory and Testimony in South American Theater: Upstaging Dictatorship* (New York: Routledge, 2008), p. 23.
35. Estela Golovchenko, Interview conducted in Spanish, Montevideo, 17 October 2013.
36. The dramatised reading took place as part of the Out of the Wings Festival 2017 at the Cervantes Theatre, London. Full details: 'Ready or Not', *Out of the Wings Festival*, (2017) <ootwfestival.com/ready-or-not/> [accessed 29 September 2020]. Cast: Mother: Kate Eaton; Father: Dermot Canavan; Daughter: Lucy Phelps; Santiago: Elliott Bornemann.
37. Lessa, p. 133.
38. Lessa, p. 134. The chapter in Lessa's book on 'Transitional Justice in Uruguay (1985–2012): Latecomer or Unique?' (pp. 131–61) tracks the introduction and impact of the Ley de Caducidad, the pressure from activists and civil society to repeal it, as well as changes in the international context as trials of military leaders began to take place in Argentina and in Europe. She also analyses and provides a detailed account of the ways in which the law was reinterpreted by the left-wing Frente Amplio Governments to enable some action and prosecutions to take place.
39. Lessa, p. 135.
40. Lessa, p. 137 referring to the Text of the Ley de Caducidad N.15.848.
41. Golovchenko, Interview.
42. Ibid.
43. Puga, p. 19.
44. Lessa, pp. 147–48.
45. Puga, p. 19.
46. Johnston, 'Professing Translation', p. 381.

CHAPTER 6

❖

Ready or Not by Estela Golovchenko

Information about the rehearsed reading can be found on p. 136.
Information about the cast is included in Chapter 5 (p. 158 n. 36).
For details of the original text in Spanish, see p. 156 n. 1.

Characters

MOTHER
FATHER
DAUGHTER
SANTIAGO

I.

In the refuge — an isolated place that is used only as a hiding place — a pale light delineates the space. The FATHER *is alone smoking a cigarette.*

FATHER (*To the* MOTHER *who enters the scene*) She's not awake yet?
MOTHER No. I'm going to wake her.
FATHER (*Stopping her*) Wait a bit, it's still early.
MOTHER You've got to go.
FATHER I know I do. What if we let her sleep and when she wakes up, you tell her...
MOTHER No. You have to say goodbye.
FATHER She knows I'm leaving. We talked about it last night.
MOTHER You promised her you were going to say goodbye. When she wakes up and finds you're not here, she'll blame me for not waking her up. You know what she's like.
FATHER (*Hugs her*) Like you.
MOTHER Like you as well.
FATHER She's beautiful.
MOTHER She's intelligent.
FATHER The best thing we've done. (*Pause*) You know, last night I was looking at her whilst she was sleeping and I thought, someone like her, with her character, how bright she is, she'll achieve what she sets out to do. Don't you think?

MOTHER She's very gifted. It's a shame her lot has been to live through such a difficult time.

FATHER It doesn't matter. She has all she needs inside. And the most important thing is that she's fearless.

MOTHER If only that were enough.

FATHER Do you know what she said to me last night?

MOTHER What?

FATHER That if I wanted, she would come with me.

MOTHER Did she say that? She's very close to you.

FATHER And I said to her: what about Mum? And she said that you'd understand. She knows I'm the weak one, that I'm nothing without you both.

MOTHER She must have sensed something, because I thought it too.

FATHER What?

MOTHER That she should go with you.

FATHER We can't take that risk.

MOTHER I don't know what's more risky. Sometimes I think it's best if we do the complete opposite of what we plan to do. They know how to put themselves in our shoes and they move quickly.

FATHER (*Gently*) Are you afraid?

MOTHER Of course I am. Just like you and everyone else.

FATHER You don't seem it. You're always so calm. You never lose it.

MOTHER That's a luxury we can't afford.

FATHER If it were my choice I wouldn't go. I don't want to leave you all alone.

MOTHER Or rather, you don't want to go alone.

FATHER No. (*Pause*)

MOTHER We already discussed it. We can't go with you. It's pointless to put all three of us at risk like that.

FATHER I won't rest until I hear from you.

MOTHER We'll work out how we can talk soon enough. We have to wait a bit, until you're settled and have things sorted.

FATHER If you two went...

MOTHER You're more committed; you can't stay.

FATHER I know.

MOTHER Nothing is going to happen to us.

FATHER I'm going to miss you both (*they embrace*).

MOTHER And we'll miss you.

FATHER I love you.

MOTHER Me too. Take care of yourself.

FATHER Take care of our daughter.

MOTHER With all my strength.

THE LITTLE GIRL (*Entering*) Daddy?

The DAUGHTER *appears at the back of the stage and she waits in the half-light. When they see her, her parents stop hugging and go towards her. But they don't reach her, they continue until they disappear into the darkness.*

2.

In the Senator's office in the Legislative Palace. The DAUGHTER *enters and is clearly wary. She carries a rucksack on her shoulder and her untidy appearance contrasts with* SANTIAGO*'s. When they both enter, the light gets brighter.*

SANTIAGO Your father isn't here at the moment but please come in. Take a seat.

DAUGHTER Will he be long?

SANTIAGO I don't know. Those meetings are awful. You can never tell when they'll end. But don't worry, I've let him know you're here.

DAUGHTER What is the meeting?

SANTIAGO It's with the Treasury. It's about the proposed new law. You know the latest?

DAUGHTER Yes, of course. And he's voting against, as always.

SANTIAGO Well, yes... Why would he go about complicating things at this stage?

DAUGHTER (*Ironically*) Of course, what would be the point in that... (*Awkward pause*) And who are you? The secretary?

SANTIAGO No. Lucía is the secretary. I'm more of an assistant.

DAUGHTER Ok. And have you worked with him for long?

SANTIAGO Since the Doctor has been in this seat. At the moment I'm working part time whilst I'm preparing for my next exam.

DAUGHTER You study Law?

SANTIAGO Yes. How did you know?

DAUGHTER Educated guess.

SANTIAGO How come?

DAUGHTER Well... it's from the way you look. How can you stand wearing a jacket and tie? Aren't you hot?

SANTIAGO No. I'm used to it. Besides, here you have to look the part.

DAUGHTER (*As if she doesn't understand*) What part's that?

SANTIAGO I mean you have to be well dressed.

DAUGHTER Ok.

SANTIAGO So, it's the first time you've come here...

DAUGHTER Yes. (*To herself*) And the last, I hope.

SANTIAGO It's strange that you never wanted to come, out of curiosity. Or did your father not invite you?

DAUGHTER To be honest, it's not because of either of those reasons.

SANTIAGO I'm never going to forget the first time I came here. Working here seemed like a dream. (*He sits in the Senator's chair and strokes it.*)

DAUGHTER Clearly you like the 'little seat' as well.

SANTIAGO And you don't?

DAUGHTER Are you mad? I'm against all politicians.

SANTIAGO You're against your father, then?

DAUGHTER Exactly!

SANTIAGO If you could see him working every day like I do.

DAUGHTER He earns a good little wage for it. And what about you, how did you get this job?

SANTIAGO Eh?

DAUGHTER Did you know him?

SANTIAGO Your father? Yes. He and my dad have been friends for years. He asked for a little job for me, 'to get me started', he said. Your dad's a good guy. He's always willing to do someone a favour. Well, around here everything is mutual, you see.

DAUGHTER (*Ironically*) I see. Do you have a cigarette?

SANTIAGO No. But if you want one, your father has some...

DAUGHTER No! Don't go and ask him.

SANTIAGO (*Taking a packet out of the desk*) Here you are. He always has several packets on the go. He opens one, leaves it somewhere and opens another.

DAUGHTER He must buy bulk loads.

SANTIAGO Actually, people give them to him. See? They're imported. (*He offers her a cigarette.*)

DAUGHTER (*To herself, taking one*) Oh right. They must be in exchange for the 'favours'.

SANTIAGO Keep the packet if you like. He won't even notice it's missing.

DAUGHTER (*Dropping the packet as if it were burning her*) No thanks.

SANTIAGO Do you need a light?

DAUGHTER No. I've got one. (*She takes out a lighter and lights it.*)

SANTIAGO Do you want something to drink? We have everything.

DAUGHTER Will he be long?

SANTIAGO I don't know. (*Opening the bar*) There's whisky... there's rum... cognac... tequila... if you like I can order you a coffee.

DAUGHTER Give me a whisky, why not...

SANTIAGO (*Taking out a bottle*) Don't worry. This is already in the budget. Your father told me to look after you. I'm in charge of receiving visitors. And given that most of them have to wait...

DAUGHTER You entertain them with your chat.

SANTIAGO Sometimes I don't even speak. It depends. I learnt that from your father, you know? In this job you have to have to understand psychology. (*Pouring*) Ice?

DAUGHTER No. Just as it is. Aren't you having a drink?

SANTIAGO I don't drink during work hours.

DAUGHTER Well, you're missing out. (*She drinks.*)

SANTIAGO (*Smiling*) Your father always says the same.

DAUGHTER Does he drink?

SANTIAGO (*Lowering his voice*) Quite a bit, lately. But more than that, he smokes. God, he smokes like a man on death row. (*Silence*)

DAUGHTER What's he like?

SANTIAGO Who? Your father?

DAUGHTER Yes.

SANTIAGO (*Surprised*) What? Don't you know him?

DAUGHTER I haven't seen him for a very long time. In person, I mean. I've seen him a few times on TV. But I haven't spent time with him for years.

SANTIAGO Really? I don't believe you...

DAUGHTER I swear. He never said anything to you?

SANTIAGO No. He told me that you were coming, that's all. And that I should look after you whilst he was getting out of his meeting. But the truth is, I never thought that...

DAUGHTER What's he like?

SANTIAGO He is... calm. He never raises his voice. He always listens carefully when you're speaking to him. He must be one of the few people who actually listen. Occasionally he asks my opinion on something or the other and it makes me, I don't know... but he takes it into account. And he has a good personality. He gets on well with everyone. People here respect him a lot. From all parties. And that's saying something.

DAUGHTER Did he ever mention me?

SANTIAGO Always. From my first day here.

DAUGHTER (*For a moment, she is surprised and flattered*) What did he say to you?

SANTIAGO That he had a daughter about my age. But he never said anything to make me think that you were estranged, well, that you didn't see each other. I thought that you were a family.

DAUGHTER He said that to you?

SANTIAGO What?

DAUGHTER That we were a family?

SANTIAGO Well, not exactly. But the way he talked... somehow made me think that. Or I imagined it, I don't know. (*Still unable to convince himself*) Oh, but this really is news to me...

DAUGHTER Is he old?

SANTIAGO He was always in good spirits. Although recently I think he's been very down. He stops by the window with his arms folded, his body more hunched than ever before and that look in his eyes... as if he wasn't looking at all, or more like, as if he was looking inwards.

DAUGHTER (*Sarcastic*) I don't think he can be looking inwards. He wouldn't be able to stand it. If he begged me to come here so much, then he must be feeling older than ever. They say that old people forget the recent past but their experiences from twenty years ago are more vivid than ever. They remember every little detail.

SANTIAGO Why did he call you? Sorry, if you don't mind me asking?

DAUGHTER No, no, it's fine. He said that it was about a legal matter and I don't know what else. At first, I told him to fuck off, but then he insisted, he said it was important, that there was cash involved and, you know what? I thought of my Nan. I've been living with her since... Well, Nan can't even stand to look at him, but now she's old and I agreed to come for her. Obviously she doesn't know anything about it. It wouldn't even enter her mind, poor Nan. But she hasn't got a thing in the world and so it would be no bad thing if a few quid came her way.

SANTIAGO Do you have siblings?

DAUGHTER No.

SANTIAGO Then you're the sole inheritor. You can't complain. I wish I had a father like yours.

DAUGHTER I don't know what your father is like, but if he is still with you then I can assure you that he's better than mine.

SANTIAGO I'm talking about his economic status.

DAUGHTER Is he loaded?

SANTIAGO The Senator?

DAUGHTER Yes.

SANTIAGO You could say that.

DAUGHTER Bastard!

SANTIAGO Why does it bother you that he's rich if you're going to inherit it all?

DAUGHTER Don't you worry, I'm not going to touch a penny from him. It's bound to be dirty money.

SANTIAGO Why do you say that?

DAUGHTER Because he's corrupt and he's a traitor, that's why.

SANTIAGO You're hard on him. If you knew him.

DAUGHTER I know him much better than you do. Did he ever speak to you about his past?

SANTIAGO No.

DAUGHTER I guessed not. You don't know anything about his history?

SANTIAGO No. But from what you're saying, you don't know anything about his present either, do you?

DAUGHTER The little that I do know is enough and what I don't know doesn't interest me. (*Pause*) So he never told you anything about his past. He completely forgot everything that he was. That makes me feel sick, you know. Your father didn't say anything to you either? If they are friends then he must know the whole story.

SANTIAGO No. I don't know... we never spoke about that.

DAUGHTER And you never asked?

SANTIAGO Me? What was I going to ask?

DAUGHTER Of course, what does it matter to you?

SANTIAGO Your father matters to me. He's an important man.

DAUGHTER Obviously you don't know him.

SANTIAGO Obviously you don't either.

DAUGHTER I know him well. That's why I chose not to see him all these years.

SANTIAGO And why did you come now?

3.

In the refuge. The MOTHER *and the* DAUGHTER, *as a little girl, play a simple game together.*

DAUGHTER I want to see him.

MOTHER Who?

DAUGHTER Daddy. Who else?

MOTHER He's fine, don't worry.

DAUGHTER Is he alone?

MOTHER He's with some of his friends.

DAUGHTER So he's happy?

MOTHER Of course. He has us.

DAUGHTER But we never see each other.

MOTHER It's not because he doesn't want to, but because he can't.

DAUGHTER But why can't he come here?

MOTHER Because he's hiding.

DAUGHTER (*Treating it like a game*) So, let's go and find him!

MOTHER We can't. We're hiding too.

DAUGHTER Who from?

MOTHER (*Lowering her voice*) From the people who are counting.

DAUGHTER (*Imitating her*) Let's go and hide with Daddy then.

MOTHER But if we go to hide with him, we'll give him away and no one is allowed to know where he is.

DAUGHTER Just like Santiago. He came to hide with me behind the tree and they found us both. He should have stayed where he was. They would have only found him and then I would have freed him. (*MOTHER smiles*)

MOTHER Who's Santiago?

DAUGHTER (*Secretly*) Santiago is my boyfriend.

MOTHER Oh, is he? Santiago... (*The DAUGHTER covers her mother's mouth.*)

DAUGHTER It's a secret. Don't tell Daddy, or Nana, or anyone. (*The MOTHER shakes her head.*) Promise me?

MOTHER (*Moving her daughter's fingers away from her mouth*) I promise. How long has he been your boyfriend?

DAUGHTER I don't know. He never said it. But I know that he's my boyfriend.

MOTHER How do you know?

DAUGHTER Because he always wants to play with me. (*Pause*) Is Daddy your boyfriend?

MOTHER Yes.

DAUGHTER Do you love him?

MOTHER Of course I do.

DAUGHTER Do you miss him?

MOTHER Every day.

DAUGHTER I can hardly remember Daddy.

MOTHER What do you mean you can hardly remember him? Let's see, what colour are his eyes?

DAUGHTER Green. (*Insert the colour of the actor's eyes.*)
MOTHER See, you do remember. What else?
DAUGHTER He has long hair and a beard. (*She wriggles*) And it tickles me when he kisses me. (*She laughs*) And do you know what we play?
MOTHER What?
DAUGHTER Taking a really big breath and farting with our mouths. Like this. (*She takes a breath to fill her cheeks and squeezes them to make the sound.*)
MOTHER How do you do that? (*They start playing at squeezing each other's cheeks. They laugh out loud. They calm themselves and there is a pause.*)
DAUGHTER Who's coming to get you?
MOTHER What?
DAUGHTER You said to Nan that they could come for you at any time.
MOTHER (*After a brief uncomfortable silence*) It's true. The soldiers could come for me.
DAUGHTER What for?
MOTHER To ask me some questions.
DAUGHTER And why would they have to take you away? They can ask you whatever they want, here, at home.
MOTHER It's not the same. They have to take me away.
DAUGHTER How long for?
MOTHER I don't know.
DAUGHTER And who will I be left with?
MOTHER Nana.
DAUGHTER And when will Daddy be back?
MOTHER When all this is over, he's going to come.
DAUGHTER Where will they take you?
MOTHER I don't know. I'd rather not know.
DAUGHTER But I would, so I can come visit you.
MOTHER It's best if you don't.
DAUGHTER How will we let Daddy know?
MOTHER He'll find out, don't worry.
DAUGHTER But you'll come back, won't you?
MOTHER Of course.
DAUGHTER Will you bring me a present?
MOTHER What would you like me to bring you?
DAUGHTER A doll! One that has eyes that open and close and real hair, like yours. (*She strokes her mother's hair.*)
MOTHER If Daddy can't come when I go, you'll stay with your Nana, ok. But don't be angry with Daddy if he doesn't come. It's not because he doesn't love you. He adores you, just like I do, but there are times when we can't be with you.
DAUGHTER Why?
MOTHER Because we have things to do.
DAUGHTER What things?
MOTHER Things...
DAUGHTER Bad things?

MOTHER Do you think that Daddy and I could really do something...
DAUGHTER (*Interrupting her*) Shhh... be quiet.
MOTHER What?
DAUGHTER Listen. I think I can hear him coming.
MOTHER Who?
DAUGHTER Daddy.

4.

The FATHER comes up to the office surreptitiously. Without being seen, he observes his daughter and he is evidently moved but holds back his emotions. Then he enters properly.

FATHER Hello.
DAUGHTER (*Without really looking at him*) Hello.
SANTIAGO (*Trying to break the ice*) At last, Doctor! We were running out of conversation.
FATHER I got held up a bit. I'm very sorry to have made you wait.
DAUGHTER It's fine.
SANTIAGO Don't worry. As you know, I am an expert at entertaining visitors.
FATHER (*To SANTIAGO, making a gesture for him to leave*) Can I ask you to...
SANTIAGO Of course, Doctor. Excuse me. (*He leaves.*)

(*Once SANTIAGO leaves the office, the awkwardness between FATHER and DAUGHTER is palpable. Both characters take the opportunity, when the other one is distracted, to examine the other closely, trying to identify in their features, gestures and words the ties which unite them. In this confrontation the FATHER never loses his characteristic serene air. His attitude is more one of submission. Deep down he wants his daughter to attack him, to destroy him, to free him from guilt.*)

DAUGHTER (*Ironically*) That young man will go far.
FATHER He's gifted.
DAUGHTER He's pretentious. You can tell he learnt from you.
FATHER You're being prejudiced.
DAUGHTER No, he showed his true colours. We had a nice long chat. I was surprised that he knew very little about our relationship, and stranger still, he knew nothing about your previous life.
FATHER You told him about it?
DAUGHTER No. It would take too long. Besides, I don't think he's interested. In any case, you should have told him.
FATHER I don't go around telling my life story to everyone.
DAUGHTER I never realised that silence could be such an anaesthetic. Obviously, I live in a different world to you. You close the door and you're on to the next thing. Now I understand why he's never going to ask you anything. He doesn't have principles, he doesn't have contact with the past. He won't even ask you

out of curiosity. Tell me, honestly, don't you ever want to tell him why you lost so many years of your life?

FATHER I don't want us to talk about the past. There are things that we cannot change, we both know that.

DAUGHTER Yes, you're right.

FATHER I know that this is a difficult situation so I'm grateful to you for coming.

DAUGHTER It's no problem. I'm an adult and I know how to respond when I'm needed.

FATHER I hadn't thought about it like that but the truth is that I do need you. After everything that's happened, you're all I have.

DAUGHTER I'm the one thing you don't have.

FATHER You're my daughter.

DAUGHTER Biologically. But I don't have a father. Or rather, the father I remember is nothing like the person who is standing in front of me now.

FATHER You don't know me.

DAUGHTER I'm the only one who knows what you're really like. I know your absence, your back, your silence. That's why it drives me mad when they speak so well of you. Nobody would ever imagine that behind your generous and kind appearance, there's a complete bastard.

FATHER You talk...

DAUGHTER The way I learnt to. You weren't there to teach me.

FATHER Someone full of bitterness and hate taught you.

DAUGHTER Hate grows of its own accord. It didn't need anyone to nurture it. Besides, that someone you mentioned saved my life. If it wasn't for Nan I wouldn't be here, that's for sure.

FATHER I know. I'll always be grateful to her for that. It's a shame she brainwashed you.

DAUGHTER And who brainwashed you? Because you didn't used to be like this, from what mum told me and the few things I remember.

FATHER I'm the same as always.

DAUGHTER If you were the same then you wouldn't be here, sitting in that seat that makes your bum and your brain go to sleep.

FATHER I had to do what I did. It was the only way for me to feel like I was alive again. There are no halfway points in this, you're either for or against. And I wasn't prepared to carry on losing.

DAUGHTER With people like you, we're going to lose forever.

FATHER At this stage in my life I can tell you that nothing is forever. You don't win or lose for eternity.

DAUGHTER To think that the last time you called me I created a whole argument to try to understand you, not to justify your actions, there's no justification for what you did. And you know what? In some ways I understood you. I said to myself: it's fine, he did his own thing, found a way to make a living. At the end of the day, he has the right to live as he pleases. You never bothered me. Fine. But for you to erase history, our history, you who were the protagonist.

That I can't understand. That's why you're nothing like my father, or at least nothing like the father I remember.

FATHER Let's not talk about me. I've had enough of my things.

DAUGHTER From what I can tell, things are going very well for you. Not at all like they are for me.

FATHER That's why I called you. I know that you and your grandmother are going through a difficult time and...

DAUGHTER Since I was born I've been going through a difficult time. And do you know who is responsible?

FATHER (*Raising his voice for the first time*) I am responsible! (*Pause*) We have to talk. We have to do it calmly. It's now or never.

DAUGHTER (*Getting ready to leave*) I don't think there's any point in me staying here a minute longer. It's a waste of time.

FATHER There's something I want to give you and I'd like you to accept it. Please, for the father I once was.

DAUGHTER The one I knew didn't have anything to give except love and what's more, he demanded social justice. And now what are you? A stranger. A second-rate politician who votes against the very things that he once risked his life for. I don't want anything from him.

FATHER Would you have preferred me dead?

DAUGHTER You don't know how many times I wished you were.

5.

In the refuge.

DAUGHTER Is Daddy dead?

MOTHER Where did you get that idea?

DAUGHTER Santiago at school told me that Daddy must be dead.

MOTHER Who told him that rubbish?

DAUGHTER His mum told him.

MOTHER It's a lie.

DAUGHTER And how do we know he's alive?

(*The* MOTHER *takes out a plain piece of paper and pretends to read an imaginary letter from the* FATHER.)

MOTHER Because he sent us a letter.

DAUGHTER (*Trying to take it*) Let me see...

MOTHER (*Holding it out of her reach*) Let me read it to you.

DAUGHTER I want to read it. (*Trying to grab it*)

MOTHER You won't be able to read his writing. You know what his writing's like when he's in a rush.

DAUGHTER What does it say?

MOTHER To my darling daughter...

DAUGHTER He didn't write it to you?

MOTHER Let me read. To my darling daughter and beloved wife...

DAUGHTER Beloved means more than darling, doesn't it?

MOTHER It's the same.

DAUGHTER No, it's not the same to say someone is your darling as it is to say they are your beloved.

MOTHER Ok, it's not the same but it means the same thing.

DAUGHTER (*To herself*) Well he must love you more than he loves me.

MOTHER Hold on: I read it incorrectly. It says: to my darling wife and my beloved daughter... (*The* DAUGHTER *smiles approvingly*)... I'm writing this letter to let you know that I'm fine. I need to be here for a little while longer but when I come back, I'll bring some presents with me. A doll with real hair and eyes that open and close...

DAUGHTER For me!

MOTHER For my (*emphasising the word*) beloved little girl, who I miss every day and can't wait to see very soon. (*She breaks off, moved.*)

DAUGHTER Doesn't he say anything else?

MOTHER No.

DAUGHTER He doesn't say where he is?

MOTHER No.

DAUGHTER Why?

MOTHER It's a secret. Just like the one you told me.

DAUGHTER Which one?

MOTHER (*Lowering her voice*) The one about Santiago.

DAUGHTER (*She covers her mother's mouth*) Shhh! Don't say anything. So Nana doesn't find out. Are we going to write to Daddy?

MOTHER Ok. (*She takes out a piece of paper and a pen. They both get ready to write.*) What are you going to write to him?

DAUGHTER (*Writing*) My darling Daddy,

MOTHER Only darling?

DAUGHTER (*Screwing up the sheet of paper*) Give me another one. I made a mistake.

MOTHER Oh, no. You'll take a long time if you carry on like that. (*She passes her another sheet.*) There you go.

DAUGHTER (*Writing again*) To my beloved Daddy, when are you coming back? Mummy and I are waiting for you...

Whilst the DAUGHTER *continues writing and speaking the words softly, the* MOTHER *speaks aloud, as if she were reading her own letter to the* FATHER.

MOTHER We miss you so much. Sometimes I wonder if all this is worth it. So much suffering, so much anxiety and nothing changes. Don't think I'm feeling defeated. I'm not. I still gladly fight for the cause. But at night, when our daughter holds my hand tightly and I hear her breathing, I think, how much longer? I want to wake up with you next to me, to stroke your beard, your smiling mouth. I want to walk outside without a care in the world, look at the sky and not worry about anything, breathe in the air. I want to live. When we decided to resist, we knew full well what could happen to us. Now that I'm living the reality of it every day in my own skin, your skin and especially in the skin of our daughter, which is what hurts the most, the feeling of helplessness overwhelms me and I feel like I'm going to faint. My only comfort is thinking that she will survive us, that she will make sure to tell the world what we fought for.

6.

In the office.

SANTIAGO (*Entering*) Excuse me, Doctor. Senator Ugalde would like to speak to you for a moment, he says it's just a quick question.

FATHER (*To the DAUGHTER*) I'll be back in moment. Please, wait for me. (*He leaves. The DAUGHTER gathers her things and prepares to leave.*)

SANTIAGO (*He blocks her way*) What happened?

DAUGHTER What could happen? It's pointless, I'm leaving.

SANTIAGO (*Stopping her*) Don't leave. Stay.

DAUGHTER It's not worth it. We don't get each other.

SANTIAGO Wait. You came all the way here, why don't you make an effort?

DAUGHTER (*Hiding tears*) What? More of an effort than I made all these years not to see him. And now...

SANTIAGO Now you're here. If only you knew how he waited all day for you.

DAUGHTER I've waited for him all my life.

SANTIAGO He needs you.

DAUGHTER Now is the time when I abandon him.

SANTIAGO Your father is ill. He's going to have an operation on Tuesday. I'm sorry for telling you like this but I've just found out myself. Mr Ugalde has just told me everything.

DAUGHTER Who is Mr Ugalde?

SANTIAGO He is the notary who drew up your father's will. He clearly wants to give it to you in person. Perhaps I shouldn't be the one to tell you but I'm sure that he won't let anything slip. Please, I'm asking you to make an effort and stay to wait for him.

DAUGHTER And I'm asking you not to meddle in what doesn't concern you.

SANTIAGO The Senator concerns me.

DAUGHTER Well he doesn't concern me. (*She tries to leave.*)

SANTIAGO Well if you won't stay for him, stay for yourself. Why don't you give yourself the chance to speak to him? You might not get another. (*The DAUGHTER stops. Silence.*)

DAUGHTER Is it serious?

SANTIAGO Lung cancer.

DAUGHTER Is he going to die?

7.

In the refuge. They speak in a low voice.

FATHER Don't be scared. Nothing is going to happen to me.

DAUGHTER So why don't you stay, then?

FATHER We already talked about that.

DAUGHTER I want to go with you...

FATHER No, darling, you can't. Besides, you can't leave Mum on her own, can you?

DAUGHTER Nana can stay with Mum.

FATHER It's not the same.

DAUGHTER Why?

FATHER Because you're her daughter and Nana is her mother. (*Pause*)

DAUGHTER Why?

FATHER (*Softly*) Why again? Why what?

DAUGHTER Why is it that when parents get divorced the kids always have to stay with their mums?

FATHER Mum and I aren't getting divorced.

DAUGHTER Ok, when they split up.

FATHER (*Getting impatient*) Listen to me, Mum and I are not splitting up in the way that you think we are. We love each other very much and we love you very much. We just need to split up for a while. It's for our safety, so that nothing happens to us. And especially so that nothing happens to you. But it's just for a short time, that's all, do you understand?

DAUGHTER No.

FATHER Well, it doesn't matter, one day you will understand.

DAUGHTER I don't think so.

FATHER (*Insisting*) We're going to move. I'm looking for a place for us to live and then you'll come and join me. That's all.

DAUGHTER Why didn't you tell me that first?

FATHER But you can't tell anyone at school because it's a secret, ok?

DAUGHTER A secret?

FATHER Or more like a surprise. One day, when no one suspects anything... shoom! We'll disappear from the neighbourhood as if by magic.

DAUGHTER And where will we reappear?

FATHER Somewhere new.

DAUGHTER Where?

FATHER Ah. That's another secret.

DAUGHTER And no one will know where we are?

FATHER No one.

DAUGHTER Not even Nan?

FATHER Not even her.

DAUGHTER But, why?

FATHER (*Firmly*) Because that's just the way it is. And from that day onwards we're never going to split up again.

DAUGHTER Promise me?

FATHER I promise you. And now go to bed because it's late. (*He kisses her. Then he goes towards the door.*)

DAUGHTER Daddy.

FATHER Yes?

DAUGHTER Will you read me a story? (*The FATHER looks at his watch.*)

FATHER Of course, darling. (*He leaves the part of the stage that is lit and returns with a book in his hand for the following scene.*)

8.

In either space. The MOTHER can be part of this scene.

FATHER When I found out that they had taken Mum I cursed myself thousands of times for not having been there with her, with both of you. It was just a few hours before we were due to meet in Buenos Aires, like we planned. Just a few hours. We never saw each other again. No one can understand how it feels. I did everything I could but it was useless. There came a point when I couldn't bear so much sadness. I never felt like a coward. I had to make lots of difficult decisions and many times I risked my own life. But the absence of your mother made me feel invisible. Do you know what it is to be invisible? We use that word a lot. We use it to insult, we use it to comfort ourselves, we use it for so many things that it has lost all meaning. To be invisible is to be a living corpse, it is someone who has been crushed to the point of exhaustion, who has lost their way. Your mother and I were a special couple. There aren't many couples like us, do you understand? I can't stop thinking that if we had met at another time, if what happened to us hadn't happened, we would have been a great family, fantastic parents. But we can't turn back time.

DAUGHTER Nan told me that they killed her but we never saw her dead. It's just the opposite; she was always around, in the house, making noise everywhere. But she never spoke to us. One day I did the Ouija board at home with some friends. I asked to speak to Mum and she appeared, said her name and nothing else. We asked if she could speak and she didn't reply. She was there the whole time, watching us play without saying a word. And in my dreams, she's always silent too. Nan says that when the dead don't speak in our dreams it's because we still haven't really let them die. That's what she says.

FATHER She never stopped following me. I still see her in the middle of a crowd of people in the street, on a bus or in a taxi that flashes by like lightening. When I go to bed I sense that she opens the door and seeps in like a beautiful angel with her long hair and dark, shining eyes. She draws close slowly and kisses me. I feel her breathing, the warmth of her lips and I know that I'm not dreaming. She leaves me signs everywhere, in all the corners of the house, on every street corner. Sometimes I sense she's so close I could hold her. But when I stretch out my arms she disappears again.

DAUGHTER I have all her things. Her clothes, her perfume, her photos cover the house. I have boxes, shoeboxes, drawers of keepsakes. I kept everything that you could possibly keep: newspaper cuttings, letters, censored books, postcards, bits of string, stones, beads, lip liner, brooches, records, everything. The house I live in is a museum to the memory of Mum.

FATHER I cut myself off completely. Even from you. I got rid of everything that belonged to your mother. Even my wedding ring. I distanced myself from everything that was a link to her. I rejected our friends, our comrades, the ideals we shared. I couldn't stand all those things that reminded me of her.

DAUGHTER Nan and I took it upon ourselves to look for her. We're still looking for her now. We won't stop until we know where she is.

FATHER I was scared of hating you with all my soul for reminding me of your mother. That's why I distanced myself. Guilt killed me. The same guilt that's killing me now I see you again.

9.

In the office. The FATHER *re-enters, slightly agitated. He fears that his daughter has left.*

FATHER (*To the* DAUGHTER) Are you leaving? (SANTIAGO *prepares to leave. To* SANTIAGO) You can stay if you want.

SANTIAGO No, I...

FATHER Stay, please. It's better for everyone. (*He takes out a cigarette.*)

SANTIAGO Are you going to smoke, Doctor?

FATHER Pour me a whisky. (*He lights the cigarette.*)

DAUGHTER (*Sitting down*) I'll have one as well.

(*The* DAUGHTER *takes another cigarette from the pack belonging to her* FATHER. SANTIAGO *pours whisky for both of them. He hesitates a moment and then pours himself one as well. Then he sits down. There is a moment of complete silence.* SANTIAGO *coughs.*)

FATHER (*To the* DAUGHTER, *gently*) You're just like your mum.

DAUGHTER Why did you change so much?

FATHER It's the only way I found to survive. And you?

DAUGHTER I found my way.

FATHER Good. Do you work?

DAUGHTER Yes, in the bakery.

FATHER And, are you happy there?

DAUGHTER Sort of. I didn't even finish secondary school. I couldn't stand the rules. And I never thought about doing a degree.

FATHER And what would you like to study?

DAUGHTER I don't know. I never thought about it. I had to go out to work so I didn't bother finding out what I'd like to do.

SANTIAGO It is hard to know what you really want to do. My dad always wanted me to be a lawyer but there are times when I think that...

DAUGHTER (*To the FATHER*) And how did you end up in that seat?

FATHER They came for me at home. By that stage I had fought with everyone in the world. I didn't give it much thought. I needed to believe in something else.

DAUGHTER And do you believe in this?

FATHER Of course I do. I'm not that much of a hypocrite.

DAUGHTER You even use hair gel.

SANTIAGO bursts out laughing.

DAUGHTER And what are you laughing at?

SANTIAGO I'm laughing because I was the one who told him to use hair gel, wasn't I, Doctor? (*To the DAUGHTER*) Does it look really bad?

DAUGHTER He looks like a ...

SANTIAGO A 'suit'...

DAUGHTER No, like a twat. (*All three laugh.*)

DAUGHTER (*To her FATHER*) Deep down I'm a bit jealous of you.

FATHER Jealous?

DAUGHTER Yes. Because of the way you worked everything out.

FATHER What?

DAUGHTER Cutting everything, everyone off. Whereas I look back and I see myself fighting with kids at school because of what they were saying about my parents. And then at secondary school, sitting on the floor in the head's office, tearing up my notebooks and holding back tears. Whenever a boy came up to me because he wanted to go out with me, I always asked him to tell me about his family tree. And poor guy, if he had any military in his family, I would just about strangle him! You know, even now I can't bear to see an officer. One day a soldier asked me for the time and I gave him such a piece of my mind that he just stood there staring at me. (*The FATHER laughs*) I swear, he didn't understand a thing, poor bloke. And he was a kid, younger than me, I think.

FATHER It was hard for me too. But forgetting is an exercise and after a while, you see the results. When we get past that hurdle, of forgetting, we're all the same. Like now. If for a moment we forget our feelings of resentment, we seem so close.

DAUGHTER We seem...

FATHER I envy you too. I envy your anger.

DAUGHTER I have an awful personality, don't I?

FATHER More than that. Anger makes you alert. That makes me admire you more than envy you. Do you have... a partner?

DAUGHTER No, I'm useless. I don't attract anything.

FATHER Me neither.

DAUGHTER I've never met anyone who understands me, who understands what I had to go through, who shares what I feel.

FATHER Whereas there are certain things that I don't want to share with anyone. I keep them to myself...

DAUGHTER I'm used to solitude now.

FATHER Me too.

SANTIAGO (*Who does not understand the meaning of the conversation*) I also really like being alone. Listening to music, reading...

FATHER (*Still looking at his daughter firmly in the eyes*) We're talking about something different. (*Silence*)

DAUGHTER Why did you make me come here?

FATHER I know that your grandmother is unwell, that she had to sell the house and so on.

DAUGHTER So you're aware of everything?

SANTIAGO There's always someone willing to pass on the gossip.

DAUGHTER And what gossip did you get about me?

FATHER (*Smiling*) I know that you're a good person. That's all that matters to me.

DAUGHTER I never let anyone tell me your news. But I always found out something or other.

SANTIAGO Of course, the Senator is a public figure.

DAUGHTER Everything that I did, I did it and thought what you'd say about it.

FATHER Really?

DAUGHTER Yes, but I always did the complete opposite.

FATHER I got, sometimes the two of you got mixed up in my mind. Your mother and you. I always depended on your mother for everything, even buying the smallest thing. So I thought: what would my daughter say if she saw me wearing this tie?

DAUGHTER That it looks awful on you. (*They laugh*) You used to dress differently, before. I remember your beard. When you came to give me a kiss every night before bed.

10.

In the refuge.

DAUGHTER Daddy was here last night.

MOTHER Where?

DAUGHTER Here, home. He came into my room, he talked to me for a while, he gave me a kiss... oh, and he read me a story.

MOTHER Are you sure? It couldn't have been a dream?

DAUGHTER No. I was awake.

MOTHER And he left?

DAUGHTER Yes. But before he went I told him a secret.

MOTHER Can you tell it to me?

DAUGHTER It's a secret about magic.

MOTHER Oh.

DAUGHTER I can do magic.

MOTHER Can you?

DAUGHTER That's how I made Daddy come here, by magic.
MOTHER Oh, is that it? How did you do it?
DAUGHTER I closed my eyes really tight until I could see little stars. Try it, you'll see. (*The* MOTHER *closes her eyes*) Can you see the little stars?
MOTHER No.
DAUGHTER But you have to close your eyes really tight. Can you see them now?
MOTHER Yes, now I can see them.
DAUGHTER What colour are they?
MOTHER Blue.
DAUGHTER No. They have to be orange. Close them tighter. Can you see them? (*The* MOTHER *keeps her eyes tightly shut.*)
MOTHER (*Amazed*) Yes... I can see them... thousands of orange stars.
DAUGHTER (*Satisfied*) You see. Now make a wish. Go on.
MOTHER What should I wish for?
DAUGHTER I don't know. For Daddy to sleep next to you tonight. (*Silence*) Go on. Say it.
MOTHER I wish for Daddy to sleep next to me tonight.
DAUGHTER That's it. Now you just have to wait for night-time to come.
MOTHER Where did you get that from?
DAUGHTER Someone taught me to do it.
MOTHER Who? Daddy?
DAUGHTER No. Santiago.

II.

In the office.

FATHER (*To* SANTIAGO) Santiago, could you take these papers to Mr Ugalde? Tell him he just needs to sign them. My daughter will take them with her now.
SANTIAGO Yes, Doctor. (*He takes the papers and leaves.*)
DAUGHTER What did you call him?
FATHER Who?
DAUGHTER Him. What was his name?
FATHER Santiago.
DAUGHTER Oh, I thought so. Do you remember Santiago, the boy who used to live nearby? Do you remember that he went to school with me and we used to play together?
FATHER It's the same one.
DAUGHTER Who?
FATHER He is Santiago.
DAUGHTER (*Surprised*) My Santiago?
FATHER Your Santiago. You see it's impossible to cut off everything?
DAUGHTER So he is Santiago, who'd have thought it?
FATHER He's a good lad.

DAUGHTER He's ignorant. Lots of airs, lots of books, but he lacks sense. He still needs to see the world. He needs to go to my neighbourhood, see how people live, see the poverty, and then he'll stop worrying so much about his tie.
FATHER He is aware of it all.
DAUGHTER He hides it well.
FATHER He doesn't express it in the same way you do and he works differently.
DAUGHTER As far as I'm concerned, there is only one way to work.
FATHER I used to think the same thing too. But let's not argue about that again.

SANTIAGO enters with the documents.

SANTIAGO It's all here, Doctor. You just need to sign them.

The FATHER signs several copies in silence whilst SANTIAGO puts the papers in order.

DAUGHTER (*To SANTIAGO*) So you are Santiago...
SANTIAGO Yes.
DAUGHTER Do you remember me?
SANTIAGO Well yes, we were talking just a moment ago.
DAUGHTER From before.
SANTIAGO No. (*Looking towards the FATHER*) What? You're telling me that we already knew each other?
DAUGHTER From when we were little. From school, don't you remember? We were in primary school together. Then I went to live with my Nan and we didn't see each other again.
SANTIAGO I haven't a clue.
DAUGHTER (*To the FATHER*) You didn't tell him either?
FATHER No.
DAUGHTER Am I the only one here with any memory?
FATHER It seems that way.
SANTIAGO It was so many years ago.
DAUGHTER It's not about how many years ago it was, don't you get it? It's about what you want to remember! And to think that you were my boyfriend!
SANTIAGO Me?
DAUGHTER Yes, you, forgetful.
SANTIAGO (*To the FATHER*) What do you think of all this?
FATHER It seems that you were my daughter's boyfriend.
SANTIAGO When?
FATHER When you were eight years old.
SANTIAGO As if I could have been anyone's boyfriend. I've never had a girlfriend.
DAUGHTER (*Ironically*) That's obvious.
SANTIAGO (*To the FATHER*) What's wrong with her?
FATHER She is offended because you don't remember her.
DAUGHTER (*To the FATHER*) Whereas I remember him perfectly. I even kept a pencil sharpener he gave me.
SANTIAGO Really?

DAUGHTER Yes. You were wonderfully annoying. You followed me around like a love-struck idiot, desperate for my attention.

SANTIAGO And you still have the pencil sharpener?

DAUGHTER Of course I have it. I have everything. I'm a depository of keepsakes. But you know something, when I get home I am going to chuck it all out. I don't know what use all these things I've kept have been to me.

SANTIAGO No. Don't throw it away. Give it back to me.

DAUGHTER Why do you want it?

SANTIAGO I don't know. To have a little piece of my history.

DAUGHTER And you're about to start worrying about your history now? History isn't kept in drawers, it's in here (*she points to her head*) and here (*she points to her heart*).

SANTIAGO (*To the FATHER, confused*) What do you think? It was her who told me just a minute ago that she kept the pencil sharpener. I never kept anything in my life.

DAUGHTER That's obvious. The only thing you think about is writing a guide with instructions on how to reach that seat as quickly as possible.

SANTIAGO (*To the FATHER*) Why is she taking it out on me? I didn't do anything to upset her.

FATHER (*To SANTIAGO*) We did, yes. We did things to upset her. (*SANTIAGO leaves. The FATHER passes a folder to the DAUGHTER.*) This is yours. And thank you for coming here today.

DAUGHTER What is it?

FATHER Contracts. As of now you are the owner of two apartments, a house on the coast and a bank account.

DAUGHTER What makes you think I'll accept them?

FATHER Because you need them. And your grandmother does too.

DAUGHTER Nan isn't going to want anything from you.

FATHER We already discussed it. And came to an agreement.

DAUGHTER With Nan? You spoke to Nan?

FATHER Yes.

DAUGHTER And she accepted?

FATHER Yes.

DAUGHTER You can tell she's getting old. For a while now she's been saying that she's frightened of dying. But it's not because she is frightened of death but because she doesn't want to leave me alone in the world.

FATHER That makes perfect sense to me.

DAUGHTER (*Taking the documents*) And all of this, how did you do it?

FATHER Hard work. Don't even think otherwise. Those were different times.

DAUGHTER In this country corruption makes work.

FATHER That may be true but it's not been the case for me.

DAUGHTER And do you feel you deserve all of this?

FATHER Honestly, yes.

DAUGHTER And what am I going to do with it all?

FATHER Whatever you want.
DAUGHTER You aren't placing any conditions on it?
FATHER None. I'm sure that you'll put it to good use.
DAUGHTER Even if you dislike everything I do with your money?
FATHER It doesn't matter to me what you do, providing you don't do it out of spite or to get revenge on me. That's why I insisted on your coming here. I wanted you to see me for what I am: a poor old man.
DAUGHTER And what about you? Aren't you going to need anything?
FATHER I have a good salary, I'm renting. Besides, if I need some cash, don't worry, I can ask you for a loan.
DAUGHTER (*Ironically*) I don't think so, you're a Senator of the Republic, after all.

SANTIAGO enters euphorically.

SANTIAGO (*To the DAUGHTER*) If you close your eyes really tight you'll see a thousand tiny orange...
SANTIAGO AND DAUGHTER Stars!
SANTIAGO Then you can make a wish. It will definitely come true.

The DAUGHTER looks her father in the eyes. She sees him as a poor old man and she feels extremely sorry for him. She wants to hug him, to take care of him. SANTIAGO leaves. The DAUGHTER packs away the papers, smiling. She moves slowly towards the exit, turns on herself and, still smiling, asks the FATHER a question.

DAUGHTER Tell me, Senator, will you vote for or against the law?

The FATHER goes up to her and kisses her tenderly on the cheek. The DAUGHTER doesn't move and allows him to kiss her.

12.

In the refuge. The DAUGHTER turns around and receives a kiss from her mother. The MOTHER is anxious, she has a bag in her hand and she looks outside, scared.

DAUGHTER Mum! Are you leaving?
MOTHER Yes.
DAUGHTER But they haven't come for you yet.
MOTHER But they're going to come and I don't want them to find me here.
DAUGHTER Why?
MOTHER Because of what I told you before, do you remember?
DAUGHTER About hiding?
MOTHER Yes. I don't want them to find you or Nan.
DAUGHTER I don't mind being found. Anyway, I like doing the counting.
MOTHER So you can start counting now. I'm going to hide. But don't look for me. I'm going to be hiding somewhere around here for a long time. But I'll always be watching you, so you have to be good and do as your Nan tells you. Ok?

DAUGHTER And, what if I find you?

MOTHER If you find me, don't say anything, pretend you haven't seen me. Because otherwise, I'll have to count.

DAUGHTER So what?

MOTHER I don't like counting.

DAUGHTER You like hiding, like Daddy?

MOTHER Yes. Come on, give me a kiss and start counting.

DAUGHTER Up to what?

MOTHER (*Crying*) Up to fifty... no, up to one hundred.

DAUGHTER One, two, three, four, five, six, seven, eight... (*To the MOTHER who has still not left, she looks at her confused*) Mum, who else is playing hide and seek with us?

MOTHER Keep, keep counting.

The MOTHER disappears. The DAUGHTER continues counting even when the light fades completely and the scene is in total darkness.

DAUGHTER Ready or not, here I come. Mum, where are you? Daddy?

CONCLUSION

The Role of the Theatre Translator: Interpret, Intervene, Instruct

Vitez states that: 'Translation no more than the theatre cannot be considered in isolation.'[1] At the beginning of this study, I referred to some of the challenges posed by working with, writing and thinking about international theatre in translation at a time when the UK had voted to leave the European Union. I now find myself writing this final reflection on Uruguayan theatre in translation in 2020, in the context of a global pandemic, at a time when the prospect of going to the theatre in London or beyond still feels too far out of reach. At this time, I cannot help but reflect on the fact that this is another significant change which has posed an unexpected challenge to society and provoked many questions about the ways in which we connect with others in our local, national and international communities. It has caused us to reflect on the ways in which we communicate with and tolerate others and drawn into sharp relief the ways in which local, national and international leaders act in the face of a global crisis. It has forced us to consider how we understand ourselves and others. Once again, there has been a focus on borders. There has also been some focus on language and the need to translate government and National Health Service guidance into community languages. These issues and questions remain in the air as I write and I suspect that they will continue to echo in our society in the coming months and years. The need to listen to, to learn from, and to work with others is evident and essential as we face these challenges.

Despite the difficulties currently faced by the arts sector, which are immense, I have been inspired by the ways in which artists and theatre companies have responded by creating work which brings people together at a time when we feel very separated, even isolated. Many theatres around the world have made recordings of live performances available and it has been exciting to see plays from Spain, Uruguay, the UK and beyond that I would not have been able to see otherwise.[2] A lot of new ways of working have emerged too, with theatre companies and groups transforming their practices to create ways of connecting and working online. Out of the Wings monthly table reads have been taking place via an online platform and recordings of a series of monologues by Abilio Estévez, translated by Kate Eaton, have been produced as a meditation on solitude.[3] I was able to test the version of my translation of *The Library* included in this book with a dispersed group of actors via Zoom and this experience enabled me to focus on listening to the rhythm and the humour of the exchanges in the script and how they change over the course of the three acts. Foreign Affairs have conducted their theatre translator training programme online.[4] Theatre company Cut the Cord used Arts Council England funding to create an international play-reading group who came together online every week for a workshop or panel about a translated play.[5] This involved partnerships with theatre publishers, playwrights, directors and facilitators. I was invited to lead a workshop on Uruguayan theatre and culture when the participants read *The Rage of Narcissus* by Sergio Blanco (original: *La ira de Narciso*) translated and directed by Daniel Goldman and performed at the Pleasance Theatre, London, in 2020.[6] In the workshop we discussed Uruguayan theatre traditions, the idea of national theatre, artistic exchange between Uruguay and Europe, and ways of storytelling, including autofiction.

Very few of the plays featured as part of the programmes or initiatives mentioned above were written specifically for or about this moment of the global pandemic (although there are exciting initiatives to commission and translate new plays which deal with the topic of the pandemic, such as the Poor Connection project).[7] But theatre and theatre in translation have a role to play in helping us to examine and explore the challenges we face and the ways in which we might respond. The worlds we encounter on stage from different times and places can shed light on and help us to understand our contemporary experiences. Through the close analysis of six plays, this study has shown how topics and themes including the bureaucratic disease, the intergenerational divides and the types of violence and repression experienced in Uruguay, depicted on stage, can connect with contemporary discourses and experiences in the UK. This study has also shown that when theatre is translated, we almost always view, interpret, understand and engage with it from the place in which we find ourselves at that time: our current situation has an impact on how we read and receive narratives from other places. It also means that our interpretation may change at different moments in time as different issues and concerns arise in the target culture. The interpretation can be changed and informed by the types of dramaturgical and scholarly research detailed in this book, which enables the translator to understand the original work in context and this can inform and transform the way it is then presented to target audiences. The tendency to view and interpret translated theatre from where we are now is not a bad thing. By interpreting theatre from our current place, we can make connections with theatre experienced by others at other moments and enable the voices and ideas to speak afresh and anew into our current situation. As translators work to reactivate those voices, we engage with concepts, actions and ways of responding to crises that have originated in other places at other times but which are relevant to us today. In doing this, translators create an afterlife for the dramatic text in a new context as we explore and extend the meanings generated by the original. We allow the play to intervene in the target context and the discussions, discourses and issues 'in the air' in the theatre.[8] It is not only plays about the health crisis and pandemic that will help us to understand it and to respond to it in creative, thoughtful and productive ways. Plays about isolation, failures in communication, illness, families and ingrained inequalities can all provide insights into what we are experiencing now. Audiences may be surprised, shocked and stimulated to find that voices from contexts which may initially have seemed distant and different can speak meaningfully and forcefully into the target situation.

It is for this reason that I argue that theatre in translation creates a laboratory, to echo another idea from Vitez: it is a space in which to encounter new concepts, challenge the status quo and experiment with ways of finding solutions to the challenges and crises that we face.[9] It is a space in which to test, trial, refine and encounter. The emphasis placed throughout this study on making connections, forming points of contact, and developing a language for the translated play which echoes discourses in the target context, all reinforce the idea that theatre in translation can open up new ways of thinking about ourselves. At the same time, through thinking both critically and creatively about how, as translators, we can work with the concepts of distance and proximity throughout the translation process, I've shown how we gain insights into other stories and experiences. We can learn about and from others and aspects of, for example, the trials of modernisation, the repression of dictatorship and the confusion caused by the transition to democracy in Uruguay. The translation can serve both to expose an aspect of the source culture and also to provoke discussions about a similar topic or related one in the target culture. Those new insights provided by translated theatre are significant. It is for this reason that theatre in translation can help us to understand and reflect on the global pandemic and the issues, opportunities and inequalities that it has caused, beyond the threat to our mental and physical health. Theatre and translation cannot be considered in isolation.

This study has illustrated the frames of analysis, the types of research, the modes of experimentation, as well as the dialogues and practice undertaken with theatre practitioners, that enable the theatre translator to create a robust translation of a dramatic text. It has demonstrated translation as a creative practice in which the theatre translator is a writer for the stage. I have emphasised the processes of close reading, scholarly analysis and research as fundamental in understanding the play in its original context. This process of interpreting the play is detailed in Chapter 1 and enables the translator to understand the language, culture and context of the original. The knowledge of how a play is located and how it functions in the original context equips the translator to identify points of contact which enable the play to become mobile and move into the target context. The steps in the theatre translation process outlined in this study specify the different types of analysis and questioning to which the original dramatic text is subjected during the translation process. This is not intended as a guide but rather to show how a conceptualisation of the different aspects of the process, and the multiple types of analysis and interpretations involved, can transform theatre translation practice by creating productive links between approaches to theory and practice. This study has identified key questions generated at each stage of theatre translation. I have illustrated the range of research and collaborative practice undertaken as the translator works to resolve some of these problems.

If, as I have already stated, we cannot think of translation in isolation, then it is important to recognise that translation processes are constantly shaped by other factors and influences including budgets, deadlines, translating for specific casting requirements and theatre spaces, collaborations with directors and theatre companies. In this study, I have discussed different ways in which the translator collaborates with theatre companies and creative teams. There are also instances where a translator may be asked to translate for a very specific mise-en-scène and to work with the director from an early stage and this can significantly shape the translation. For every instance of translation, the processes outlined in this book will take place in different ways and priority will be given to different stages at different times, depending on the project and the translator. However, in all instances, the ways of conceptualising these processes, the connections between the thematic and the theoretical, and the experimentation through practice equip the translator to choose an effective translation strategy and create a robust translation in the target language.

Through the process of analysis, the theatre translator is able to create fruitful links between the themes arising from the play and theatre translation theory, which will inform their approach to the translation. In Chapter 3, I examined how an exploration of the experiences of afterlife depicted on stage by Raquel Diana and Mario Benedetti respectively enabled me to understand the protagonists as serving a spectral function. These characters inhabit a provocative and challenging in-between space which serves as a 'productive opening of meaning'.[10] By connecting the depiction of the theme of afterlife to theories in Translation Studies of the translated text as the afterlife of the original, I developed a translation strategy which focussed on the idea of the translation as an extension of the original which serves to open new meanings in the target context, rather than to communicate a specific message. This enabled me to focus on rendering into the English: the sense of an in-between space which was both recognisable and strange; the ways in which, through the protagonists, the playwrights established a sense of proximity to the audience in order to provoke challenging questions; the emphasis on the experiences depicted on stage as unfinished which created a connection back to the original context but also suggested future iterations.

I have argued that the translator carries out the role of a dramaturge by analysing the text in depth as a piece to be performed and identifying the dramatic core of the play around which the narrative centres. As part of the process, they also identify the micro-structures of the dramatic text which both sustain and amplify the issues, ideas and narratives present in the dramatic core. Johnston refers to this as the 'architecture of the piece' and this is useful in conceptualising how the translator creates a framework for the play in the target language in which they then work to create the language of the play for the target audience.[11] There are no fixed meanings but through a process of inhabiting the dramatic text the translator acquires knowledge of the scope of possible meanings generated by the text in the original language and context. This enables them to create a network of meanings, which they transfer into the target language, and this network informs their translation choices. It equips them to make decisions as to how to convey to the target audience what is at stake for the characters. The engagement with the text as the basis for performance through the dramaturgical analysis enables the translator to creatively imagine a possible future performance of the translated text. Some of the strategies proposed in this study as a way to conceptualise the performance of the dramatic text in the target culture include: the preverbal imagining of a projected future performance, the creation of images and diagrams that help to map out the scenography and the movements within it, and the focus on transitions between different times and spaces. An awareness of the ways in which the dramatic text contains instructions in the form of stage directions, scenography, and the rhythm and pace created in the dialogue in the original enables the translator to transfer these elements into the translated dramatic text. In this way, the translated text provides instructions and indications to the creative teams who will work on it to create the performance, whilst also leaving space for their interpretations.

Having undertaken the work to translate the dramatic text, the theatre translator is equipped to articulate and demonstrate the links between source and target cultures, and between theory and practice, by contributing to rehearsals. I have shown how this equips them to act as dramaturge in the rehearsal room and to engage in critical discussions with actors and directors about representing the play. I've illustrated how the academic and their work can move beyond the academy through a series of collaborations which are enriching for both academics and theatre companies. Every time I am in a workshop or rehearsal with actors, I am constantly noting and later reflecting on the types of questions that they ask to explore if they could be incorporated into my own process at an earlier stage. I have learnt an immeasurable amount from these interactions and they have informed the types of questions that I ask the text as I enter into a dialogue with it. This has also been a process of learning about the different stages of creating a translated play because some of their questions are not to be resolved by me; they are part of the process of staging; they are questions to be resolved by the director; they are questions about a character the actor is playing which they need to make decisions about. The translated text provides a basis for and paves the way for the work of the creative teams who develop it for performance.

As translators, we must attempt, in our own way, to inhabit the world of the dramatic text. This is an idea emphasised throughout Chapter 5 where I outlined the ways in which, as translators, we can see ourselves as moving into a text and finding creative and productive ways to engage with the 'sediment' which remains from previous 'tenants'.[12] Rather than focus exclusively on how we move the text (which necessarily happens during the translation process as it moves into the target context), I show how we can focus on moving into the dramatic text in order to become attuned to the multiple voices, realities and experiences that it tells us about. This multiplicity is complex but it forces us to recognise that there are many narratives, ideas, concepts and critiques contained within the dramatic text. Creative teams may choose to accentuate these in particular ways in order to respond to specific concerns affecting society at the time of production. This was the case for the 2016 performance in London of *Pedro and the Captain*, examined in Chapter 3, which underscored the need for us to recognise and engage with contemporary human rights violations.

In my own process, an important aspect of inhabiting the dramatic text has involved conversations with playwrights about their ideas, the inspiration for their work and their creative practice. The majority of these conversations started in Uruguay where I have lived and carried out research trips. I am grateful for these opportunities to discuss work with authors, which have continued over email, and these discussions have always sparked my imagination and creativity. These interactions with playwrights did not focus on ideas around the author's intention but rather around their process. It is for this reason that this book has explored the work of the translator as an imaginative, creative and writerly process. The discussions with playwrights have always helped me to clarify and focus my ideas about the plays that I was translating at the time. They have never made me instantly modify or change my translation; however, they have often provided new possibilities and new ways of imagining how the text could function in translation for the target audience. Their insights have always contributed to the network of meanings that I outlined in Chapter 1; they have enabled me to conceptualise, evaluate and understand the scope of possible meanings of the play. This has shaped and enhanced the framework in which I have worked to render the text into English. As a result, these exchanges with playwrights have always been fruitful and exciting and this has been another way to make contact with aspects of the culture of the original text.

The insights gained from speaking to playwrights were enriched by opportunities to carry out research at universities, theatres and libraries with the help of many generous and knowledgeable scholars, subject specialists and playwrights. They were also enhanced by the experience of going to the theatre in Uruguay to see some of the plays included in this book, as well as many others. My creative process as a theatre translator has been enriched by knowledge of, awareness of, and contact with the spaces in which Uruguayan theatre takes place and the different encounters, exchanges and conversations that have taken place in theatre queues, lobbies and auditoriums. It is important for me to acknowledge that inhabiting these dramatic texts has been informed by inhabiting many different theatre and performance spaces in Uruguay and I have been inspired and transformed by these experiences. These are perhaps the less tangible aspects of the research carried out but they are and always will be incredibly important for my process.

The three chapters of analysis included in this book demonstrate how translation demands close reading and scholarly analysis of the dramatic text. As a result, translation for performance creates an approach that demands a rigorous examination of the text which is productive in generating new insights into the play in the original language. The types of analysis, questions and exchanges which take place throughout the translation process can form the basis of literary and theatre criticism and scholarship. This scholarly work can enhance and support engagement with theatre from different cultures and pave the way for new translations and productions of plays that were previously unknown. The frames of analysis of theatre translation outlined in this book provide tools to critically understand the theatre and literary traditions of different countries.

The dramaturgical and scholarly research is essential to understand the play and the context from which it emerged but it is important to recognise that it does not provide all the answers (and the translator should not expect it to). We cannot possibly attempt to uncover every single reference, allusion and place referred to in the original. Research is an essential step in inhabiting the dramatic text, moving into it as tenants, to echo Aaltonen, along with a range of other collaborators who will bring the text to life for the stage.[13] An awareness and understanding of the context in which the original dramatic text was created and what was at stake at the time, as well as a critical understanding of what is at stake in the dramatic text itself, underpin the translation process. The latter is fundamental and underscores the translator's ideas and vision for how the text functions as a play and this will inform the way in which they translate. However, we must always be prepared to be surprised (and we should enjoy it): we know that dramatic texts can shock, critique, ridicule, disguise and invent. We must constantly endeavour to be open to the multiple voices within any one dramatic text and be aware that texts rarely say or speak about just one thing. Working with actors, directors and reading groups in the ways set out in this book raises awareness of the capacity of dramatic texts to be multiple as each of these practitioners interprets the script, characters and situations portrayed in their own way, thus giving rise to many different readings. Translators and theatre artists will inhabit the text and understand it based on their current ideas, prejudices, concerns and views. This is why the idea of the dialogue and the constant questioning of the text — 'bombard[ing] it with questions' — is so important.[14] We have to be open to the text and to what it might be speaking about, especially in ways that challenge our expectations both about the source context and language and about the target situation. We have to be aware that the play is an imagined world and, in that world, many ideas and concepts can coexist.

Therefore, the translated play in performance can become a laboratory in which ideas presented though the dramatic action interact with the concerns in the air of the theatre and can challenge expectations, provide alternative discourses and create new narratives. The insights into the experiences of others from different times and places that we gain through seeing the worlds depicted on stage can challenge and inform the way we see them, what we know about them and our understanding of the ways in which their experiences connect to our own. Theatre translators and creative teams work to enable these narratives to generate questions for the target context that provoke the audience to learn about others, and in doing so, to learn about themselves.

Notes to the Conclusion

1. Patrice Pavis, ed., 'The Duty to Translate: An Interview with Antoine Vitez', in *The Intercultural Performance Reader* (London: Routledge, 1996), pp. 121–30 (p. 124).
2. There has been some debate about whether the release of so many recordings is fair and beneficial to the artists because, in some cases, they may not be remunerated for such wide dissemination of this work.
3. 'Ceremonias Pandémicas', *Out of the Wings Festival*, <https://ootwfestival.com/ceremonias-pandemicas/> [accessed 26 October 2020].

4. *Foreign Affairs*, <http://www.foreignaffairs.org.uk/> [accessed 31 July 2021].
5. 'Plays by Post', *Cut the Cord*, <https://www.cutthecordtheatre.com/plays-by-post> [accessed 31 July 2021].
6. Sergio Blanco, *The Rage of Narcissus*, trans. by Daniel Goldman (London: Oberon Books, 2020).
7. A series of short plays about connecting virtually with others commissioned by the Argentine Association of Translators and Interpreters (AATI) and the Diplomatura en Dramaturgia at the Centro Cultural Paco Urondo de la Facultad de Filosofía y Letras at the University of Buenos Aires. The plays were translated into English by international teams of translators, facilitated and supported by the Arts and Humanities Research Council Open World Research Initiative projects *Language Acts and Worldmaking* and Cross-Language Dynamics: Reshaping Community, and in collaboration with Out of the Wings. For more information see: 'Poor Connection: Online Rehearsed Readings of New Plays from Argentina', *School of Advanced Study*, <https://modernlanguages.sas.ac.uk/events/event/22875> [accessed 26 October 2020].
8. David Hare, *Writing Left-Handed* (London: Faber and Faber, 1991), p. 24.
9. Pavis, ed., 'The Duty to Translate', in *The Intercultural Performance Reader*, p. 127.
10. Colin Davis, *Haunted Subjects: Deconstruction, Psychoanalysis and the Return of the Dead* (Basingstoke: Palgrave Macmillan, 2007), p. 11.
11. David Johnston, 'Translation for the Stage: Product and Process', *NUI Maynooth Papers in Spanish, Portuguese and Latin American Studies*, 6 (2002), 1–28 (p. 14).
12. Sirkku Aaltonen, *Time-Sharing on Stage: Drama Translation in Theatre and Society* (Clevedon: Multilingual Matters Ltd, 2000), p. 47.
13. Ibid.
14. Patrice Pavis, *Theatre at the Crossroads of Culture*, trans. by Loren Kruger (London: Routledge, 1992), p. 138.

BIBLIOGRAPHY

AALTONEN, SIRKKU, *Time-Sharing on Stage: Drama Translation in Theatre and Society* (Clevedon: Multilingual Matters, 2000)

ABBONDANZA, JORGE, 'Una leyenda criolla', in *Teatro uruguayo contemporáneo: antología*, ed. by Roger Mirza (Madrid: Fondo de Cultura Económica: Centro de documentación teatral, 1992), pp. 477–81

ALBUQUERQUE, SEVERINO JOÃO MEDEIROS, *Violent Acts: A Study of Contemporary Latin American Theatre* (Detroit, MI: Wayne State University Press, 1991)

BARTHES, ROLAND, *Image, Music, Text*, ed. and trans. by Stephen Heath (London: Fontana Press, 1977)

BASSNETT, SUSAN, 'Still Trapped in the Labyrinth: Further Reflections on Translation and Theatre', in *Constructing Cultures: Essays on Literary Translation*, ed. by Susan Bassnett and André Lefevere (Clevedon: Multilingual Matters, 1998), pp. 90–108

BENEDETTI, MARIO, *Literatura uruguaya siglo XX* (Montevideo: Arca, 1988)

—— *Montevideanos* (Montevideo: Centro Editor de América Latina, 1968)

—— *Pedro and the Captain: A Play in Four Parts*, trans. and intro. by Adrianne Aron (San Francisco: Cadmus Editions, 2009)

—— 'Pedro and the Captain (translation from Spanish)', trans. by Freda Beberfall, *Modern International*, 19.1 (1985–87), 33–52

—— *Pedro y el capitán* (Montevideo: Editorial Planeta S.A. / Seix Barral, 2011)

—— *Pedro y el Capitán (Pieza en cuatro partes)* (Mexico City: Editorial Nueva Imagen, 1979)

BENJAMIN, WALTER, 'The Task of the Translator: An Introduction to the Translation of Baudelaire's *Tableaux Parisiens*', trans. by Harry Zohn, in *The Translation Studies Reader*, ed. by Lawrence Venuti, 2nd edn (New York: Routledge, 2004), pp. 75–85

BLANCO, SERGIO, *The Rage of Narcissus*, trans. by Daniel Goldman (London: Oberon Books, 2020)

—— *Thebes Land*, translated and adapted by Daniel Goldman (London: Oberon Books, 2016)

BOYLE, CATHERINE, 'On Mining Performance: Marginality, Memory and Cultural Translation in the Extreme', in *Differences on Stage*, ed. by Alessandra de Martino, Paolo Puppa and Paola Toninato (Newcastle upon Tyne: Cambridge Scholars Publishing, 2013), pp. 207–23

BRANDO, OSCAR, 'Florencio Sánchez: vida y obra en tres actos', in *El 900*, ed. by Oscar Brando, 2 vols (Montevideo: Cal y Canto, 1999), I, 239–52

BRODIE, GERALDINE, *The Translator on Stage* (London: Bloomsbury, 2018)

CASTRO, GRISELDA, *Sainetes: análisis de obras de Florencio Sánchez y Armando Discépolo* (Montevideo: Editorial Técnica S.R.L., 1988)

'Ceremonias Pandémicas', *Out of the Wings Festival*, <https://ootwfestival.com/ceremonias-pandemicas/> [accessed 26 October 2020]

CHON, WALTER BYONGSOK, 'Intercultural Dramaturgy: The Dramaturg as Cultural Liaison', in *The Routledge Companion to Dramaturgy*, ed. by Magda Romanska (Oxford: Routledge, 2015), pp. 136–40

Cordones-Cook, Juanamaría, 'Entrevista a Carlos Maggi', *Latin American Theatre Review*, 20.2 (1986–87), 107–12

'Dancing Alone Every Night', *Out of the Wings Festival*, (2016) <https://ootwweb.wordpress.com/dancing-alone-every-night/> [accessed 27 October 2020]

Davis, Colin, *Haunted Subjects: Deconstruction, Psychoanalysis and the Return of the Dead* (Basingstoke: Palgrave Macmillan, 2007)

Derrida, Jacques, *Specters of Marx: The State of the Debt, the Work of Mourning and the New International*, trans. by Peggy Kamuf (New York: Routledge Classics, 2006). Proquest Ebook Central

Despeyroux, Denise, *Black Tenderness: The Passion of Mary Stuart*, trans. by Simon Breden, ed. and intro. by Margherita Laera (Imola: Cue Press, 2017)

—— *La Realidad / Reality*, trans. by Sarah Maitland (Madrid: Ediciones Antígona, 2019)

Di Stefano, Eugenio Claudio, *The Vanishing Frame: Latin American Culture and Theory in the Postdictatorial Era* (Austin: University of Texas Press, 2018)

Diana, Raquel, *Bailando sola cada noche, Dramaturgia Uruguaya*, (2008) <http://www.dramaturgiauruguaya.uy/obras/bailando-sola-toda-la-noche/> [accessed 17 September 2020]

—— *Bailando sola cada noche: comedia más bien negra y patética* (Montevideo: Yaugurú, 2013)

—— 'Her Open Eyes', trans. by Sophie Stevens, *The Mercurian: A Theatrical Translation Review*, 8.2 (2020), 186–206 <https://themercurian.files.wordpress.com/2020/11/the-mercurian_8.2_fall-2020_final-1.pdf> [accessed 12 July 2021]

Diccionario de la lengua española, 21st edn (Madrid: Real Academia Española, 1992)

Diccionario del español del Uruguay (Montevideo: Ediciones de la Banda Oriental, 2011)

Duffau, Marcelino, and Gabriela Gómez, eds, *Premio Autor Nacional COFONTE: Dramaturgia 2002–2005–2006* (Montevideo: COFONTE, 2011)

Escalante, Laura, ed., *50 años de teatro uruguayo: antología*, 2 vols (Montevideo: Ministerio de Educación y Cultura, 1988–90)

Foreign Affairs, <http://www.foreignaffairs.org.uk/> [accessed 31 July 2021]

Frega Ana, 'La formulación de un modelo: 1890–1918', in *Historia del Uruguay en el siglo XX (1890–2005)*, ed. by Ana Frega and others, 2nd edn (Montevideo: Ediciones de la Banda Oriental S.R.L: Ministerio de Relaciones Exteriores: Facultad de Humanidades y Ciencias de la Educación, 2008), pp. 17–50

Gago, Soledad, 'Muertas No Sueñan', *El País*, <servicios.elpais.com.uy/especiales/digital/2018/muertas-no-suenan/> [accessed 31 July 2021]

García Lorca, Federico, *Doña Rosita la soltera*: *Doña Rosita the Spinster*, ed. and trans. by Gwynne Edwards (London: Methuen Drama; A. & C. Black, 2008)

Gates-Madsen, Nancy, 'Tortured Silence and Silenced Torture in Mario Benedetti's *Pedro y el capitán*, Ariel Dorfman's *La muerte y la doncella* and Eduardo Pavlovsky's *Paso de dos*', *Latin American Theatre Review*, 42.1 (2008–09), 5–31

Gené, Juan Carlos, *Teatro* (Buenos Aires: Centro Editor de América Latina, 1983)

Global Voices Theatre, <https://globalvoicestheatre.com/> [accessed 31 July 2021]

Golovchenko, Estela, *Estela Golovchenko: teatro*, ed. by A. Rodríguez, intro. by Emilio Irigoyen (Montevideo: Editorial Fin de Siglo, 2021)

—— *Punto y coma*, 'Dramática Latinoamericana', *CELCIT*, (2003) <https://www.celcit.org.ar/publicaciones/biblioteca-teatral-dla/?q=golovchenko&f=&m=> [accessed 18 October 2020]

—— *Punto y coma, Dramaturgia Uruguaya*, (2003) <https://dramaturgiauruguaya.uy/punto-y-coma/> [accessed 17 October 2020]

—— 'Teatro Interior', in *Dramaturgia Interior: proceso de creación de cinco dramaturgos en red*, ed. by Mariana Percovich and Ariel Mastandrea (Montevideo: Ministerio de Educación y Cultura; Dirección Nacional de Cultura, 2009), pp. 17–23

Gregory, Stephen W. G, 'Humanist Ethics or Realist Aesthetics? Torture, Interrogation and Psychotherapy in Mario Benedetti', *La Trobe University — Institute of Latin American Studies, Occasional Paper*, 12 (1991), 1–43

Güiraldes, Ricardo, *Don Segundo Sombra*, ed. by Sara Parkinson de Saz, 13th edn (Madrid: Ediciones Cátedra, 2009)

Hare, David, *Writing Left-Handed* (London: Faber and Faber Ltd, 1991)

'Historia', *Teatro El Galpón*, <https://www.teatroelgalpon.org.uy/historia/> [accessed 6 September 2020]

Hutcheon, Linda, with Siobhan O'Flynn, *A Theory of Adaptation*, 2nd edn (Oxford: Routledge, 2013)

Johnston, David, 'Professing Translation: The Acts-in-between', *Target*, 25.3 (2013), 365–84 <doi 10.1075/target.25.3.04joh>

—— 'Securing the Performability of the Play in Translation', in *Drama Translation and Theatre Practice*, ed. by Sabine Coelsch-Foisner and Holger Klein (Frankfurt a.M.: Peter Lang, 2004), pp. 25–38

—— 'Translation for the Stage: Product and Process', *NUI Maynooth Papers in Spanish, Portuguese and Latin American Studies*, 6 (2002), 1–28

Kaiser, Susana, *Postmemories of Terror* (New York: Palgrave Macmillan, 2005)

Las Hermanas de Shakespeare: perspectivas de género en el teatro (Montevideo: Intendencia de Montevideo, 2018), <https://montevideo.gub.uy/sites/default/files/biblioteca/publicacionsimposiolashermanasdeshakespeare_0.pdf>

Legal Aliens Theatre, <https://www.legalalienstheatre.com/> [accessed 31 July 2021]

Legido, Juan Carlos, *El teatro uruguayo: de Juan Moreira a los independientes, 1886–1967*, (Montevideo: Ediciones Tauro, 1968)

Lessa, Francesca, *Memory and Transitional Justice in Argentina and Uruguay: Against Impunity* (New York: Palgrave Macmillan, 2013)

Machín, Antonio, *A Barbacoa me voy*, online audio recording, YouTube, 8 November 2014 <https://www.youtube.com/watch?v=SZSB2Zhf4qE> [accessed 31 July 2021]

Mackey, Theresa. M., 'Reverse Stockholm Syndrome in *Pedro y el capitán*: Paradigm for the Cycle of Authoritarianism in Latin America', *Literature and Psychology: A Journal of Psychoanalytic and Cultural Criticism*, 43.4 (1997), 1–15

Maggi, Carlos, *La biblioteca*, in *50 años de teatro uruguayo: antología*, ed. by Laura Escalante, 2 vols (Montevideo: Ministerio de Educación y Cultura, 1988–90), I, 113–60

—— *The Library*, in *Voices of Change in the Spanish American Theater: An Anthology*, ed. and trans. by William Oliver (Austin: University of Texas Press, 1971), pp. 105–69

Maitland, Sarah, *What is Cultural Translation?* (London: Bloomsbury Academic, 2017)

McSherry, J. Patrice, *Predatory States: Operation Condor and Covert War in Latin America* (Lanham, MD: Rowman & Littlefield, 2005)

Mirza, Roger, 'De la desacralización liberadora a la denuncia: I', *La Escena Latinoamericana*, 2 (1989), 52–56

—— 'Escenificaciones de la memoria en el teatro de la postdictadura: *Pedro y el Capitán, Elena Quinteros. Presente* y *Las cartas que no llegaron*', in *La dictadura contra las tablas: teatro uruguayo e historia reciente*, ed. by. Roger Mirza and Gustavo Remedi (Montevideo: Biblioteca Nacional, 2009), pp. 37–81

—— 'El naturalismo y sus transgresiones', in *Teatro uruguayo contemporáneo: antología*, ed. by Roger Mirza (Madrid: Fondo de Cultura Económica: Centro de documentación teatral, 1992), pp. 11–64

—— 'El Teatro Como Fiesta Popular', *La Semana de El Día*, 12 September 1981, p. 21

—— ed., *Teatro uruguayo contemporáneo: antología* (Madrid: Fondo de Cultura Económica: Centro de documentación teatral, 1992)

Moliner, María, *Diccionario de uso del español*, 2nd edn (Madrid: Gredos, 1998)

Morello-Frosch, Marta, and Martha Morello-Frosch, 'El diálogo de la violencia en "Pedro y el capitán" de Mario Benedetti', *Revista de Crítica Literaria Latinoamericana*, 18 (1983), 87–96

Nancy, Jean-Luc, *Being Singular Plural*, trans. by Robert D. Richardson and Anne E. O'Byrne (Stanford, CA: Stanford University Press, 2000)

'Normativa y Avisos Legales de Uruguay, Ley N° 19580', *IMPO: Centro de Información Oficial*, 9 January 2018, <www.impo.com.uy/bases/leyes/19580-2017> [accessed 31 July 2021]

ONS, <https://www.ons.gov.uk/peoplepopulationandcommunity/crimeandjustice/bulletins/domesticabuseinenglandandwalesoverview/november2019> [accessed 10 October 2020]

Out of the Wings, <http://www.outofthewings.org> [accessed 9 September 2020]

Pavis, Patrice, ed., 'The Duty to Translate: An Interview with Antoine Vitez', in *The Intercultural Performance Reader* (London: Routledge, 1996), pp. 121–30

—— *Theatre at the Crossroads of Culture*, trans. by Loren Kruger (London: Routledge, 1992)

'Plays by Post', *Cut the Cord*, <https://www.cutthecordtheatre.com/plays-by-post> [accessed 31 July 2021]

Podestá, José J., *Medio siglo de farándula: memorias* (Córdoba: Rio de la Plata, 1930)

'Poor Connection: Online Rehearsed Readings of New Plays from Argentina', *School of Advanced Study*, <https://modernlanguages.sas.ac.uk/events/event/22875> [accessed 26 October 2020]

Puga, Ana Elena, *Memory, Allegory and Testimony in South American Theater: Upstaging Dictatorship* (New York: Routledge, 2008)

Rea, Lauren, *Argentine Serialised Radio Drama in the Infamous Decade, 1930–1943: Transmitting Nationhood* (Farnham, Surrey: Ashgate, 2013)

'Ready or Not', *Out of the Wings Festival*, (2017) <ootwfestival.com/ready-or-not/> [accessed 29 September 2020]

Rein, Mercedes, and Jorge Curi, *El Herrero y la Muerte*, in *50 años de teatro uruguayo: antología*, ed. by Laura Escalante, 2 vols (Montevideo: Ministerio de Educación y Cultura, 1988–90), II, 429–64

—— *El herrero y la Muerte*, in *Teatro uruguayo contemporáneo: antología*, ed. by Roger Mirza (Madrid: Fondo de Cultura Económica: Centro de documentación teatral, 1992), pp. 483–534

—— *El herrero y la Muerte*, in *Teatro uruguayo contemporáneo: antología*, ed. and introd. by María Nélida Riccetto (Buenos Aires: Colihue, 1993), pp. 123–68

—— 'El herrero y la muerte: Leyenda criolla de Mercedes Rein y Jorge Curi', *Escenario: Revista Teatro Circular de Montevideo*, Serie Autores Nacionales, 1 (July, 1982), 1–43

Remedi Gustavo, *Carnival Theater: Uruguay's Popular Performers and National Culture*, trans. by Amy Ferlazzo (Minneapolis: University of Minnesota Press, 2004)

Reta, Adela, 'Prólogo', in *50 años de teatro uruguayo: antología*, ed. by Laura Escalante, 2 vols (Montevideo: Ministerio de Educación y Cultura, 1988–90), I, 5

Riccetto, María Nélida, ed., *Teatro uruguayo contemporáneo: antología* (Buenos Aires: Colihue, 1993)

[Rodríguez Monegal, Emir (?)], 'Dramaturgo con ambiciones', *Espectáculos*, 21 December 1962

Ruiz, Esther, 'El "Uruguay próspero" y sus crisis. 1946–1964', in *Historia del Uruguay en el siglo XX (1890–2005)*, ed. by Ana Frega and others, 2nd edn (Montevideo: Ediciones de la Banda Oriental S.R.L; Ministerio de Relaciones Exteriores; Facultad de Humanidades y Ciencias de la Educación, 2008), pp. 123–62

Sánchez, Florencio, *M'hijo el dotor*, in *Teatro*, 7th edn (Buenos Aires: Editorial Sopena Argentina, 1972), pp. 243–82

—— *M'hijo el dotor*, study and notes by Mabel V. Manacorda de Rosetti and Rosa Palma de Carpinetti, ed. by María Hortensia Lacau, 7th edn (Buenos Aires: Editorial Kapelusz, 1979)

—— *Representative Plays of Florencio Sánchez*, trans. from the Spanish by Willis Knapp Jones, UNESCO Collection of Representative Works, Latin American Series (Washington, DC: Pan American Union, 1961)

STEVENS, SOPHIE, 'Distance and Proximity in Analysing and Translating *Bailando sola cada noche* [Dancing Alone Every Night] into English', *The Mercurian: A Theatrical Translation Review*, 6 (2016), 81–99, available online at <https://the-mercurian.com/2016/11/16/distance-and-proximity-in-analysing-and-translating-bailando-sola-cada-noche-dancing-alone-every-night/>

—— 'Representations of Transition, Memory and Crisis on Stage in *Punto y coma* [Ready or Not] by Uruguayan Dramatist Estela Golovchenko', in *Theatre, Performance and Commemoration: Staging Crisis, Memory and Nationhood*, ed. by Alinne Balduino P. Fernandes, Miriam Haughton and Pieter Verstraete (London: Bloomsbury, forthcoming)

TAYLOR, DIANA, *Disappearing Acts: Spectacles of Gender and Nationalism in Argentina's 'Dirty War'* (Durham, NC: Duke University Press, 1997)

'Translation, Adaptation, Otherness: "Foreignisation" in Theatre Practice' (project), <www.translatingtheatre.com> [accessed 26 October 2020]

'Translation Plays, Intercultural Workshops', *King's College London*, <https://www.kcl.ac.uk/Cultural/-/Projects/Translation-Plays> [accessed 13 October 2020]

VERSÉNYI, ADAM, 'The Dissemination of Theatrical Translation', in *The Routledge Companion to Dramaturgy*, ed. by Magda Romanska (Oxford: Routledge, 2015), pp. 288–93

—— *Theatre in Latin America: Religion, Politics, and Culture from Cortés to the 1980s* (Cambridge: Cambridge University Press, 1993)

—— 'Translation as an Epistemological Paradigm for Theatre in the Americas', *Theatre Journal*, 59.3 (2007), 431–47 <http://dx.doi.org/10.1353/tj.2007.0173>

'Violencia doméstica: una mujer murió cada 15 días', *El País*, 24 November 2014, <http://www.elpais.com.uy/informacion/violencia-domestica-mueren-mensualmente.html> [accessed 31 March 2015]

WALKER, BEATRIZ, *Benedetti, Rosencof, Varela: el teatro como guardián de la memoria colectiva* (Buenos Aires: Ediciones Corregidor, 2007)

YÁÑEZ, RUBEN, 'El teatro actual', *Capitulo oriental: la historia de la literatura uruguaya*, 31 (1968–69), 479–98

Film

MORLEY, CAROL, dir., *Dreams of a Life* (Dogwoof, 2011)

INDEX

www.ingramcontent.com/pod-product-compliance
Lightning Source LLC
Chambersburg PA
CBHW080542090426
42734CB00016B/3180
9781781883143